Children *and the*
Great Hunger
in Ireland

D1627756

Children *and the* Great Hunger *in* Ireland

Edited by

CHRISTINE KINEALY
JASON KING
GERARD MORAN

QUINNIPIAC UNIVERSITY PRESS

Published by:
Quinnipiac University Press
275 Mount Carmel Ave
Hamden, CT 06518–1908
www.quinnipiac.edu
for

Ireland's Great Hunger Institute:
www.qu.edu/institutes-and-centers/irelands-great-hunger-institute/
Cork University Press:
www.corkuniversitypress.com

Copyright: IGHI 2018
ISBN: 978-0-9904686-9-1

Cover Image: *The Claddagh, Galway* by John Leech
Designed by the Office of Integrated Marketing Communications

Typesetting by Marsha Swan
Printed by GRAPHYCEMS

Contents

This publication is dedicated to our children, who make everything worthwhile: Siobhán and Ciarán; Aislinn, Nathalie, and Fergus; Eoghan, Cian, Cillian and Caoimhe.

Christine Kinealy, Jason King, Gerard Moran

Foreword
THE GREAT SILENCE

Marita Conlon-McKenna

Growing up in Ireland there seemed to be a resounding silence about the Great Irish Famine. As school students, we learned little about this dark and tragic time in our history books or even from our history teachers, as the focus was on what were considered greater periods in both Irish and European history. Perhaps there was shame and an element of not wanting to resurrect memories of such a catastrophic time in Ireland's troubled history. This evasion was both disappointing and baffling, but only served to rouse the curiosity of generations of students and history lovers.

Fortunately, times have changed, and Ireland recognizes fully 'The Great Hunger' as a major part of our history, which not only has had a deep and lasting affect on generations of Irish people but also has helped shape modern Ireland. The Great Irish Famine is commemorated annually with a large event held in various counties, both north and south, to remember the million people who died and the million who emigrated. Strokestown Park House in Roscommon now houses The National Famine Museum and in West Cork, Skibbereen's Heritage Centre includes both a Famine exhibition and a local research centre. Across Ireland, workhouses, soup kitchens and even Famine graves are being restored and protected and the study of the Great Irish Famine is now on the school curriculum.

Ireland's Great Hunger is of interest to millions around the world, not only Irish people or those who may have Irish family roots, but those with a curiosity and knowledge of history and of Ireland.

However, despite all this renewed interest in *An Gorta Mor*—The Great Hunger, the tragic effect it had on the lives of children has mostly been overlooked. Little has been written of the hundreds and thousands of children who died during the Great Irish Famine years of 1845 to 1852, and who were often buried in unmarked graves, their deaths unrecorded. Or of those young people who were forced to emigrate to America and Canada, or other less familiar places.

In Ireland, the population had grown to over eight million, with the 1841 census showing that children under 15 years of age represented 40.5 percent of the population. Yet this important cohort of young victims of the Great Irish Famine has merited scant attention.

With the publication of *Children and the Great Hunger,* it is heartening to see editors Christine Kinealy, Jason King and Gerard Moran bring together renowned academics, historians, experts, writers and researchers who have turned their attention to these so-called forgotten ones—the child victims of the Great Hunger, and examined various aspects of these lost lives, researching and discovering fresh information about this tragic time in so many children's lives.

The chapters give a broad and varied perspective on all aspects of these children of the Famine, their lives, outcomes and how they are remembered, from Christine Kinealy writing extensively on the impact on children growing up in Famine Ireland, to Gerard Moran and Simon Gallaher's insightful work on the ill-treatment of the young in Irish workhouses and the trauma suffered by them both during and after the Famine, and Jonny Geber's study on the bioarchaeology of child experiences during the Great Hunger, which uses forensics to examine the physical damage often wreaked on child inmates of these charitable institutions.

Extensive research also has focused on young emigrants with a particular interest taken by Mark McGowan, Jason King and Koral Lavorgna in young children and orphans who found themselves transported by ship to Quebec and Montreal and other British North American cities. Lavorgna's focus is on the education of such Famine orphans; McGowan gives a new perspective to the reality of the adoption of these children by Canadian families, while King follows the determined quest of Irish orphan Robert Walsh to find his sister. All give a critical analysis of the kind of care child emigrants received, and the psychological damage inflicted on them as they coped with loss of family, home, land and even language in a new world. Eileen Moore Quinn expands on this, writing that though much of an emigrant's native Gaelic language might be lost, certain Irish words and phrases were remembered and with constant use became a relevant part of their new language.

Consideration is also given to how the story of the young people caught up in the Great Hunger and emigration has been reflected in published literature over the intervening century; from Stephen Butler writing on the very popular fiction of Irish Canadian author Mary Anne Sadlier in the 19th-century, with her didactic stories of Irish orphans and emigrants, which had a massive appeal to a huge readership, to Robert A. Young Jr writing of the extensive and growing library of books published over the recent decades for young readers written about Ireland's Great Hunger. Maureen Murphy deals with the huge task of introducing the Great Irish Famine on the secondary school curriculum in New York, and the wide-ranging areas of study it encompasses, which enables American students to not simply examine the past, but discover how it relates to current global issues of hunger and migration.

Salvador Ryan writes of the vital importance of the Irish Folklore Commission's *Schools' Collection* of stories and memories of the Famine, collected by children from their family and neighbours across Ireland in 1937. It is fascinating to read the children's accounts on all aspects of the Famine. This is an invaluable resource that certainly deserves this new attention. Irish-born writer, Michael Collins tells of the modern-day emigrant's lament for the far-reaching effect of the Famine and how it continues to be voiced. His words reflect on the complexities of simply being Irish.

With a focus on children during the Great Irish Famine, it is important to remember that in Ireland of the 1840s life was precarious for children at the best of times for their families eked out a living on the land they rented, which had usually been sub-divided again and again among tenant families who struggled to pay the rent to the landlord's agent. The British authorities grew concerned about the increasing population, and the dependence of so many on what they considered unsustainable small holdings.

The potato people—as such families were known—were totally dependent on the potato crop, which grew easily and abundantly in the small fields they rented. Potatoes formed their main food as they could be easily cooked and stored and provided a healthy, if bland, diet.

The arrival of potato blight, *"the murrain,"* which affected as much as a third of the potato crop of 1845, not only in Ireland but in Scotland and parts of England and Europe, brought severe hardship to many.

Irish hero and M.P. Daniel O'Connell, and members of the Mansion House Committee in Dublin made an appeal to Queen Victoria for emergency measures to be implemented in Ireland as families and children began to suffer. Rents went unpaid, livestock were sold, the little clothing and possessions the poor had were pawned or sold to buy meal and, later, much-needed seed potato to plant in the spring.

However, in late August 1846 it was clear that the potato blight had returned. This time the consequences were disastrous for the entire Irish potato crop was destroyed, with even early potatoes that had been stored rotting in their pits.

For families across the country, all hope was lost for they had nothing left to sell or pawn, no money for rent and no food to feed their children as winter approached. The already weakened people were soon ravaged by hunger.

Desperate appeals to parliament and the landlords were made as relief was needed urgently. Charles Trevelyan, the head of the British Treasury, seemed immune to the suffering of Irish people as food and livestock continued to be exported to British ports, while people starved. Trevelyan had a belief that God and nature had somehow intervened to solve the *Irish problem.*

Public works schemes were set up to employ local men on building roads in return for a payment, which was barely enough to buy food for his family. Thousands were employed on such schemes, but many were hungry and too malnourished for such heavy labor and they soon fell ill with "road fever." Workers were often not paid for weeks and the winter of 1846 and into 1847 brought snow and cold and ice, as poorly clad men, women and even children broke stones and labored building roads that led to nowhere in return for only a few pennies.

As the situation deteriorated Dr. Dan Donovan, known as the Irish Famine Doctor, from Skibbereen in West Cork, began to write his "Diary of a Dispensary Doctor," which was published in *The Southern Reporter*, a Cork newspaper, giving an accurate account of the horrific suffering experienced in his own region. Many of his harrowing reports on the worsening situation were also carried in overseas papers, as were reports of other concerned observers.

Donovan wrote of a mother who had visited his dispensary and wished that all her children were dead:

> Bad luck to them for children! I have five of them sick, and I would think myself lucky, if they were all dead by morning.

Donovan admonished her for being cruel, but she went on to explain to him:

> This time twelve months ago I would as soon lose my heart's blood as one of my children, but it is killing me now to see them starving and crying.

It was Donovan who showed the illustrator James Mahony of *The Illustrated London News* in February 1847 the awful conditions that prevailed on the streets and in the hovels and lanes of the town where people lay dying of hunger and fever, with children often the only ones left to tend the sick. Mahony's images, many of which were of starving children, were published worldwide to a shocked readership. Another visitor to the town was Elihu Burritt, the American humanitarian who accompanied Donovan as he attended to the dying in Skibbereen. Burritt wrote:

> I have seen how much beings, made in the image of God, can suffer on this side of the grave, and that too in a civilised country.

The people were suffering, broken by starvation and sickness, in that long, harsh, freezing winter of 1846 and early 1847. The corpses of the dead lay on the streets and roads and ditches, many buried in mass graves and burial pits.

The ageing and ailing Liberator, O'Connell, left his Famine-torn Kerry to attend the new parliament in London, where he made his last speech on 8th February 1847, to plead once more for his people:

> Ireland is in your hands. She is in your power. If you do not save her she can't save herself. And I solemnly call on you to recollect that I predict with the sincerest conviction that one quarter of her population will perish unless you come to her relief.

Parliament did little and only weeks later a heartbroken and unwell O'Connell set out for Rome to plead his case with the Pope, however, *en route* to the Vatican, he died in Genoa.

Driven by despair and hunger, people flocked to the hated Poor Law Union Workhouses. There were 130 of them, many of which had only opened a few years earlier. Built to house those that were utterly destitute in districts around Ireland, with their harsh and austere surroundings they offered little comfort, with inmates expected to work for their keep and abide by their strict rules.

Desperate mothers, believing the workhouse was their only hope of survival, begged for admittance for two or three of their starving children; husbands pleaded for their wives and offspring to be allowed to enter. They were refused as the admission rules were strict. Individual family members could not enter the workhouse; they were only permitted to enter as a whole family unit.

The irony was that once they did so, the family members were immediately separated and parted from their loved ones. Males and females were segregated with husbands and wives parted, brothers and sisters divided, and mothers and infants separated once the baby reached two years of age. For children, this separation was particularly hard as they missed their parents and siblings and were alienated from all they had ever known.

Those admitted to the workhouse soon discovered that disease and sickness were rampant in the overcrowded and unhygienic conditions, infirmaries and fever sheds filled with inmates sick with typhus and dysentery. Instead of saving them, the workhouse often hastened their end. Overwhelmed, a number of the workhouses, which were financed by local ratepayers, were forced to close their doors, as the wretched and starving thronged the towns and roads.

William Forster, a British Quaker working on behalf of the Central Relief Committee, was shocked at the terrible sights he witnessed, especially the condition of the children:

> ... like skeletons, their features sharpened with hunger and their limbs wasted so that little was left but bones, their hands and arms, in particular, being much emaciated, and the happy expression of infancy gone from their faces.

Under huge international pressure, Trevelyan finally gave the order for Temporary Outdoor Relief to be extended to those who were not in a workhouse with the introduction of the Soup Kitchen Act.

In the spring of 1847, soup kitchens were set up across the country to feed the needy. Many would walk miles for the soup and a serving of bread or some grain or gruel. The quality of the soup was poor but it helped three million people to survive. Young children and the very old and weak often perished for they were unable to manage such a walk and lining up for hours to be fed, many who were too weak to walk, crawling on all fours.

Conditions to obtain relief in June 1847 were changed with a stringent amendment to the Poor Law Act—the Gregory Clause, which insisted that anyone receiving relief in a workhouse or soup kitchen must not have a holding of more than a quarter of an acre of land. Small tenants were immediately forced to give up their homes and land if they wanted to feed their families. Landlords quickly used this law to enable them to evict their tenants, tumbling their cottages and using the land for livestock and tillage. Emigration, often with assisted passages offered by the landlords or the guardians of the local union workhouses, was for many destitute their only hope of a new life.

So began the mass migration of children and families across the wild Atlantic to the new world in the United States and Canada. Fares were cheaper to British North America so many opted to journey there. Some, already ill and weak, were lost on such journeys with no food, air or sanitation in overcrowded cramped conditions, which aided the spread of typhus and dysentery and ship fever. Many were lost at sea or did not survive the imposed quarantine on Grosse Île and Partridge Island.

One of the largest groups to receive such "assistance" was the 1,490 tenants evicted from Major Denis Mahon's Strokestown Park House Estate in Roscommon, many of them widows and children. They were made to walk from Roscommon to Dublin to board ships to Liverpool, and then on to Canada. Half of them perished. It is hard to imagine the scale of such a mass movement of people but in 1847 alone, 400 ships filled with poor Irish emigrants landed in Quebec.

For exhausted children in filthy rags arriving in a strange land, with a language they did not know, it must have been a truly frightening experience. Most struggled to adjust to life in a new country where home, family and their native Gaelic language were all lost to them. Often, they were dependent on the charity of the Catholic Church and the good people of their new country.

The legacy of the Great Hunger for many would be silence, for they did not want to recount or remember the horrors and degradation they and their families had endured. Relatives recalled that the dark days of the Famine were simply not discussed or rarely mentioned.

For other survivors, like Fenian leader Jeremiah O'Donovan Rossa, "the hunger" would prove a catalyst. Having not only witnessed the death of his father from road fever in 1847 and seen his mother and brothers and sisters evicted from their family home in West Cork, the young O'Donovan Rossa was determined to take revenge. He joined the Young Irelanders, later becoming a leading force in the Fenian movement both in Ireland and in America, where he was deeply involved in the long fight against British imperialism.

> *The famine came and filled the graves*
> *I saw my father die –*
> *The bit of ground was gone*
> *The bailiff with 'the notice' came*
> *I saw the rooftree in a flame*
> *The crowbar work was done*
> *With neither house nor hod, nor bread*
> *The workhouse was my doom*
> *And on my jacket soon I read*
> *The Union of Macroom*
> Lyric for Fenian Ballad written by Jeremiah O'Donovan Rossa

The children of the Great Hunger witnessed sights that no young person should ever witness. Alongside immense physical deprivation, many must have suffered emotional and psychological distress, as a result of their traumatic experiences, over those long Famine years 1845 to 1852.

The Great Irish Famine was one of the greatest humanitarian disasters of 19th-century Europe. Complex issues of class, religion, land ownership and politics all contributed to the scale of loss, which was enormous in a country like Ireland. However, it was man's inhumanity to man and injustice that were the two true Colossi of the Great Irish Famine.

Unfortunately, little has been learned from history for these two giants still preside over modern-day calamities of natural disasters, epidemics, war, conflict and the large-scale migration of refugees, which affect millions of people, many of them children globally.

The deep-rooted scars created by the Great Hunger continue to linger on as we remember all those, both young and old, who died so tragically during those terrible Famine years, and the millions of Irish emigrants who left behind both home, place and family on their perilous journey to a new life. However, we also must remember a generation of children, in Ireland, America, Canada and Australia, who fought to survive and, grabbing on to hope, somehow had the courage to begin again.

Introduction

WALKING SKELETONS OF DEATH

Christine Kinealy, Jason King
and Gerard Moran

The emergence and growth of Childhood Studies since the 1990s has helped
to promote interest in the experiences and agency of children.[1] Within Ireland,
the appearance of this discipline is of recent origin. The creation of the History
of Irish Childhood Research Network in 2014 recognized the importance of
this area, its aim being "to provide a fresh forum for researchers to discuss
topics and themes related to the history of children and childhood (including
adolescence) over the centuries both in Ireland and beyond its shores."[2] They,
in turn, date their intellectual origins to the publication in 1962 of *Centuries of
Childhood*, the English translation of Philippe Ariès's *L'enfant et la vie familiale
sous l'Ancien Régime*.[3] The historiography is still in its infancy with relatively
few studies by Irish scholars. However, in the same year that the Network
was founded the publication of *Children, childhood and Irish society 1500 to the
present*, edited by Maria Luddy and James Smith, marked an important step
in "addressing this lacuna."[4] The interdisciplinary approach adopted in this
volume reflects the approach taken by Childhood Studies and its commitment to drawing from research from a range of scholarship.

Regardless of the emerging interest in the history of children and child-hood, and the sustained scholarly interest in the history of the Irish Great Famine that has taken place since 1995, the historiography of how children suffered, survived or perished during the tragedy of the Great Hunger remains sparse to non-existent. This is perhaps surprising given that in any famine, and Ireland was no exception, children are one of the groups most vulnerable to excess mortality. Children and the aged accounted for one-third of the Irish population in the 1840s, but three-fifths of the deaths.[5] Yet, their individual stories remain largely invisible. In contrast, in imagery of famines, as Margaret Kelleher so poignantly pointed out in 1997, children, together with their starving mothers, are well represented.[6] Moreover, works of fiction on this topic, notably since the 1960s, have been especially prolific in terms of children's literature, and these books have overwhelmingly viewed the Famine through the eyes of young people.[7] Scholars, however, have proven more reluctant to focus on this key demographic group. Even the groundbreaking, comprehensive and size-able *Atlas of the Great Irish Famine* first published in 2012, did not include any section devoted to children. Consequently, their stories remain little known, they appearing as passive and tragic specters within a heart-rending landscape, whose experiences, contributions, lives and deaths, remain as auxiliary and silent. An aim of this publication is to rescue some of their narratives.

While children have been sidelined in written accounts, one of the most iconic images of the Famine comes from the *Illustrated London News*, namely, the depiction of Bridget O'Donnel and her two children from County Clare. James Mahony, the illustrator, graphically shows the impact that hunger and famine was having on the O'Donnel children. Unfortunately, it is not known what happened to the O'Donnel children after this report was published on 22 December 1849, but the plight of the family in many ways highlights the vicissitudes that their peers endured during this period. Significantly, the O'Donnels were not just symbols, but actual people, with a real story. The family had been evicted from their four-acre farm, their house knocked down, their corn taken and two children had already died. Young lives terminated, a family devastated, a generation lost—and a narrative that was being duplicated throughout the island.

For high art, however, representing the Famine presented a number of challenges that resulted in few contemporary paintings. Irish artist Daniel Macdonald is unusual in that his 1847 painting, "An Irish Family Discovering the Blight of Their Store," directly engages with the unleashing of the event.[8] It does not, however, confront the painful consequences of what the potato failure meant to the Irish peasantry. Ironically, but perhaps not surprisingly, this loss is most captured by an artist in Canada, commissioned by a Bishop who survived "famine fever," to provide a contemporary and authentic view of the impact of the starvation of people who escaped from Ireland.[9] Théophile Hamel's "Le Typhus," created in 1847 in Montreal, is one of the few contemporary, and consequently, most chilling, views of the impact of the Great Hunger.[10] Unusually, possibly uniquely, it depicts the death of Irish emigrants, including that of children. It is a powerful reminder that the suffering caused by the Famine was not confined to the island of Ireland.

From an official, administrative perspective, children were regarded distinctly from adults: Poor Law legislation separated those aged 14 or under from their parents; the Soup Kitchen Act gave half rations to those who were 9 and under; emigration regulations computed anybody aged 14 and under as a "half" emigrant. For all other purposes, however, children did not receive any special treatment or privileges. Similar to the adults, they had no special right to relief or, as it turned out, to life. There is no doubt that children fared worse than adults during this tragedy. This is evident from the mortality rates in the workhouses, which the essays by Gerard Moran, Jonny Geber and Simon Gallaher highlight. After they were separated from their parents, such "children then went out of life like bubbles bursting on the stream," recalled Denis C. O'Connor in *Seventeen years' experience of workhouse life* (1861),[11] a remarkable statement explored further in Gallaher's chapter. If children perished in these institutions, built for the purpose of providing relief, how did they fare outside of them? Asenath Nicholson, an American philanthropist who traversed Ireland in 1847, providing food and an unsentimental eyewitness testimony, identified another form of loss that preceded death—the demise of childhood. The sounds associated with young lives also disappeared and were replaced by an unnatural form of silence:

> The dogs ceased their barking, there were scarcely any cocks to be heard crowing in the morning, and the gladsome mirth of children everywhere ceased. O! ye, whose nerves are disturbed by the glee of the loud-laughing boy, come to this land of darkness and death, and for leagues you may travel, and in house or cabin, by the way-side, on the hill-top, or upon the meadow, you shall not see a smile, you shall not see a sprightly foot running in ecstasy after the rolling hoop, leaping the ditch, or tossing the ball. The young laughing full faces, and brilliant eyes, and buoyant limbs, had become walking skeletons of death.[12]

Other eyewitness accounts illustrate the impact that famine and hunger had on those who were most vulnerable. The Mayo magistrate, Michael O'Shaughnessy, told the Select Committee on the Poor Law in May 1849, that on his travels around the county:

> it was quite inflicting to see the state of the children; they were nearly naked, with a few rags upon them, the hair standing to an end from poverty; their eyes sunken, their lips pallid, and nothing but the protruding bones of their little joints visible. I could not help exclaiming as I passed them, 'Am I living in a civilized country and part of the British empire?'[13]

O'Shaughnessy was not unique in asking the question of how such suffering could take place at the heart of the richest empire in the world. Moreover, it was an empire that had access to ample resources of food. The short-lived implementation of the Temporary Relief Act in the summer of 1847, when over three million people each day received free supplies of soup and bread, was palpable evidence of the government's ability to provide food to those who needed it.[14] But providing gratuitous relief—even to children— was deemed both politically and ideologically unacceptable to those who governed Ireland; starvation was a preferable alternative. The chapter by Christine Kinealy provides more examples of eyewitness accounts, set against a backdrop of relief polices that repeatedly failed to make special provision for young people.[15] This indifference was not unique to the Famine period, but was part of a longer continuum, recently categorized as part of "the grim history of children in Irish social policy."[16]

Although not specifically explored in this small volume, the experiment of the Earl Grey Scheme, from 1848 to 1850, provides a telling microcosm of how female young adults were viewed and treated.[17] The sending of work-house girls, aged between 14 and 18, to a British colony on the far side of the world, like so much emigration, was simultaneously escape and exile. Although they were orphans (in the sense that they had lost one, but not necessarily two, parents), moving to Australia threw them into an overwhelming male, sparsely-populated, but convict-rich, society. When the scheme was brought to an early close, over 4,000 girls had already participated. Regardless of disappointment with their domestic skills, these young women married, and gave birth to a new generation of Irish-Australians. If their origins were humble, their experiences harrowing, and their reception often hostile, the Earl Grey orphans were trail-blazers, who are increasingly being recognized as a vital part of the story of the Irish in Australia.[18]

More renowned is the cultural memory and myth of the Irish Famine orphans who were adopted into French-Canadian families after the loss of their parents on the coffin ships and in the fever sheds of Grosse Île and Montreal in 1847. Mass mortality among the adults created a generation of orphans, whose Irish identity was often lost during the adoption process. Canada, also a British colony that was overtly Protestant, gave refuge to a predominantly Catholic influx of weak and dying people. At the forefront of this caregiving effort were the remarkable Grey Nuns, a French-Canadian order.[19] In her celebrated "Cherishing the Irish Diaspora" address (1995), Ireland's President Mary Robinson paid tribute to those "French-Canadian families who braved fever and shared their food, who took the Irish into their homes and into their heritage."[20] In doing so, she echoed John Francis Maguire's claim in *The Irish in America* (1868) that "the orphan children were gathered to the homes and hearts of the generous Canadians".[21] In fact, it was Maguire who first popularized the memory of Famine orphan adoptions in Quebec, and especially the fact that they were allowed to keep their Irish surnames.[22] Their retention of their Irish family names is always emphasized in both English and French language recollections of the arrival of Quebec's Famine orphans in 1847.[23] Indeed, this cultural memory is so widely shared that author Suzanne Aubry could cast her eponymous orphan protagonist Fanette's would be benefactor—in the first of seven novels—as a false protector simply because "she couldn't remember [her family name] and said that orphans don't need one anyway!" Later, the heroine's newly adoptive mother insists that "you will keep your family name, Fanette O'Brennan,"[24] and thereby confirms her rightful place in the French-Canadian family and society at large.

And yet, as Mark McGowan makes clear in this volume, the majority of Irish Famine orphans in Quebec became child laborers rather than cherished members of the family. Moreover, even when the orphans were genuinely loved as blood relations, their stories did not always end happily. For instance, Jason King tracks the return journey of Robert Walsh from Quebec, where he lost his parents in 1847, back to Ireland in 1872, where he went in search of his baby sister who had been left behind. "My sister, my dear sister, if she exists," he had written in 1857, "when she would learn that she has a brother and sisters in Canada who are thinking of her she would write to them... We will see then we are not alone in the world, and it is this thought that will give us courage to endure our separation here."[25] Walsh never found her and died soon after his journey had ended in failure. Koral LaVorgna's remarkable study of the education of Irish Famine orphans in Saint John, New Brunswick, provides a different insight into how children fared in institutions outside of Ireland. Clearly, the experience of child emigrants in Canada was often harrowing in spite of the orphans' myth, but it was diverse as the chapters by LaVorgna,

McGowan and King all demonstrate. South of the Canadian border also, thousands of Irish American orphans were a legacy of the mass exodus. The reception given to a number of these children who were fortunate enough to be taken into care, has been explored in our sister volume, *Women and the Great Hunger*.[26] Regardless of these pioneering studies, the fate of the majority of children who left Ireland during the Great Hunger remains largely unexplored, but as all of these chapters suggest, there are many primary sources waiting to be located and mined.

Outside of institutions, what happened to children who survived the rigors of emigration? Steve Butler's chapter on the writings of Mary Anne Sadlier provides an insight into how an idealized—and Catholic—interpretation of life in the new world was being created. These children of the Famine were the nationalist leaders of the future, and of a new nationalism that spread far beyond the island of Ireland. Commenting on Ireland, Declan Kiberd has argued that children were being fashioned into the inheritors and guardians of the nationalist cause, he suggesting that:

> Like the Americans of the same period, the Irish were not so much born as *made,* gathered around a few simple symbols, a flag, an anthem, a handful of evocative phrases. In the process, childhood—like Ireland itself—had to be reinvented as a zone of innocence, unsullied and intense, from which would emerge the free Irish protagonist.[27]

While the above examples are located within a Catholic narrative of the cultural influences on children of the Famine and subsequent decades, other forces were at work. Although not new, the Famine had unleashed a more intense program of Protestant proselytizing that cast a long shadow over the districts thus targeted.[28] Children were the main focus of the proselytizers, enticed by promises of food, education, employment and salvation. In the post-Famine decades, the work of the Protestant missions continued, although on a smaller scale and under attack from an emboldened and increasingly powerful Catholic church. Again, children were specially targeted, notably through the pages of *Erin's Hope: The Irish Church Missions' Juvenile Magazine*. Throughout the 1850s and 1860s, it used stories and anecdotes to promote the benefits of the missionary schools compared with the horrors of the "poor house" or education in a convent.[29] Clearly, children continued to be in the center of the battle for hearts and souls in Ireland, and further afield.[30]

The interplay between memory, myth and folklore in regard to children and the Famine is explored in chapters by Eileen Moore Quinn and Salvador Ryan. Quinn explores how the Irish language was remembered, and forgotten, within America by the children and grand-children of Famine emigrants. Ryan brings to light a much under-used resource, that is, the Irish Folklore Collection held in University College, Dublin.[31] Of special interest is the Schools' Folklore Collection, an innovative project that was carried out between 1937 and 1939, in what was then called the Free State. This scheme put schoolchildren at the heart of collecting and thus preserving the memories of the Famine, or as survivors often termed it, *an drochshaol*. Ryan expertly explores a number of these stories, while explaining why folk memory—even at a distance of time—is important.

Unfortunately, it is not known what the impact of acting as chroniclers of the Famine had on the Irish schoolchildren in the 1930s. They, however, would having been reaching adulthood at the centenary of the first appearance of the potato blight in 1945. Although this anniversary resulted in a scholarly volume, commissioned by Éamon de Valera (which appeared belated in 1956),[32] and an art exhibition in Dublin, academic interest in this topic remained muted in the decades that followed. However, a powerful, if largely forgotten, legacy of the centenary was a number of visual representations created in honor of the anniversary of the Hunger. This included "Gorta" by Lucy Davidson in 1946, also known as "Burying the Child," which captures some of the unspeakable agony of losing a child.[33] According to art historian, Niamh Ann Kelly:

> The wretchedness of the figures, the burnt grass, the images' shadowy tones
> and cheerless palette reflect on the grim scenario depicted. A tiny bundle of an

infant prematurely dead from Famine is wrapped in a brown woolen blanket, and is about to be buried. The grief stricken family have created a grave in an open countryside. There is no cemetery or plot marker; the place is unremarkable; perhaps it is the site of a *cillin,* an unconsecrated burial ground for unbaptized children and people on society's margins. For this child there is no ceremonial shroud, no mourning neighbours, no keeners, no grave-diggers.[34]

One hundred years after the Famine, the death of a child remained one of the most evocative reminders of its inhumanity and horror.

Regardless of the interest shown in commemorating the 100th anniversary of the Famine, the scholarly silence on this topic remained. Not even Cecil Woodham-Smith's powerful, and provocative, *The Great Hunger,* published in 1962, could ignite interest.[35] It was not until the sesquicentenary that both scholarly and popular interest in the Famine exploded—with little signs of diminishing over 20 years later. One of the outcomes of this revival of interest was a fresh engagement with how to teach the Famine in schools. Again, this debate was not confined to Ireland, with educators in the U.S. often leading the way. Maureen Murphy's chapter on the introduction of the Famine Curriculum in New York, which includes examples of some of the lessons, provides a fascinating glimpse into the pedagogical and practical considerations that shaped this curriculum. The approach taken by Murphy and her colleagues was to see the Great Famine—and all famines—as rooted in issues of social justice. In this way, one of the greatest tragedies of the 19th century, becomes relevant to young people across the globe in the 21st century.

If children, like women, have suffered from scholarly neglect in regard to Irish Famine studies, they have been at the center of creative writing directed at children and usually centered on children. One of the most successful and talented of this generation of writers is Marita Conlan-McKenna who took time out of her own writing schedule to provide a Foreword reflecting on the chapters in this volume. Conlon-McKenna also features in the chapter by Robert Young, a Librarian at Quinnipiac University, which, within its Great

Hunger collections, holds a corpus of Children's Literature relating to this topic. Young explores how the writing of youth fiction has changed over the decades, partly mirroring the growth of scholarship on children's literature and the Great Hunger. The volume concludes with an original piece of writing by novelist, Michael Collins, exploring how a writer finds his "voice" when tackling a topic such as the Famine. In this chapter, Collins gives a sense of the differentiation between the sensibilities of writers versus that of historians.

Class, religion, gender and location all played a part in how people experienced, died or survived during the Great Hunger. Age was also a key factor. Children, the most vulnerable group in any crisis, were afforded little additional protection in the cauldron of suffering that existed in Ireland between 1845 and 1852. Those who survived shaped not only post-Famine Ireland, but societies much farther afield. The chapters that follow tell some of their stories. They reveal the richness of sources available even, as Jonny Geber shows, literally beyond the grave.

NOTES

1. In the U.S., Childhood, or Children's, Studies were generally thought to have originated in Brooklyn College, part of the University of the City of New York, in 1991.
2. The Network was established by the committee members of the History of Irish Childhood Conference in St. Patrick's College, Drumcondra, Dublin, in June 2014.
3. See notification of conference to be held by the Network in 2018: irishchildhood .wordpress.com/2017/11/03/cfp-centuries-of-childhood-dcu–2018/, accessed 15 February 2018.
4. Maria Luddy and James Smith (eds), *Children, childhood and Irish society, 1500 to the present* (Dublin: Four Courts Press, 2014).
5. Phelim P. Boyle and Cormac Ó Gráda, 'Fertility Trends, Excess Mortality and the Great Irish Famine,' in *Demography,* vol. 23, 4 (November 1986), pp. 543–562.
6. Margaret Kelleher, *The Feminization of Famine: Expressions of the Inexpressible?* (Durham: Duke University Press, 1997).

7. See Chapter 12 by Robert Young.

8. The work of Daniel Macdonald (1820–53), curated by Niamh O'Sullivan, was exhibited at Ireland's Great Hunger Museum in 2016.

9. 'Le Typhus' is installed in the ceiling at the entrance to Notre-Dame-De-Bonsecours Church in Montreal.

10. This image of the Famine was the central feature of Ireland's Great Hunger Institute exhibition, 'Saving the famine Irish. The Grey Nuns of Montreal' curated by Christine Kinealy and Jason King, which opened at Quinnipiac University in 2015 and, at the time of publication of this volume, is on display at the Russell Library in Maynooth University. Also see, Jason King, 'Mortuary Spectacles: The Genealogy of the Images of the Famine Irish Coffin Ship and Montreal's Fever Sheds,' in Marguérite Corporaal, Oonagh Frawley, and Emily Mark-Fitzgerald (eds), *The Great Irish Famine: Visual and Material Cultures* (Liverpool: Liverpool University Press, 2018), pp. 88–110.

11. Denis C. O'Connor, *Seventeen years' experience of workhouse life: with suggestions for reforming the poor law and its administration* (Dublin, 1861), p. 48.

12. Asenath Nicholson, *Annals of the Famine in Ireland in 1847, 1848 and 1849* (New York: E. French, 1851), pp. 82–83.

13. *Eighth Report from the Select Committee on Poor Laws (Ireland),* HC 1849 (237), xv, p. 40, q. 6503.

14. For more on the Temporary Relief Act, or Soup Kitchen Act, see Christine Kinealy, *A Death-Dealing Famine* (London: Pluto Press, 1997).

15. According to Declan Kiberd, 'The manipulation of childhood by sentimental Victorians was just another example of such functional hypocrisy,' *Inventing Ireland*, p. 104.

16. Fiona Dukelow, Mairéad Considine, *Irish Social Policy. A Critical Introduction* (Dublin: Gill and MacMillan, 2009), p. 307.

17. These young females were explored in a chapter in *Women and the Great Hunger* and in the Emmy-winning documentary 'The Great Hunger and the Irish Diaspora' both by Rebecca Abbott.

18. 'The Kerry workhouse girls who became Australian pioneers,' *Irish Times*, 1 December 2014; 'Some 4,000 Irish girls sent to Australia under orphan scheme,' *Irish Times*, 10 August 2016.

19. See Jason King, 'The Famine Irish, the Grey Nuns, and the Fever Sheds of Montreal: Prostitution and Female Religious Institution Building,' in Christine Kinealy, Jason King, and Ciarán Reilly (eds), *Women and the Great Hunger* (Hamden, Connecticut:

Quinnipiac University Press and Cork: Cork University Press, 2016), pp. 95–108; Jason King, "The Remembrance of Irish Famine Migrants in the Fever Sheds of Montreal," in Marguerite Corporaal, Christopher Cusack, Lindsay Janssen and Ruud van den Beuken (Eds.), *Global Legacies of the Great Irish Famine. Transnational and Interdisciplinary Perspectives* (Bern: Peter Lang, 2014), pp. 245–266; Jason King, Irish Famine Archive, faminearchive.nuigalway.ie, accessed 23 March 2018.

20. oireachtas.ie/viewdoc.asp?fn=/documents/addresses/2Feb1995.htm, accessed 23 March 2018.

21. John Francis Maguire, *The Irish in America* (Montreal and New York: D. & J. Sadlier, 1868), p. 148.

22. See Jason King, "Remembering Famine Orphans: The Transmission of Famine Memory between Ireland and Quebec," in Chris Noack, Lindsay Janssen and Vincent Comerford (eds.), *Holodomor and Gorta Mór: Histories, Memories and Representations of Famine in Ukraine and Ireland* (London: Anthem Press, 2012), pp. 115–144.

23. See Jason King, 'Staging Famine Irish Memories of Migration and National Performance in Ireland and Québec,' *CLCWeb: Comparative Literature and Culture* 18.4 (2016): pp. 1–8. Available at: doi.org/10.7771/1481–4374.2907.

24. Suzanne Aubry, *Fanette (Volume I): Uptown Conquest* (*Fanette – Ā la conquête de la haute ville*, 2008). Translated by Martina O'Brennan. Montreal: O'Brennan Publications, 2015. Location 824, 995.

25. Archives du Séminaire de Nicolet, F091/B1/5/2 & F091/B1/5/3. Translated by Jason King.

26. In *Women and the Great Hunger*, Turlough McConnell explores the fate of the children looked after by Sisters of Charity in New York. See Christine Kinealy, Jason King and Ciarán Reilly, *Women and the Great Hunger* (Quinnipiac University Press and Cork University Press, 2016), pp. 185–192.

27. Declan Kiberd, 'Childhood and Ireland' in *Inventing Ireland. The Literature of the Modern Nation* (Harvard University Press, 1996), pp. 101–102.

28. See Christine Kinealy, *Charity and the Great Hunger* (London: Bloomsbury, 2013), chapter twelve.

29. Lauren Clark, 'Gendering the Irish Child reader as buyer,' in *Journal of Historical Research in Marketing*, vol. 6, issue 1, 8–28, pp.15–16. Available at: doi.org/10.1108/JHRM–07–2013–0036, accessed 4 March 2018.

30. By the final decades of the 19th century, the battle had become more one-sided in favor of a cultural nationalism that was generally Catholic. In the 1880s, the largest

children's association was the Irish Fireside Club, which had its origins as a news-paper column in the *Weekly Freeman*. The Club lasted from 1887 to 1924. See Ríona Nic Congáil, '"Fiction, Amusement, Instruction": The Irish Fireside Club and the Educational Ideology of the Gaelic League,' in *doras.dcu.ie/21565/1/115*. Available at: file:///C:/Users/aoife/AppData/Local/Temp/115_SCAN-1.pdf, accessed 7 March 2018.

31. Drawing on information in the Folklore Archive, one of the strongest chapters in the 1956 publication by R.D. Edwards and T.D. Williams was by Roger McHugh, 'The Famine in Irish Oral Tradition,' R. Dudley Edwards and Desmond Williams (eds), *The Great Famine: Studies in Irish History 1845–52* (Dublin: Browne and Nolan, 1962), pp. 404–405. McHugh (1908–1987) was a professor of English at University College, Dublin. He was one of the first scholars to make use of the oral history memories of the Famine from a questionnaire circulated in 1945 to collect the oral traditions of the Famine.

32. A lively account of the vicissitudes that accompanied the publication of Edwards and Williams's, *The Great Famine*, cited above, is provided in Cormac Ó Gráda's, 'Making History in Ireland in the 1940s and 1950s: the saga of the Great Famine,' in *The Irish Review*, No. 12 (Spring/Summer 1992).

33. This painting is currently owned by Quinnipiac University and displayed at Ireland's Great Hunger Museum in Hamden.

34. Niamh Ann Kelly, *Ultimate Witnesses: The Visual Culture of Death, Burial and Mourning in Famine Ireland* (Hamden, CT: Quinnipiac University Press and Cork: Cork University Press, 2017), p. 7.

35. For more on Woodham-Smith's contribution to the historiography, and the reasons why she was largely shunned by the Irish academic community, see Kinealy, '"Never Call Me a Novelist": Cecil Woodham-Smith and the Great Hunger,' in Kinealy, King and Reilly, *Women and the Great Hunger,* pp. 15–36.

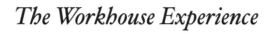

The Workhouse Experience

CHAPTER ONE

ATTENUATED APPARITIONS OF HUMANITY

The innocent casualties of the Great Hunger

Christine Kinealy

Pale mothers, wherefore weeping? 'Would to God that we were dead,
Our children swoon before us, and we cannot give them bread!'
Little children, tears are strange upon your infant faces,
God meant you but to smile within your mother's soft embraces.
'Oh! we know not what is smiling, and we know not what is dying;
But we're hungry, very hungry, and we cannot stop our crying.
And some of us grow cold and white—we know not what it means;
But as they lie beside us we tremble in our dreams.'[1]

In any famine, the elderly and the young are two of the most vulnerable groups. This situation was no different during the Great Hunger when children under the age of 10 and people aged 60 and over were disproportionately represented amongst the Famine dead. Although these two groups only accounted for one-third of the population, they represented over 60 percent of Famine deaths.[2] There were a number of reasons. Pregnant and nursing mothers were particularly susceptible to fluctuations in food availability, leading to high infant mortality.[3] In addition to lack of food, depleted energy levels made personal hygiene more difficult to maintain, which, in turn, led to increased infections.[4] It also meant "poorer childcare, less effective care for the ill and the elderly, and possibly less fuel and clean water, all of which relied on physical effort."[5] Young children were vulnerable to diarrhea, intensified by the lack of proper hydration. In Ireland, the winter of 1846 to 1847 was one of the coldest for a century, with snow falling as late as April. Yet, descriptions of children repeatedly show them as being dressed in rags or being almost naked. Seeking relief in a workhouse provided little protection. The doctor in Castlerea workhouse in County Roscommon, for example, lamented the lack of "warm clothing and shoes…for the children—the cold in the feet having a great effect in producing dysentery."[6] Appeals were generally ignored. This chapter examines a number of accounts describing the condition of children after 1845 and asks why so little was done to help these innocent casualties of the Great Hunger.

Even before the Famine, attitudes toward the Irish poor had been grounded in the belief that their poverty was due to indolence, not circumstance. George Nicholls, the English Poor Law Commissioner who was responsible for overseeing the introduction of a Poor Law to Ireland, showed little sympathy during a brief visit to the country in 1836, reporting to his superiors in London:

> The Irish peasantry generally have an appearance of apathy and depression … their cabins are slovenly, smoky, dirty, almost without furniture, or any article of convenience or common decency. On entering a cottage, the women and children are seen seated on the floor surrounded by pigs and poultry, the man is lounging at the door, which can only be approached through mud and filth. Yet he is too indolent to make a dry approach to his dwelling.[7]

The Irish Poor Law of 1838 was therefore designed with the intention of not just relieving destitution, but of bringing about social transformation in Ireland. After 1846, many of the relief policies introduced by the British government shared the same aim of moral reform and social regeneration.[8]

The 1838 legislation said relatively little in regard to destitute children, categorizing them along with "destitute poor persons as by reason of old age, infirmity, or defect may be unable to support themselves."[9] However, no special provision was made for children in regard to their treatment within the workhouses, except that children were compelled to attend the workhouse school. A child was deemed to be somebody under the age of 15. At Nicholls's insistence, as had been the case with legislation introduced in England during the reign of Elizabeth I, the Irish Poor Law required that parents should support their children, and that children should support their parents.[10] In keeping with this, only complete family units, not individuals, could enter a workhouse. By 1845, 118 of the 130 workhouses planned for Ireland were open and admitting paupers. The harsh regime within these institutions, based on strict regimentation and classification, and the separation of families by gender and by age, meant that few of the poor availed themselves of this form of relief.

Frederick Douglass, who was visiting Ireland at the end of 1845, was no stranger to hardship. He had escaped from slavery at the age of 20, fleeing to the northern states of America. However, as a "fugitive" slave, he remained in danger of recapture and return to slavery, hence his journey to Ireland and Britain where he would be safe. Douglass stayed in Ireland from the end of August 1845 to the beginning of January 1846. He was appalled by the poverty that he observed, even in the vicinity of Dublin, likening the conditions he witnessed as being similar to those on slave plantations. He was especially shocked by the state of Irish women and children, describing the former as being:

> ... barefooted and bareheaded, and only covered by rags which seemed to be held together by the very dirt and filth with which they were covered—many of these had infants in their arms, whose emaciated forms, sunken eyes and pallid checks, told too plainly that they had nursed till they had nursed in vain.[11]

Douglass went on to say:

> The spectacle that affected me most, and made the most vivid impression on my mind, of the extreme poverty and wretchedness of the poor in Dublin, was the frequency with which I met little children in the street at a late hour of the night, covered with filthy rags, and seated upon cold stone steps, or in corners, leaning against brick walls, fast asleep, with none to look upon them, none to care for them. If they have parents, they have become vicious, and have abandoned them. Poor creatures! They are left without help, to find their way through a frowning world—a world that seems to regard them as intruders, and to be punished as such. God help the poor![12]

While Douglass's visit coincided with the first appearance of potato blight, at this stage nobody realized that its reappearance in 1846 would turn the food shortages into a devastating famine.

The impact of the second potato failure was swift and deadly, as it impacted on a population already worn down by one year of shortages. In the summer of 1846, Sir Robert Peel, leader of the Conservative Party, resigned as prime minister. He was replaced by Lord John Russell, a weak leader who came into power at the head of a minority government. Regardless of the greater need of the Irish poor as they faced a second year of food shortages, the new Whig government made relief provisions more stringent and dependent on carrying out hard, physical labor.

Public works had first been introduced by Peel's government. They were re-introduced by the Whig government in August 1846, but with harsher conditions attached. Wages were deliberately kept below local wage rates, despite rising food prices, while payment was based on piece-work, thus penalizing those who were already weak. Although originally intended to provide employment for men, one of the consequences of the low wages was that women and children sought employment on the works, despite the fact that they received even lower wages than men. One report from Fermanagh stated that the only people employed on the works were either young boys or feeble men, who were only able to work for half a day.[13]

As news of the suffering in Ireland spread, with newspapers throughout the world carrying graphic reports of the distress of the Irish poor,[14] a massive international fundraising project got underway.[15] A number of philanthropists visited the country in person to give relief. One of the first groups of outsiders to traverse the west of Ireland was the Society of Friends, or Quakers. They included the veteran English Quaker, William Forster, who travelled with Joseph Crosfield, a young Quaker from Liverpool, and 27-year-old James Hack Tuke from Yorkshire.[16] Writing in December 1846, Forster expressed his shock at the condition of the children who:

> exhibit the effects of famine in a remarkable degree, their faces looking wan and haggard with hunger, and seeming like old men and women. Their sprightliness is entirely gone, and they may be seen sitting in groups by the cabin doors, making no attempt to play or to run after the carriages.[17]

Forster's reaction was mirrored in the correspondence of a number of relief officials. Captain Wynne, writing from west Clare in December 1846, informed his superiors that:

> Although a man not easily moved, I confess myself unmanned by the extent and intensity of suffering I witnessed, more especially amongst the women and little children, crowds of whom were to be seen scattering over the turnip fields, like a flock of famishing crows, devouring the raw turnips, mothers half naked, shivering in the snow and sleet, uttering exclamations of despair, whilst their children were screaming with hunger. I am a match for anything else I may meet here, but this I cannot stand.[18]

Regardless of Wynne's private compassion, he subsequently gained a reputation for ruthlessly cutting people from relief lists, thus adding to mortality throughout Clare.[19]

Following the first appearance of blight, the Poor Law had been kept distinct from the special relief introduced, Peel's government wanting to draw a line between ordinary and extraordinary relief. Following the second failure, such distinctions became blurred as the poor flocked to their local workhouses. Under the terms of the 1838 legislation, however, relief could only be provided within the confines of the workhouses and their total capacity was for 100,000 inmates. Even when a workhouse became full, outdoor relief was not permitted. However, the lowness of the wages on the public works threw pressure on the workhouses—pressure that they, in turn, could not meet. At the beginning of February 1847, the inspecting officer for Leitrim made a heart-rending plea for a food depot to be established in the town. In the preceding week, 30 people had died in the local workhouse. Moreover, "Two cartloads of children, whose parents died from starvation I suppose, were sent to the poor-house but could not be taken in, the fever prevailing to such a dreadful extent there."[20] There is no record of what happened to these orphans. Crosfield observed a similar case occurring in the Carrickmacross workhouse when the Board of Guardians were considering applications for admission:

> A most painful and heart-rending scene presented itself; poor wretches in the last stages of famine imploring to be received into the house; women who had six or seven children, begging that even two or three of them might be taken in, as their husbands were earning but 8d. per day; which, at the present high price of provisions, was totally inadequate to feed them. Some of the children were worn to skeletons, their features sharpened with hunger, and their limbs wasted almost to the bone.[21]

Because only whole family units could be admitted to the workhouses, regardless of the palpable need and suffering of many children, they could not receive any relief from the Poor Law.[22]

William Bennett was one of the many English Quakers who became involved in providing relief. While most of the activities of the Society of Friends was aimed at establishing soup kitchens or distributing much-needed clothing, bedding and fuel to the poor, Bennett directed his energies to providing them with "small seed," in order to help in their longer-term survival. Bennett landed in Ireland in the spring of 1847, accompanied by his eldest son, with the intention of "touring the worst-hit areas." Their arrival coincided with the closing of the public works, which had left many people with no means of support. During this hiatus in relief provision, private charity provided a vital lifeline to the poor.[23] Unfortunately, Bennett's visit also coincided with an unusually hard and prolonged winter, with recurring frost and snow adding to the suffering of the poor.[24] Initially, Bennett had intended to visit only counties Mayo and Donegal but he decided to extend his stay and travel to counties Tipperary and Kerry.

Bennett published a narrative of his visit, which was composed of letters written to his sister in London, who herself was a member of the Ladies' Irish Clothing Committee.[25] Bennett's book was published only four months after his return to England. The income from sales was to be used for "Irish relief," while he hoped the contents would encourage more donations to be sent to Ireland.[26] Despite the health risks, Bennett had visited the homes of the sick and dying. As the following extract shows, it was not always possible to identify gender:

> We entered a cabin. Stretched in one dark corner, scarcely visible, from the smoke and rags that covered them, were three children huddled together, lying there *because they were too weak to rise,* pale and ghastly, their little limbs—on removing a portion of the filthy covering—perfectly emaciated, eyes sunk, voice gone, and evidently in the last stage of actual starvation. Crouched over the turf embers was another form, wild and all but naked, scarcely human in appearance. It stirred not, nor noticed us.[27]

Bennett returned to the state of the children on a number of occasions:

> Perhaps the poor children presented the most piteous and heartrending spectacle. Many were too weak to stand, their little limbs attenuated,—except where the frightful swellings had taken the place of previous emaciation,— beyond the *power of volition when moved.*

Unusually, Bennett was one of few observers to name those whom he witnessed. When he and his son visited the island of Arranmore off the coast of Donegal, an island that contained approximately 1,500 inhabitants, he identified multiple families and children who were in a desperate situation, including:

> Widow Mooney, with five orphans—her husband and one child had been buried the day before our visit. That they died of starvation we readily believed, as the widow asserted there had not been *any food whatever* in the house for several days. The children, even under their fresh affliction, presented a gaunt, unmeaning, vacant stare, characteristic of inanition; their very lips having become blanched and shrivelled from prolonged destitution.[28]

And:

> Edward Gallagher, of Leabgarrow, whose family consisted of six, had his arm broken. The appearance of the children was wonderfully similar; their prominent jaw-bones and sunken cheeks fearfully indicating the progress of starvation. A very sickly infant sat up in its cot, whilst we remained in the house; the face was deadly pale; it was endeavouring, with a beseeching look and melancholy whine, to attract the attention of its anxious mother, who was heedless to it for a moment, in her anxiety to secure our sympathy for her famishing offspring. Long will it be ere the anguish of that infant's languid eye, expressive only of mortal agony, will fade from our memory.[29]

In 1846, Elihu Burritt, "the learned blacksmith" from Connecticut, had travelled to Europe to promote world peace. Like many who had read of the extreme suffering in Skibbereen and its environs, he felt compelled to visit west Cork and view the suffering first-hand. He spent three days in Skibbereen at the end of February 1847, but when he became ill, he departed immediately. His account, which he published, however, conveys his own sense of general horror and the fact that he was unprepared for what he saw despite having read newspaper accounts. Burritt provided a poignant account of a man trying to provide for his seven small children by taking them to the nearest food depot, which offers an insight into the difficulties of obtaining relief even when it had been made available. In order to make it to the depot, "the miserable skeleton of a father had fastened his youngest child to his back, with four more by his side." On arrival, he had "staggered up to the door, just as we entered the bread department of the establishment." The father was clearly ill, "The hair upon his face was nearly as long as that upon his head. His cheeks were fallen in, and his jaws so distended that he could scarcely articulate a word," but it was the condition of the children that bothered Burritt most:

> His four little children were sitting upon the ground by his feet, nestling together, and trying to hide their naked limbs under their dripping rags. How these poor things could stand upon their feet and walk, and walk five miles, as they had done, I could not conceive. Their appearance, though common to thousands of the same age in this region of the shadow of death, was indescribable. Their paleness was not that of common sickness. There was no sallow tinge in it. They did not look as if newly raised from the grave and to life before the blood had begun to fill their veins anew; but as if they had just been thawed out of the ice, in which they had been imbedded until their blood had turned to water.[10]

While the extreme thinness of children was frequently commented on, the impact of starvation could affect the body in other ways by causing a painful swelling.[31] This unnatural bloating was witnessed by Burritt:

> The cold, watery-faced child was entirely naked in front, from his neck down to his feet. His body was swollen to nearly three times its usual size, and had burst the ragged garment that covered him, and now dangled in shreds behind him.[32]

Burritt admitted that the vision of the child continued to "haunt" him, "like Banquo's ghost."[33] If Burritt, having spent only three days in Skibbereen, felt thus haunted, how did other eyewitnesses and survivors ever rid themselves of similar ghastly specters?[34]

The swelling also was commented on by a number of relief officials. One Poor Law inspector reporting from County Sligo on "extreme destitution" noted:

> The children were bloated in their faces and bodies, their limbs were withered to bones and sinews, with rags on them which scarcely preserved decency, and assuredly afforded no protection from the weather. *They had been found that day, gnawing the flesh from the bones of a pig which had died in an out-house.*[35]

As a system of providing emergency relief, the public works failed on a number of levels. They did not save lives and they exacerbated the deteriorating condition of the poor. From the government's perspective they were both bureaucratic and expensive; therefore, in January 1847, a decision was made to close them in spring and instead to make an extended Poor Law responsible for all relief in Ireland. From a British perspective, the attraction of doing this was that the Poor Law was financed by local poor rates, meaning that all relief would be financed from Irish taxation. The amended Poor Law was to become operative in August 1847 and, in the intervening period following the closure of the public works, a Temporary Relief Act was introduced. The Temporary Relief Act, or Soup Kitchen Act, was one of the most successful measures introduced during the Famine, at its height providing more than three million people a day with free rations of food. Children received half rations.[36] It was a tremendous logistic feat that demonstrated the ability of the British government to provide relief, and to do so relatively cheaply. Unfortunately for the Irish poor, giving gratuitous relief—even to children—was deemed to be ideologically unacceptable.

The food provided in the government's soup kitchens required that all recipients had to attend in person with the exception of "the sick, the impotent, and children under nine years of age."[37] Children over this age had to walk to the nearest depot and then to queue, sometimes for hours. Nonetheless, in July 1847 when the demand for soup peaked, 3,020,712 persons received separate rations, of whom 2,265,534 were adults and 755,178 were children.[38] Children, therefore, represented one-third of the recipients of this type of relief. Following the harvest of 1847, the Poor Law, which had been amended to allow outdoor relief, became responsible for saving the lives of the Irish poor. As the chapter by Gerard Moran demonstrates, it was children who were the most vulnerable group in this reconfigured system of relief.

The change to Poor Law relief following the harvest of 1847 was to have a detrimental impact on a population facing its third consecutive year of food shortages. The new legislation included the draconian Quarter Acre Clause, which deemed that no person who occupied more than one-quarter of an acre of land was eligible to receive relief.[39] This forced people who had survived the first two years of famine to make the painful decision to relinquish their homes and holdings if they wanted to obtain relief for their families. No special provision was made for children and the transfer to Poor Law relief did not protect them either inside or outside the workhouses. Moreover, by increasing the level of poor rates, it provided an added incentive to landlords to evict their poorest tenants. Evictions were one of the cruelest aspects of the latter stages of the Famine. Children were generally present, one sympathetic observer commenting that "the children screamed with agony at seeing their homes destroyed and their parents in tears."[40] A similar remark was made by a priest who witnessed approximately 700 people being evicted and their homes destroyed in one day in County Cavan. He noted it was accompanied by, 'the wails of women, the screams of children, the agony of men'.[41] The next day, the priest administered the last rites to four of the homeless.

Could more have been done to help children? An example of a successful system of providing relief to young people that was both practical and efficacious was pioneered by Pawel de Strzelecki of the British Association for the Relief of Distress in Ireland and the Highlands of Scotland.[42] Strzelecki, a Polish explorer, had volunteered his services to the newly formed Association at the beginning of 1847. He immediately travelled to Westport in County Mayo, his journey hindered by heavy snowfalls. On arrival, he informed the London Committee that:

No pen can describe the distress by which I am surrounded. It has actually reached such a degree of lamentable extreme that it becomes above the power of exaggeration and misapprehension. You may now believe anything you hear and read, because what I actually see surpasses whatever I read of past and present calamities.[43]

Strzelecki also informed them that:

Of the fate, gloomy and awful, which overhangs the whole population, that of the poor children, and the babies at the breasts of their emaciated and enervated mothers, excites the deepest feelings of commiseration.[44]

Two months later, Strzelecki was joined by Mathew Higgins, who based himself in Belmullet in north Mayo. Higgins found the streets "full of people in a dying state." Like his colleague, he was deeply affected by the plight of the children but realized that he had to manage his limited resources. Nonetheless, he informed the London committee:

I cannot express to you how painful it is to witness the wretched children, actually expiring in the streets, and to be disbarred from assisting them; but if I were to do so once, I could not walk around the town.[45]

Strzelecki was aware that children were particularly defenseless and "in the general run and scramble for food have been left behind," and he was determined to do something practical on their behalf. He also wanted to protect them "from the afflicting scenes in which they have been partly spectators, partly actors."[46] In spring 1847, Strzelecki pioneered a system of feeding schoolchildren in the Westport Union. Under his scheme, 1,460 children aged between 5 and 14 were provided with new clothing and one meal a day. Moreover, the local supervisors were "requested to require that water, towels, soap, and combs are provided at each school at which relief is afforded, and that no children be allowed to partake of this ration without having first well washed."[47] The scheme was an immediate success, winning praise in the local press, and not only helping the children, but taking pressure off parents who no longer had to share their scant resources. Moreover, the emphasis put on cleanliness was important in protecting the children from disease.

The success of the scheme against a backdrop of the chaos and suffering resulting from the change to Poor Law relief, led Strzelecki in October 1847 to request permission to extend the project to other areas. This was granted, the London Committee, acting under the guidance of the British Treasury, receiving permission to extend the schools scheme to the 22 unions that had been officially declared to be "distressed" by the government.[48] By the end of the year, the schools scheme was operating in unions from Skibbereen in County Cork to Glenties in County Donegal; for the next seven months, over 200,000 children received free rations of food daily, and were appropriately clothed.[49] In recognition that his funding would dry up by the end of summer 1848, Strzelecki made a personal appeal to the prime minister to continue with the schools project. Although Russell agreed to do so, the decision was overturned by Charles Trevelyan, the chief civil servant at the Treasury, who argued that the scheme fell outside the scope of government relief.[50] Consequently, the scheme came to an end in August 1848. In this same year, Trevelyan was knighted for his services to the Irish poor and he received a salary bonus of £2,500 for his "extraordinary labours during that trying time."[51] Strzelecki, in contrast, refused to accept any payment for the work that he had done in Ireland. He was knighted some months after Trevelyan, leading one London newspaper to aver that the Polish man's efforts on behalf of the Irish poor were "in no degree inferior to those of Mr Trevelyan." It further pointed out, "Moreover, they were voluntary and gratuitous, and they involved much personal danger and discomfort."[52] Strzelecki's scheme was an example of what could have been done on behalf of the poor children of Ireland. According to William O'Brien, writing in 1896, long after Strzelecki had passed away, within the west of the country, "The name of this benevolent stranger was then, and for long afterwards, a familiar one, if not a household word, in the homes of the suffering poor'.[53]

While the majority of visitors to Ireland had come in 1847 in the wake of the second potato failure, eyewitnesses from the later period were less usual. The *Illustrated London News,* however, sent a correspondent, the Cork-born artist, James Mahony, to the west of Ireland in both 1847 and again in 1849. In 1847, Mahony had been commissioned to visit Skibbereen and its environs— a district that had achieved a grim notoriety in the media for reports of suffering and starvation. The paper was unusual among the English press in that it expressed sympathy with the Irish poor. Moreover, because it was illustrated, the paper provided a view of the suffering through a visual medium, some of its images becoming the most iconic and recognizable representations of the Famine. "Boy and Girl at Cahera" and "Bridget O'Donnel and Children" depict young people whose wretchedness was apparent in their facial expressions, unkempt hair and the shapeless, torn clothing that barely covered them.[54]

At the end of 1849, the paper again sent a correspondent to the west of Ireland, initially to Kilrush in County Clare, an area that had by-passed Skibbereen in terms of the level of evictions and mortality. Interestingly, the article commenced by saying that the condition of Ireland had been rendered "considerably worse" by the implementation of the new Poor Law—an opinion that would not have been popular in England.[55] This viewpoint, however, had also been expressed by a number of independent observers who had given evidence before a parliamentary committee on the Irish Poor Laws in the same year.[56] Detailed text accompanied the illustrations. One report outlined the fate of a child, not named, but simply referred to as "Judy O'Donnel's son." It highlighted the cruelty of evictions:

> Two wretched families have taken refuge under the bridge in a hole. They consist of two widows, one with three children, all ill of jaundice, and the other with five. The history of Judy O'Donnel, one of the widows, is worthy of being sketched. She had given evidence against a dishonest relieving officer whose relative was a driver upon the estate on which she lived, and Judy's house was very soon afterwards levelled with the ground. The wreckers

came upon it in her absence, when her son gallantly defended his home. He mounted on the roof with a bag of stones, and kept the enemy at bay till his ammunition was exhausted, when he was obliged to give in, and stand by to see the little furniture of his mother cast into the road and the house pulled down. Judy exhibited her receipts for the rent up to the last gale; and she declared the agent of the owner, to whom she had tendered what was due twice, had refused, and that she was ejected because she deposed against the dishonest public servant. Judy and Margaret O'Donnel, with their families, then retired to the hole under the bridge, represented in the sketch, and there they are now suffered to remain, holding their habitation at the mercy of the county surveyor. They are afraid of being ejected even from this spot, and dare not cross the stepping-stones shown in the Sketch lest they should be taken up for trespassing. Judy O'Donnel's son is dying of dysentery.[57]

It is hard to imagine that the young boy, the more spirited defender of his mother, survived. The paper also provided an unusual view of the actions of another child—the young daughter of the local Poor Law inspector, Captain Kennedy.[58] Arthur Edward Kennedy had been born in County Down and after studying at Trinity College in Dublin commenced a career in the army.[59] He had returned to Ireland in 1846 and taken up an appointment with the Poor Law Commission. He was sent to County Clare in late 1847. Kennedy was appalled by what he found and set about improving the administration of the Poor Law. However, he realized that much of the suffering was caused by the heartlessness of local landlords—most notably Colonel Crofton Moore Vandeleur and Marcus Keane—who were carrying out wholesale evictions. Vandeleur was not only a major landowner, he was also Chairman of the Kilrush Poor Law Guardians. Kennedy's compassion was transmitted to his young daughter, who became the subject of both an illustration and a report in the *Illustrated London News*:

Miss Kennedy (about seven years old) is the daughter of Captain Kennedy, the Poor-law Inspector of the Kilrush Union. She is represented as engaged in her daily occupation of distributing clothing to the wretched children brought around her by their more wretched parents. In the front of the group I noticed one woman crouching like a monkey, and drawing around her the only rag she had left to conceal her nudity. A big tear was rolling down her cheek, with gratitude for the gifts the innocent child was distributing. The effect was heightened by the chilliness and dreariness of a November evening, and by the wet and mire in which the naked feet of the crowd were immersed. On Captain Kennedy being appointed to the Union, his daughter was much affected by the misery of the poor children she saw; and so completely did it occupy her thoughts, that, with the consent of her parents, she gave up her time and her own little means to relieve them. She gave away her own clothes—she was allowed to bestow part of her mother's— and she then purchased course materials, and made up clothing for children of her own age; she was encouraged by her father and some philanthropic strangers, from whom she received sums of money, and whose example will no doubt be followed by those who possess property in the neighbourhood; and she devoted herself with all the energy and perseverance of a mature and staid matron to the holy office she has undertaken. The Sketch will, I hope, immortalize the beneficent child, who is filling the place of a saint, and performing the duties of a patriot.

On all sides I hear praises of the amiable child and her excellent father, and this is not without a moral for the landlords. The public officers who are appointed to administer and control the relief of the poor, have it in their power to do much for the people.[60]

Despite these pointed and public criticisms of both the operation of the new Poor Law and the actions of local landlords in Kilrush, little changed and mortality continued to rise, at a time that the impact of the Famine was subsiding in other parts of the country. Writing to the Lord Lieutenant on the eve of Christmas 1849, the local parish priest, Father Kelly, reported that of the 2,000 people in the workhouse 900 were children, and all were "in a delicate frame and constitution." For the past week, both the old and the young only had turnips to eat.[61] Again, such public, heartfelt appeals appeared to make no difference in terms of relief policies. However, in 1850, at the insistence of the radical MP, George Poulett Scrope, a select committee was appointed to enquire into the local administration of the Poor Law in the Kilrush union. His report, presented to the House of Commons in July 1850, made it clear that children were subject to the same awful conditions in the local workhouse as adults:

> Hundreds of men, women and children, kept in close confinement in crowded yards, or still more densely crowded day rooms, in rags and filth by day, at night often naked; the straw of the beds not changed for months: packed together three or four in a bed, even when suffering from dysentery: sore feet, sore hands, sore heads, ophthalmia, contagious diseases, and vermin prevalent throughout: soap, and even water, often unattainable: filth and putrid effluvia visible everywhere, within and without the house. The meals so stinted and irregular, that some have to wait till midnight for what ought to have been their mid-day meal. The dietary tables ordered by the Commissioners as much disregarded as are the numbers which the houses are limited by them to contain; women of the worst character, and afflicted with the most loathsome diseases, herded with the hitherto uncontaminated daughters of the poor peasants; no discipline, or that of the stick in the crudest hands—scarcely any superintendence, owing to a false economy in official staff.[62]

Regardless of the compelling evidence provided by Kennedy and Poulett Scrope that the system of relief put in place by the British government in 1847 was failing to save lives, no changes were made in relief provision.

Not all visitors to Ireland during the Famine were sympathetic. Thomas Carlyle, the writer and philosopher, grudgingly visited Ireland in the summer of 1849. Although a supporter of the Union and an opponent of the Repeal movement, he travelled for much of the time in the company of Charles Gavan Duffy, formerly a supporter of O'Connell but one who had sided with Young Ireland. While journeying from Mayo to Sligo in July 1849, he had a visceral reaction to begging children, and to the fact that they were almost naked:

Potatoes,—poor cottier digging his little plot of them, three or four little children eagerly 'gathering' for him: pathetic to look upon. From one cottage on the way side, issue two children *naked* to beg; boy about 13, girl about 12, 'naked' literally, some sash of rag round middle, oblique-sash over shoulder to support that, stark-naked would have been *as* decent (if you had to jump and run as these creatures did) and much cleanlier. *Dramatic,* I take it, or partly so, *this* form of begging: *strip* for your parts, there is the car coming!' Gave them nothing.[63]

Carlyle's response is not surprising given his history of anti-Irish sentiment. In 1839, he had written:

The wild Milesian features, looking false ingenuity, restlessness, unreason, misery and mockery, salute you on all highways and byways. The English coachman, as he whirls past, lashes the Milesian with his whip, curses him with his tongue; the Milesian is holding out his hat to beg.[64]

It was, therefore, probably too much to expect that the presence of famine would soften his heart to the Irish condition.

This brief overview of children reveals many common themes in how they suffered during the Famine. Severe malnutrition made them susceptible to disease. They generally lacked clothes or bedding and frequently huddled together for warmth and comfort. Unfortunately, close body contact facilitated the transmission of disease. Parents, if not dead, were too ill to look after their children, or struggling for their own survival. Mass evictions left children homeless. Dead children were buried without the usual funeral rites. These children remain nameless. Overwhelmingly also, the children described remain ageless; most commentators were not able to determine their age. Overall, the condition of the Irish children shocked those who observed them. The many eyewitness accounts—by both private and public individuals—did not shy from giving grim details, while warning that the reality was even more shocking. And the reality was painful. Those who governed from London could not claim innocence or ignorance. Even Trevelyan, in a footnote to his self-satisfied account of the government's response to the Famine in *The Irish Crisis*, admitted that:

> All the letters and proceedings of these officers showed that their predominant feeling was an anxious desire to fulfil the benevolent mission on which they had been sent. One observed that he could bear anything but the 'careless misery of the children.'[65]

Yet, even when the men in power were armed with these dreadful accounts, policies did not change and the lives of children were not spared. Just as the Poor Law of 1838 had failed to make special provision for children, the various policies introduced after 1845 did not offer any additional protection to one of the most vulnerable groups during any period of food shortages.

Children in the 19th century were regarded as the responsibility of their parents, but who was responsible if those parents were ill, or destitute, had disappeared, or were dead? When families and communities had been destroyed, who was to fill this vacuum? Neither the public works nor the Poor Law were providing sufficient relief to keep people healthy. More shockingly, they were failing to save lives. Outside of those who perished in the workhouses, it is impossible to know precisely how many people died during the Famine and what proportion of them were children. Unofficial accounting suggests a horrendous story, with excess mortality being most prevalent among the young.[66] One report from Clonakilty parish in County Cork on 27 February 1847 stated that in the preceding week, 60 children and 30 adults had died through "want of sustenance," and that the number was increasing.[67]

When did the Famine end and the suffering of the children finish? There is no doubt that its impact continued after 1852, even after good harvests had returned to Ireland. Sustained emigration and the continued drop in population were two numerical indicators of its lasting impact. There are less quantifiable indicators. What was the effect of sustained malnutrition on the children's physical and mental development. What was the impact of such trauma on young minds? Charles Gavan Duffy, an Irish nationalist who witnessed the effects of the Famine in 1847, wrote:

> The famine swallowed things more precious than money or lives ... new and terrible diseases sprung up, and children were growing idiots ... In Connaught the famine created a new race with only a distant and hideous resemblance to humanity, and a traffic of wild, idle, lunatic looking paupers—women struggling for coin like monstrous and unclean animals. I saw these accursed sights and they are burned into my memory for ever.[68]

How much more did such sights affect children? Recent studies in the field of epigenetics has revealed the trans-generational consequences of famine and trauma—mental illness being one long-term legacy. It has also shown how far into the future these scars would reach, maybe as many as five generations.[69]

During the Great Famine, children were neither protected nor privileged in the various schemes introduced by the government or local elites. Consequently, they starved, they emigrated, or they died. Those who survived shaped post-Famine Ireland, but they had paid a heavy price for their survival.

NOTES

1. 'Speranza', 'The Famine Year,' *Nation,* 27 January 1847.
2. Margaret Kelleher, in M. McAuliffe, K. O'Donnell, L. Lane (eds) *Palgrave Advances in Irish History* (Basingstoke: Palgrave, 2009), p. 88.
3. S. Scott, S. R. Duncan, and C. J. Duncan, 'Infant mortality and famine: a study in historical epidemiology in northern England' in *Epidemiol Community Health,* June 1995, 49 (3): 245–252.
4. Joel Mockyr and Cormac Ó Gráda, 'Famine Disease and Famine Mortality: Lessons from Ireland, 1845–1850' (1999) p. 27. Available at: *pdfs.semanticscholar.org/498e /2d40caf5ebe67dfc422718a200112a488f79,* accessed 4 November 2017, pp. 22–23.
5. Ibid.

6. This example was cited by Daphne Wolf in her exploration of the impact of the lack of clothing "'Nearly Naked": Clothing and the Great Hunger in Ireland' in Christine Kinealy et al, *Women and the Great Hunger* (Quinnipiac University Press and Cork University Press, 2016), chapter six.

7. 'The Author's First Report', George Nicholls, *A History of the Irish Poor Law: in connexion with the condition of the People* (London: John Murray, 1856), p.162.

8. This idea of social transformation was discussed by Christine Kinealy in, *This Great Calamity. The Great Famine in Ireland* (Dublin: Gill and Macmillan, 2006).

9. 'An Act for the more effectual Relief of the Destitute Poor in Ireland', 1 & 2 Vic. c.56, 31 July 1838, section 41.

10. The legislation was the 43rd Elizabeth. Nicholls, *Irish Poor Law*, p. 178.

11. Frederick Douglass, Scotland, to William Lloyd Garrison, 26 February 1846, reprinted in the *Liberator,* 27 March 1846.

12. Ibid.

13. Extract from Journal of Captain Hancock, Inspecting Officer, for week ending 27 February 1847, in British Parliamentary Papers (BPP) *Correspondence from January to March 1847 Relating to the Measures Adopted for the Relief of Distress in Ireland*, Board of Works, Second Part, 1847, p. 187.

14. Michael Foley, *'Death in Every Paragraph'. Journalism and the Great Irish Famine* (Quinnipiac University Press and Cork University Press, 2015).

15. Christine Kinealy, *Charity and the Great Hunger. The Kindness of Strangers* (London: Bloomsbury, 2013).

16. William Forster (1784–1854) was a renowned philanthropist and abolitionist.

17. 'Extracts from Joseph Crosfield's Report of his Journey in company with William Forster', Carrick-on-Shannon, 6th of 12th Month, 1846, in *Transactions of the Society of Friends during the Famine in Ireland* (Dublin: Hodges and Figgis, 1852), p.146.

18. Captain Wynne to Lieutenant Colonel Jones, 24 December 1846, BPP, *Correspondence from July 1846 to January 1847 Relating to the Measures Adopted for the Relief of Distress in Ireland* (Board of Work Series, vol. 1, 1847), p. 466.

19. Ciarán Ó Murchadha, *Sable Wings Over the Land: Ennis, county Clare and its wider community during the great famine* (Ennis: Clasp Press, 1998).

20. Extract from the Journal of Mr Godby, Inspecting Officer, County Leitrim, for week ending 13 February 1847, BPP, Board of Works, Second Part, p. 270.

21. Extracts from Joseph Crosfield's Report, in *Transactions of the Society of Friends,* pp. 145–146.

22. For more on the inappropriateness of the Whig's relief measures see Kinealy, *This Great Calamity*, passim.

23. Kinealy, *Charity and the Great Hunger*, pp. 277–292.

24. From *Farmer's Gazette*, 'Effects of frost and snow on vegetation', in *Newry Telegraph*, 25 March 1847.

25. In 1846 and 1847, this committee raised £9,533–4–0. See *Transactions of ... the Society of Friends* (1852), p. 46.

26. William Bennett, *Narrative of a recent journey of six weeks in Ireland, in connexion with the subject of supplying small seed to some of the remoter districts: current observations on the depressed circumstances of the people, and the means presented for the permanent improvement of their social condition* (Dublin: Charles Gilpin, 1847), p. vii.

27. Ibid.

28. Ibid., Appendix, p. 170.

29. Ibid., p. 172.

30. Elihu Burritt, *A Journal of a Visit of Three Days to Skibbereen, and Its Neighbourhood* (London: Charles Gilpin, 1847), pp. 5–6.

31. Kwashiorkor, a form of severe malnutrition and protein deficiency, and characterized by swelling, was formally identified by the medical community in 1935. It could lead to death.

32. Burritt, *Three Days*, p. 10.

33. Ibid.

34. The most famous and eloquent survivor of the Holocaust, Primo Levi (1919–1987), wrote, 'till my ghastly tale is told, This heart within me burns' ('The Survivor,' 1984). He took his own life three years later.

35. Captain O'Brien to Lieutenant Col. Jones, 2 March 1847, BPP, Board of Works, Second Part, p. 180.

36. The nutritional value of a soup diet, as based on the recipes provided by the French society chef, Alexis Soyer, was debated at the time and subsequently. Queen Victoria's own physician, Sir Henry Marsh, argued that the soup diet was only suitable for children or sedentary adults. See, Ian Miller, 'The Chemistry of Famine: Nutritional Controversies and the Irish Famine, c.1845–7', *Medical History*, October 2012; 56 (4), pp. 444–462.

37. An Act for the temporary relief of destitute persons in Ireland, 10th Vic., c. 7. It received Royal Assent on 26 February 1847.

38. Charles Edward Trevelyan, *The Irish Crisis* (London: Longman, Brown, Green & Longmans, 1848), p. 88.

39. Also known as the Gregory Clause (after Sir William Gregory who had introduced it) the Clause was the 10th section of the Amended Poor Law of 1847.

40. *Illustrated London News*, 19 January 1850.

41. J. Arthur Partridge, *The Making of the Irish Nation: And the First-fruits of Federation* (London: T. Fisher Unwin, 1886), pp. 141–142.

42. The British Association for the Relief of Distress in Ireland and the Highlands of Scotland had been founded in London on 1 January 1847 by the Jewish banker and philanthropist, Lionel de Rothschild. It received over 15,000 individual donations from all over the world.

43. Minutes of British Relief Association (BRA), 1 February 1847, National Library of Ireland, MS 2024, p. 111.

44. Strzelecki, Westport, to London Committee, 29 January 1847, *Report of the British Relief Association for the Relief of Extreme Distress in Ireland and Scotland* (London: The Association, 1849), p. 92.

45. Report of Higgins, Belmullet, 8 April 1847, *Report of BRA*, p.111.

46. Strzelecki to the Committee of the BRA, BPP, *Papers Relating to ... unions and work houses in Ireland,* seventh series, 1848, p. 4.

47. Regulations regarding relief through schools, November 1847, appendix D, *Report of the BRA*, pp. 186–187.

48. Ibid.

49. *Report of the BRA*, p. 41.

50. Memorandum of Lord John Russell, National Archives of England, T. 64/367 B, 30 April 1848; Treasury Minute, 27 June 1848, *Report of the BRA*, p. 46.

51. *Morning Chronicle*, 28 November 1848.

52. Ibid.

53. W.P. O'Brien, *The Great Famine in Ireland; and a retrospect of the fifty years 1845–1895, with a sketch of the present condition and future prospects of the Congested Districts* (London: Downey, 1896), p. 190.

54. Margaret Crawford, 'The Great Irish Famine 1845–9: Image versus reality' in Raymond Gillespie and Brian P. Kennedy (eds), *Ireland: Art into History* (Dublin: Town House, 1994), p. 81.

55. 'Illustrations of the new Poor Law', *Illustrated London News*, 15 December 1849.

56. The argument that the amended Poor Law had matters worse was argued by both Strzelecki and Audrey de Vere in Seventh Report of the Select Committee on Poor Laws (Ireland), HC 1849 (194), xv.

57. *Illustrated London News*, 29 December 1849.

58. Captain Arthur Edward Kennedy (1810–1883) had commenced a career in the army in 1827 and served in Corfu and Canada. He sold his Commission in 1848. Following the Famine, he joined the colonial service, becoming governor of Gambia in 1851, in Sierra Leone in 1852, Western Australia in 1855, Vancouver Island in 1863, governor-in-chief of the West African Settlements in 1868, governor of Hong Kong in 1872, and of Queensland from 1877 to 1883, when he retired due to poor health. He had one son and two daughters.

59. For more on Kennedy and other key characters in County Clare during the Famine see Ciarán Ó Murchadha, *Figures in a Famine Landscape* (London: Bloomsbury, 2016).

60. 'Illustrations of the new Poor Law', *Illustrated London News*, 15 December 1849, p. 404.

61. Father Kelly to Lord Clarendon, the Lord Lieutenant of Ireland, 18 December 1849, reprinted as 'Starvation in Kilrush', *Freeman's Journal*, 24 December 1849.

62. George Poulett Scrope, *Draft report proposed to the select committee of the House of Commons on the Kilrush Union, 25 July 1850* (London: James Ridgway, 1850), pp. 10–11.

63. Monday, 30 July 1849, Thomas Carlyle, *Reminiscences of my Irish Journey* (London: Gilbert & Rivington, 1882), Carlyle wrote his reminiscences in October following his return to London.

64. Thomas Carlyle, *Chartism* (London: James Fraser, 1840). The pamphlet had first been published in December 1839.

65. Trevelyan, *Irish Crisis*, p. 103.

66. Extract from Journal of Captain Hutchinson, Inspecting Officer for Co. Galway, for week ending 7 February 1847, BPP, *Board of Works*, Second Part, p. 267.

67. About 13,000 had lived in the parish. Mr King to Mr Mulvaney, 27 February 1847, *Correspondence of the Measures adopted from January to March 1847 relating to the measures adopted for the relief of distress in Ireland*, BPP, Board of Works Series, Second series, vol. x, p. 159.

68. Duffy quoted in J. Arthur Partridge, *The Making of the Irish Nation: And the First-fruits of Federation* (London: T. Fisher Unwin, 1886), p. 141.

69. See Oonagh Walsh, '"An invisible but inescapable trauma": Epigenetics and the Great Famine' in Kinealy, King and Reilly, *Women and the Great Hunger*, chapter 13.

CHAPTER TWO

"SUFFER LITTLE CHILDREN"

Life in the workhouse during the Famine

Gerard Moran

While Poor Law legislation was enacted in 1838 after a long and protracted debate inside and outside of Ireland, the practical logistics of implementing the new code were only beginning, which created a situation that was often contentious and created many difficulties. Issues such as the drawing up of boundaries for both the unions-at-large and the electoral divisions from which the elected guardians would come, and the level of poor rates levied, provoked much criticism and concern. In some cases, the official boundaries of townlands could not be determined, leading the authorities to make them up themselves. A further weakness of the legislation was the proposal to locate each workhouse in a market town covering a radius of 10 miles, which had major consequences for those who had to use the institutions, in particular children. The push for the introduction of an Irish Poor Law system came not from within the country, but from supporters of the English Poor Law in the British government, who believed that a modified form of the English system could be adapted for Ireland. It was thus modeled on the 'new' English Poor Law of 1834 with the aim to relieve destitution without encouraging dependency.[1] The Irish Poor Law of 1838 was designed to be even more stringent than its English counterpart, with no relief outside the workhouses being permitted.[2] Moreover, it was decided that conditions inside the workhouse would be of a poorer quality than existed on the outside. The criteria for admission were destitution as a result of old age, illness or handicap, or where the applicants were children. Adults, destitute because of unemployment, were the next priority category. As Dympna McLoughlin points out, every workhouse operated on an individual basis "as a result of local economies, and to a lesser extent the personalities, foibles and values of guardians and functionaries."[3]

While the Poor Law was established to look after paupers, its functions were greatly expanded as a result of the Great Famine of 1845–52. This expanded role included the provision of fever hospitals, sanitation, assisting the poor to emigrate, the provision of outdoor relief, etc., and this at a time when it was barely able to cope with the crisis that the potato failure brought. Many workhouses were barely functional when the crisis started, being in operation for less than 18 months and structures were not in place to deal with the most vulnerable group of individuals, children. John Vandelaur, in his evidence to the Select Committee on the Poor Law in March 1849, maintained that the misgovernment of the Poor Law was as a result of the incompetence of the officers appointed, as they were untrained in their duties.[4] Our knowledge of conditions in the workhouses during the Famine derives largely from the administrators who managed the system or government officials who oversaw the rules and implemented them. As Ciarán Ó Murchadha points out, we know very little about life in the workhouses during this period except from official sources.[5] There are no accounts or descriptions from the individuals who had to avail themselves of its services and who endured the harsh rules laid down for the inmates, and in particular for children. This is surprising because, in 1849, 923,000 people were admitted into the workhouses and in June 1851, over 256,000 were recorded as inmate paupers. At a local level, the Limerick house was expanded so that it accommodated 5 percent of the union's total population.[6] While Helen Burke's study of the Poor Law in the

South Dublin Union shows that most inmates were only in the workhouse for a short period—over half stayed less than two months in 1848—children stayed much longer.[7] It is difficult to determine the feelings of those who became inmates and how they coped with a system that did its best to ensure only the desperate would avail themselves of its services. The surviving records from the Poor Law unions provide little or no information on the children who entered their doors. At the same time, historians who have studied the workhouses have failed to examine the position of children and other vulnerable groups who came to depend on these institutions for survival.

Conditions within Irish workhouses were harsh. On entering, the family was broken up with children separated from their parents except those under two years who stayed with their mothers. Children between 2 and 9 years were sent to the nursery wards, while those between 10 and 15 were segregated into wards for boys and girls. The authorities argued that the enforced separation of children from their parents would reduce the likelihood of them becoming paupers in adult life.[8] Parents thus had to accept the separation of the family so that their children would have the chance to survive. Strict discipline was enforced and all personal resources had to be surrendered. The very structures showed how the system had overwhelming power over its recipients: endless rules and a strict code being in place for all. For those who had freedom prior to entering the workhouse, the regime was one of great severity for children, providing many with little hope for the future.

Prior to the establishment of the Poor Law, children who were orphaned, abandoned, deserted or illegitimate had been cared for by the Foundling Hospitals located in large urban centers such as Dublin and Cork. In 1838, these children were transferred to the workhouses. Even before the failure of the potato in 1845, children comprised about one-third of the inmate population throughout the country and, when the South Dublin workhouse opened in February 1840, one-quarter of its paupers were children.[9] Following the crisis with the potato, the numbers seeking admission into the workhouses increased dramatically so that by February 1847, 93 unions contained more pauper inmates than they had been built to accommodate and some had nearly doubled their capacity as was the case in Cork, which had been built to accommodate 2,800, but had nearly 4,800 inmates.[10] However, in a number of unions the problem of workhouse overcrowding intensified towards the end of the Famine or in the immediate years after the catastrophe had ended. This was as a result of the Quarter Acre Clause in 1847, which led to between one-quarter and one-half million people being evicted from their holdings. In Cashel Poor Law Union, the highest rate of occupancy took place in mid-1851 and it was not until 1858 that inmate numbers fell to pre-Famine levels.[11] The majority of the inmates were women and children: by November 1848, for example, children made up 63 per cent of inmates in Armagh workhouse.[12] There were 63,000 children under the age of 15 in the workhouses in February 1847 and this had increased to 91,000 by mid 1851, representing 45 percent of the total inmate population. While the overall number declined over the following years, children still made up over 40 percent of the workhouse population in 1855.[13] By the end of September 1849, there were 522 girls aged between 2 and 15 in the Kilrush workhouse out of a total inmate population of 1,634, while in Derry, in December 1847, 499 of the 974 inmates were children. In the Rathdrum workhouse in County Wicklow, 1,061 of the 1,247 inmates were women and children. In January 1850, 1,070 of the inmates in Tuam workhouse were children under 15. In a number of unions, children comprised over 60 percent of the workhouse population. In Cork, the number of children under 15 who became inmates increased from 3,337 in 1847 to 6,568 in 1850.[14]

The children who entered the workhouse system can be divided into four categories, reflecting the crisis that hit the country and individuals in the late 1840s and early 1850s. These were those who entered with their families, orphaned, abandoned or deserted children and illegitimate children. The first were members of family groups who had no alternative but to enter the workhouse when the potato failed. The second group were orphans: the definition of orphan at this stage, meant that the child had lost one parent, not necessarily two. In May 1849, there were 163 widows with 202 male and 221 female children in the Mallow workhouse, which also had 81 male and 104 female orphans.[15] Of the 300 children in Ballyvaughan workhouse in October 1852, many were orphans while others were described as deserted, their fathers having left for England in search of work leaving their wives and children to be cared for by the union. In 1849, of the 248 children under 15 years in the Donegal workhouse, 120 were deemed to be orphans.[16] In Cork, 67 percent of the children admitted to the workhouse between March 1848 and August 1850 were officially classified as orphans while another 31 percent came under the heading deserted.[17] The number of orphans also increased as a result of mothers dying while inmates in the workhouses.

The third group were those who were abandoned while their parents headed for British North America (Canada) or the United States in the hope of earning enough money to send back when they were in a position to do so, thus enabling their children to rejoin them. These tended to be the poorest who were barely able to pay their own passage fares let alone those for their wives and children. There was a question mark as to whether the Poor Law should accept 'deserted children' as it was felt the father was 'wandering in search of employment elsewhere', but most workhouses such as in Ballinasloe accepted them because of the genuine distress that existed.[18] Dympna McLoughlin argues that sending children to the workhouses was not an indication of callousness, but rather was the only way of helping them to survive in their absence.[19] An example of a husband and father who emigrated leaving the family behind was Bryan Prior from the parish of Drumreilly in County Leitrim, a tenant on Sir Robert Collins's estate, who had a wife and four children. The agent, Mr Benson, promised relief if Prior gave up his five acre farm. However, after Benson had pulled down Prior's house the only aid provided was his passage fare to Quebec, but not for the rest of the family. While Prior left in the hope of sending the fare back, the family had no alternative but to seek shelter in the workhouse.[20] In some cases, the children were never united with the parents because they had died on the voyage across the Atlantic or soon after disembarking in Canada or the United States. Often, it took a number of years before the father was in a position to save the necessary funds for the rest of the family to be able to join him. In the 12-month period up to the end of September 1853, the Poor Law provided funding for 996 children under the age of 15 to be reunited with their parents, the father having provided part or all of the passage fare.[21] In October 1851, the Mountbellew guardians agreed to pay the expenses of William Molloy, a destitute boy, and Mary Conlon and her two children, so that they could join their families in North America. All came from the Killeroran Electoral Division.[22] Those children who remained in the workhouses had few prospects and the great fear of the authorities was that they would become a permanent burden on the poor rates. Rev. Daniel Liddy, the parish priest of Abbeyfeale in County Limerick, told the Select Committee on the Poor Law in March 1849 that he knew of many farmers and poor persons who had emigrated to America and left their wives and children chargeable to the electoral divisions of the unions that they had left.[23] The workhouse thus became a safety net for those parents who emigrated in search of work and, without it, they and their families would have died. While many had not wanted to enter the workhouses, they had no other institution to turn to and so they had reluctantly taken refuge in these institutions.

Even before the Poor Law had come into existence, the number of deserted children had been high: 1 percent of infants were abandoned after birth.[24] In October 1848, the master of the Ennis workhouse reported that there were a great number of women and children in the house whose husbands had abandoned them and left for America. When they entered the workhouse, the deserted women were asked to take an oath to this effect and promised to do so, but once admitted they either refused, or it was not administered by the officials.[25] The case of Bridget McMahon highlights the problem of desertion. Her husband had held land on the Shirley estate in County Monaghan but, after they were evicted, he deserted her and their three children and they were forced to enter Carrickmacross workhouse.[26] In August 1848, Michael

Hogan got permission to leave Lismore workhouse to bury his wife who had died in the fever hospital. He did not return, leaving his six children behind in the workhouse.[27] The Poor Law Guardians were aware of the problems that deserted children created for the workhouse finances and pursued with vigor those parents who absconded. However, this was often an impossible feat as many parents left the country and could not be traced. A Galway Guardian, Mr Cullen, rushed to the docks to apprehend a man from Barna who was about to emigrate leaving his four children in the workhouse. Moreover, he had £50 in his possession. The father was forced to hand over £2–10s towards the children's upkeep before departing.[28] While some unions attempted to ascertain the number of "orphans" and "deserted" children in their work-houses, as happened in Kilrush in November 1849, it was difficult keep an accurate account.[29] Attempts to draw up such lists were largely created to try to reduce the number of ineligible children, and so the pauper population could be reduced. The authorities realized that some children were placed in the workhouses by desperate parents, although the children were neither orphans or deserted. In the Castlebar union, the guardians discovered that 16 of the workhouse children came under the jurisdiction of the Westport union, but no one knew how they ended up in Castlebar.[30] There were complaints that husbands who deserted their wives and children were not adequately punished by the law and so the Poor Law had to pick up the pieces. In January 1851, the chairman of the Castlebar Board of Guardians, the Earl of Lucan, called for magistrates to impose sentences that would deter husbands from throwing their families on the unions.[31] He was not alone. The Poor Law Unions in the northeast were prepared to go to great lengths to arrest those parents who deserted their children: descriptions of the parents were published and sent to police stations, rewards were offered and arrests were made in places as far away as England and Scotland.[32] The purpose was not to reunite parents with their children, but rather to reduce the unions' expenditures.

Illegitimate children were another group who came into the workhouses because their mothers had no place to go as their families would not provide help or support when the child was born. McLoughlin instances cases from Wexford union where girls became pregnant by their employers who, in many cases, were not prepared to provide the girls or their babies with financial help.[33] In the last six months of 1853, 671 illegitimate children were born in the Irish workhouses.[34] In July 1853, five illegitimate children were born in Galway workhouse which housed another 30 illegitimate children. Four of the children died shortly after birth. An investigation found that none of the fathers were officers or inmates of the union and three of the illegitimate children had been fathered by a tradesman from the town.[35]

The workhouses also comprised children who were returned to Ireland from Britain under the Act of Settlements. (Scotland had a separate Act of Settlement from England and Wales.) Under this legislation, persons who became destitute in Britain could be returned to Ireland, even though they had resided there for a number of years.[36] They were usually returned to the nearest port in Ireland rather than their place of birth. During the Great Famine, over 63,000 people, many of them children, were sent back to workhouses in Ireland. Catherine Ryan, a native of Friarstown in County Limerick, whose husband came from County Tyrone, was deserted with their three children in London where they had lived for 15 years. She was left with no alternative but to seek admission to Marylebone workhouse but, because of the residency requirement, she was sent with her children back to Ireland, they eventually becoming inmates in Limerick workhouse. The 1846 English legislation—Poor Removal (Amendment) Act of 1846 (9 and 10 Viet., c. 66)—had made residency five years, making this an illegal removal. It meant the children had little long-term prospects.[37] A similar fate occurred to the 12 children returned to Ireland in September 1854 under the Act of Settlement and which included Mary Flanagan who was 13 and her sister, Bridget, aged 11 years, who came originally from County Leitrim.[38]

While the Poor Law was established to look after the destitute, it quickly became a dumping ground for children and others who had no place else to go. It included orphans, deserted children and the infirm. Consequently, the workhouses in their first two decades of existence contained children who were likely to remain a long-term burden on the poor rate and regarded by the authorities as "a permanent deadweight." Discipline and controlling behavior were regarded as fundamental regulations of life in the workhouses from the outset and those who broke the rules were severely punished. George Nicholls, the architect of the Poor Law in Ireland, was a firm believer in this approach stating that if discipline was lax there would be nothing to deter those capable of self support from seeking admission or becoming permanent residents in the workhouses. Workhouse officials were allowed to carry out corporal punishment and confine the inmate children who broke the rules. The regulations were not uniformly applied: some adopted a more lax regime than others depending on the attitude of guardians and officials, many of whom were former military personnel. This brought individual unions into conflict with the Poor Law commissioners. What is evident is that some masters and matrons were prepared to enforce harsh regimes against both children and adults. The attitude and approach of these officials was important in the day-to-day experiences of the pauper children. The arrival of a new master at the Ennistymon workhouse in February 1849 was greeted favorably by the inmates as "he is doing all he can to make them comfortable, as far as the regulations of the Poor Law Commissioners will allow him." This was in contrast with the assistant master who was feared by the inmates because of his brutality and who administered the rules in a pungent manner.[39] The extreme approach in which some officials treated children can be seen in Ballinrobe workhouse when the master, William Murphy, was charged and found guilty of cruelty in his treatment of a number of children. In July 1848, he was brought before the courts for the murder of Patrick McGowan and Peggy Thornton, both 12-year-old pauper inmates.[40] In March 1854, the master of Glenamaddy workhouse in County Galway was accused of severely beating two pauper children for minor misdemeanors; while in Borrisokane the resignation of the workhouse schoolmaster was demanded because of punishments he had carried out on a workhouse boy.[41] In Limerick, the school master, Mr O'Connell, smashed the skull of a boy after an altercation with a group of juveniles, while, on another occasion, two boys were flogged in the hall for having cut a desk.[42] Young boys who stole bread from the stores were often sent before the courts resulting in periods in prison, while the "refractory ward," which in essence was a place of solitary confinement, was used for young girls who broke the rules.

While the treatment of pauper children caused concern, the conditions they encountered in the workhouses was also an issue, there being little regard for their safety. This was evident from an incident in Ennistymon. A number of the pauper children were housed in an auxiliary building at Milltown, seven miles distance from Ennistymon, and brought to the main workhouse for regular inspections. In October 1850, a group ranging in age from 6 to 15 years was sent to the Ennistymon workhouse, but received no food during the journey, resulting in the death of one of the children. The porter who was in charge of the group left nine children to their own devices, five having to find shelter behind a wall for the night because of inclement weather. They returned to Milltown the following day in an exhausted state.[43]

By the late 1840s, conditions in the workhouses deteriorated as the unions were under enormous pressure to provide accommodation because of increasing demand and rising costs. The financial difficulties which unions faced can be seen in Ennis, which had debts of nearly £13,000 by February 1849 and was unable to pay its creditors. Expenditure in the Galway workhouse for the month of February came to £1,147.[44] Dramatic measures were introduced, in particular reducing the quality and quantity of food given to inmates. Diet was scaled back for all paupers to the barest subsistence level. Prior to the Famine, children between 2 and 5 years in Cork workhouse received six ounces of bread and half a pint of milk for breakfast and two pounds of potatoes and half a pint of milk for dinner; but in June 1848, in Limerick this was reduced to four ounces of Indian meal and half a pint of milk for breakfast and four ounces of Indian meal and half a pint of milk for dinner. The diet varied from union to union: in Kilmallock they received four ounces of bread for breakfast.[45] The substitution of Indian meal only aggravated the health problems of the children, leading to intestinal ailments. As early as March 1848, the Listowel guardians substituted gruel for milk in order to save money, while in January 1850 the medical officer for Ennistymon stated that the soup that the paupers received "is nothing more than meal and water without either pepper or vegetables of any kind ... and I strongly recommend that the necessary addition be made in the preparation of it, or that it be done away with."[46] The medical inspector reported in December 1851 that the healthy children had not had milk for dinner for six weeks and those aged from 9 to 15 received a pint of an inferior type of soup and on occasions were given nothing but dry bread for their meals. In Kilrush workhouse in early 1850 none of the inmates had been given milk with their meals for months.[47] The provision of inferior, and in some cases, no milk, had health consequences for children as it reduced levels of Vitamin A, iron and protein that they required in their diet. Many children were suffering from nutritional deficiencies prior to entering the workhouse so the continuation of an inadequate diet exacerbated their condition. The quality of milk was an issue in a number of workhouses; in Castlebar, for example, chalk was added to the inferior milk.[48] At the same time, some workhouse officials abused their position to reduce the quality of food for their own benefit. There were allegations that the matron in Glenamaddy used the cream of the milk meant for the children to make butter for herself. While the Poor Law Commissioners wanted the matron dismissed, the guardians refused to do so.[49]

Children suffered in other ways as conditions deteriorated. When the Rev. S.G. Osbourne visited the Limerick workhouse in July 1850, he found hundreds of young children in the most piteous condition, existing in their rags as no other clothes were available; while in Ballinasloe workhouse, there were 60 boys and 252 girls who could not be properly clothed.[50] When the proprietor of the *Limerick and Clare Examiner*, R. Goggins, visited Kilrush workhouse in February 1850, he encountered 300 inmates, many of them children, who were just mere skeletons, "they had no flesh on their bones." He observed:

They sat listless and insensible, and seemed to be quite indifferent to every-thing passing around them; the faces of some quite yellow, those of others dark, as if even before death decomposition were settling in.[51]

The demand for additional accommodation after 1846 often meant that children were transferred to auxiliary buildings that were a distance from the main workhouse building as with the Milltown house in the Ennistymon union. Auxiliary buildings were acquired for convenience and were available at a low cost rather than conforming to suitability to housing paupers, and in particular children. Denis O'Connor, the clerk of Limerick Poor Law Union, told the Select Committee on the Poor Laws in May 1849 that it was more difficult keep discipline in the auxiliaries because of their structures and most of the children at this stage were housed in them.[52] The Sligo auxiliary workhouse, the Charter House, situated at the Mall, was comprised entirely of children under 12 years who were orphans or deserted by their parents; while in Kenmare all of the pauper children, numbering 700, were housed in a former brewery. This was to ensure better discipline within the workhouse system as officials maintained the children were more easily managed than adults.[53] One of the auxiliary workhouses in Scariff union initially only had child paupers, but as admissions increased, fever patients were transferred there in March 1850, leading to the children coming in contact with fatal diseases "and thereby inhale, without much delay, pestilence and death."[54] These buildings tended to be former grain stores, stables, breweries, etc., having been built for industrial or commercial purposes, and became opera-tional to sort out a major accommodation crisis, but were totally unsuited to house children because of inadequate ventilation and space. Children were largely confined to the bedrooms and schoolroom, seldom having access to the outdoors.

Many children were admitted to the workhouses in a poor and emaciated state, but the institutions exacerbated rather than improved their condition. Children who entered the workhouse in a healthy state soon succumbed to diseases that were rampant in the institutions. The greatest problem was the lack of adequate space for those with diseases due to overcrowding, suggesting children's health was not a priority for the guardians. Diseases such as dysentery, diarrhoea, typhus, ophthalmia and even cholera were widespread and had devastating consequences. The remedy for dysentery is proper nutrition, but this was not available in most of the workhouses as the guardians cut costs. Between 1849 and 1853, 135,000 inmates contracted ophthalmia, 95,000 of them children. Ophthalmia led to complete or partial blindness in one or both eyes and is linked to poverty, overcrowding, monotonous diet, poor nutrition, exposure to cold and wet weather, inadequate clothing and bedding.[55] Between October 1849 and 1851, 1,801 children were treated with this ailment in Kanturk workhouse.[56] In Limerick, ophthalmia was rampant as a result of up to four children sleeping in a bed and "the paupers in their own unwashed rags, two in 1 bedding vermin in the house," while in January 1848, Alderman Wallnutt visited Mount Kennedy auxiliary workhouse in Limerick and found the children huddled together lying on pillows, four of whom were dead.[57] In Fermoy, in February 1847, there were 30 children with diseases huddled together in three beds.[58] Dr Cullinan, the medical officer, told the Ennis guardians that the overcrowded state of the workhouse created the greatest danger to the health of the inmates and if remedial measures were not taken "the most alarming ravages of disease might be expected."[59] The mortality rate among children was high as a result of coming in contact with these diseases, in particular among those under two years. In 1842, 35 percent of all children admitted to the North Dublin workhouse died, few infants survived, but the authorities still claimed conditions were better than if they had remained on the outside.[60] In 1848, 38 percent of this group died in the South Dublin Union.[61] In January 1850, the inspector for Listowel union reported that when he visited the workhouse he found 11 children dying of dysentery and, in a two week period, 45 inmates had died, most of them children.[62] Between 1 October 1846 to 31 March 1847, 343 people died in Boyle workhouse, 75 being infants up to two years and 196 were children aged between 2 and 14 years.[63] In Galway, 102 of the 191 inmates who died between 1 August and 21 November 1851 were children.[64] In the Cork workhouse between 1845 and 1850, 7,825 children died with the highest mortality occurring in 1847 when 1,381 died, accounting for 53 percent of all fatalities for that year.[65]

While typhus, dysentery and diarrhoea were rampant throughout the Famine period, the outbreak of cholera in 1849 and 1850 led to increased levels of mortality and inevitable panic among the pauper population, impacting greatly on children. In the Kilmallock auxiliary workhouse, which was a former stable, there were 434 children in March 1850 of whom 244 were described as severely sick, and the report added "two-thirds of them at least will soon cease to trouble the rate payers."[66] Between 26 October and 9 December 1846 70 of the 130 who died in Skibbereen workhouse were children.[67] The *Mayo Telegraph* kept a close watch on mortality levels in the Castlebar workhouse, questioning the official figures, stating it was not the old or infirm that were the main group that were dying, but rather children who suffered because of the poor diet and contracting the fatal diseases. One mother sent her seven young children to the workhouse believing they would be safe, but within days four became fatally ill.[68] When 137 inmates were officially recorded as having died between 1 March and 12 April 1851, the newspaper provided a detailed account of each death between 10 and 30 May, and of the 40 inmates who died, 25 were under 15 years, and of these, 18 were under 10. Thomas Fay was aged 2 years and died on 10 May and Catherine Carty, aged 4 years, on 28 May.[69] Sanctuary in the workhouses was not the panacea for the problems that children faced. When Mr Reid, a tradesman in Castlebar died, his wife, who had been evicted by Lord Lucan, sent her three children to the workhouse, where they were classified as "deserted children" because the mother had decided to leave for England in search of work. One of the children died shortly after being admitted, while the other two were in a serious condition.[70]

While the workhouses may have been intended as the safety net for the survival of children, it became part of the religious struggle for children that was part of the "Second Reformation." Within the Foundling Hospitals, orphans whose religion was unknown had been brought up in the Church of Ireland and this system was continued with the establishment of the Poor Law. Prior to the massive increase in the number of children in the work-houses, the attorney general for Ireland adjudicated that where the religion of an orphan or deserted child was unknown, the child could be brought up in the religion of the state, the Church of Ireland.[71] As the number of orphans and deserted children increased after 1845, where their religious affiliation was unclear, these children were instructed in the Protestant faith, much to the anger and hostility of the Catholic chaplains and clergy. In 1851, the Catholic chaplain in Ballinrobe workhouse, Father Hardiman, accused his Church of Ireland counterpart, Rev. Anderson, of proselytizing Catholic pauper children. As late as 1857, the O'Malley case in the Tuam workhouse highlighted this problem. Constable O'Malley was a convert from Catholicism. When he died, his wife and children entered the workhouse. When the mother died, Catherine Plunkett, the sister of the Church of Ireland Bishop of Tuam, took charge of the children and raised them in the Protestant faith. When the local Catholic priest became aware of this situation, he took the children out of the workhouse and handed them over to their uncle, William O'Malley, to be raised as Catholics.[72] This law was not changed until 1862 following which such children could be registered in the faith of their godparents.

The greatest long-term concern which many unions faced was what to do with children who were a permanent burden on the poor rates and had no family to return to. By late February 1850, there were 720 girls in the Galway work-house aged between 9 and 15 years.[73] Many were orphans and they had entered the workhouses at such a young age that they knew no other life. Jane Murray was 8 years old when she entered Ballinasloe workhouse and, by 1852, had been a resident for seven years. Likewise, Ellen Egan from Castleblakeney became an inmate in the same workhouse when she was 9 years old and had been a pauper inmate for six years.[74] The problem was what would become of these paupers in the long term? There were growing indications of insubordination and disorderly conduct which on occasions led to riots. An instance of this unrest occurred in Kilrush on 3 September 1850 when 25 youths, resident in the workhouse for a long period, attacked the master, Mr Pollin, hitting him with a stone and severely injuring him. The police had to intervene and the youths were arrested. Illegal combinations among the juvenile paupers were reported also from Limerick workhouse leading to a complete breakdown in law and order.[75] The master of the Galway workhouse stated in October 1850 that some boys were out of control and he had acquired a pistol to protect himself, while in Tuam, the master indicated the juvenile boys were insubordinate and had began obstructing him from performing his duties.[76]

To overcome the problem of insubordination and to reduce expenditure many unions sought ways of getting rid of children when they came of age. Children up to the age of 12 years were educated as the unions employed teachers for both boys and girls. Afterwards, boys were trained in occupations such as shoemakers, tailors, weavers, bakers, carpenters, etc., while girls received training in sewing, knitting, washing, baking etc. However, one observer was to later complain that the girls were not given any practical experience in house work, stating:

> They acquire no knowledge of any kind of household work; they have nothing to do but attend to meals or their schools; they take what is given them, and do not know where it came from, how it is cooked, or what it cost. A great many of them have never had a knife or a fork or a plate in their hands, and, as servants, they are perfectly useless.

It was pointed out that the longer they stayed in the workhouse, the more useless they became, which meant that they were not wanted as domestic servants.[77]

A number of unions did attempt to secure positions for the boys once they came of age: Ennis, Cork, Galway and Ballinasloe workhouses tried to send groups to join the navy and army, while the Wexford union trained boys in nautical skills with those regarded as suitable being apprenticed to sea captains.[78] Positions also were sought for boys in factories in Britain and Ireland: in 1847, the Castleblaney guardians paid the travel fares of six young boys to Newcastle-upon-Tyne after George Bates, a fire brick manufacturer, promised to provide them with work at wages of 5 shillings a week, while the Ballinasloe guardians in 1852 paid for 10 boys to travel to Bristol where positions were secured as apprentices in a cotton factory.[79]

For those girls who entered the workhouse as children and were now of a working age, there were few opportunities outside of the institution. As the number of female pauper inmates greatly exceeded the work available within the workhouses, there was little to keep them occupied and Irish employers were reluctant to employ these girls as there was a female work pool outside the workhouses, which was greater than the positions available. By 1848, the guardians were increasingly concerned about what to do with juvenile girls, and when the opportunity arose of sending them to the colonies, they availed of it. In Australia, Canada and the Cape Colony, there was a demand for female labor and for wives for the colonists. The introduction of the Female Orphan Scheme in 1848, resulting in 4,114 workhouse girls having their passage paid to Australia by the colonial authorities, opened up the possibility of sending young girls to other colonial destinations, with Canada being the preferred option because transport costs were cheaper. While proponents of the schemes argued that they provided the girls with the opportunity to better themselves, the primary motive was economic: getting rid of a "deadweight," which would otherwise impact on the poor rates. Bolton Massey summed up this argument at a meeting of the Kilmallock Board of Guardians in May 1850:

> You have them immured within your walls, a drag-chain upon you, perhaps to die there; send them away, they are stalwart, and able to earn a living in a foreign land, which I regret to say they cannot do here.[80]

Even before the Poor Law was established, some institutions had sent children who were long-term inmates to the colonies. The Cork Foundling Hospital as early as 1831 had sent children to Australia, in particular girls, and in 1846, the Cork guardians decided to send 50 young girls of good character, who had previously been children in the house of industry, to the Cape of Good Hope.[81]

The possibility of a new life in the colonies was attractive for many juvenile girls and the numbers wanting to emigrate exceeded the number of places available. In December 1848, 25 females left the Athlone workhouse for Australia, aged from 13 to 16 years, even though the regulations stated the girls should be at least 16 years, while six of the girls sent from the Waterford workhouse in April 1848 were only fifteen years, one Catherine Foran had been an inmate for six years.[82] The *Dublin Evening Post* in supporting the emigration of these girls said:

> We rejoice that those poor children have been rescued from misery at home, and placed in a particular position where they have the fairest prospects of becoming ultimately prosperous settlers, useful members of a rising community, and, in every respect, a credit to their country.[83]

The emigration schemes did provide children who were long-term residents with the opportunity of a life away from the workhouses and many were happy to avail themselves of it. In the five-year period from 1851 to 1855, the Poor Law assisted 1,638 children under the age of 15 to emigrate.[84] The master of Parsonstown workhouse stated that of the female inmates under his charge, all wanted to be sent to Australia.[85] The group that left Cork workhouse in late 1849 expressed their gratitude to the guardians before they departed; while Jane and Alice Drum sent from the Sligo Union to Port Philip in 1848 informed the guardians they were doing well in Australia: one had secured a job as a house maid while the other obtained a position as a children's nurse.[86]

The fundamental weakness with the Poor Law and the workhouse system during the Famine was that it was trying to cope with a catastrophe that it was never designed for. Nowhere was this more evident than how it responded to those children who became inmates. There were people who believed that the system destroyed the child's individuality and turned those who became long-term inmates into automatons who could not function outside of the system and that this was especially the case with children.[87] Time in the workhouses created children who were without ambition, without initiative and without individuality. Independent observers who observed the pauper children branded the workhouses "chambers of horrors." John Arnott who wrote on conditions in the workhouses in the late 1850s stated, "for the young children admission to the workhouses was an entrance to the grave."[88] These children were a lost generation who were deprived of their childhood and their future role in society. This was summed up by the *Tuam Herald* in May 1850:

> If the present young generation of manhood and womanhood, is permitted to ripen into the age of manhood and womanhood, without a single feeling in common with the society around them, strangers to the decencies of domestic life, without respect of the laws of property, a drifting herd of non-descript beings, 'pariahs' in the native land, they will prey on the very vitals of well-regulated social life with the morbid hate of demons.[89]

NOTES

1. England and Wales had possessed a state system of poor relief since the late 16th century. In line with the various debates on the causes and consequences of poverty that took place in the early nineteenth century, the existing Poor Law legislation was modified and made more stringent, as codified in the new Poor Law of 1834.

2. Christine Kinealy, 'The Role of the Irish Poor Law during the Famine' in Cathal Pórtéir, *The Great Irish Famine* (Cork: Mercier Press, 1995), pp. 104–22.

3. Dympna McLoughlin, 'Superfluous and unwanted deadweight: the emigration of nineteenth-century Irish pauper women' in Patrick O'Sullivan (ed.), *The Irish Worldwide, Irish Women and Irish Emigration,* vol. iv (Leicester University Press, London; 1995), p. 69.

4. *Seventh Report of the Select Committee on Poor Laws (Ireland)*, HC 1849, HC 1849, xv, p. 44, q. 5349.

5. Ciarán Ó Murchadha, *Sable Wings over the Land: Ennis, County Clare and its Wider Community during the Great Famine* (CLASP, Ennis; 1998), p. 186.

6. *Eighth Report from the Select Committee on Poor Laws (Ireland) Act*, HC 1849 (237), xv, p. 51, q. 6650.

7. Helen Burke, *The People and the Poor Law in Nineteenth Century Ireland* (West Sussex: The Women's Education Bureau, 1987), p. 185.

8. Michelle O'Mahony, *Famine in Cork City: Famine Life at Cork Union* Workhouse (Cork: Mercier Press, 2005), p. 99.

9. Burke, *The People and the Poor Law,* p. 85.

10. Ibid., p. 79.

11. Denis G. Marnane, 'The famine in south Tipperary – pt 3' in the *Tipperary Historical Journal* (1998), p. 73.

12. Virginia Crossman, *The Irish Poor Law, 1838–1948* (Dundalk: Studies in Irish Economic and Social History 10, 2006), pp. 21–2.

13. Joseph Robbins, 'Emigration of workhouse children to Australia' in John O'Brien and Pauric Travers (eds), *The Irish Emigrant Experience in Australia* (Dublin: Poolbeg Press, 1991), p. 34; Burke, *The People and the Poor Law,* p. 163.

14. Kilrush Poor Law Union Minutes, dated 30 September 1849 in *Kilrush Union Minute Books, 1849* (Ennis, 1997), p. 87; Patrick Durnin, 'Aspects of Poor Law administration and the workhouse in Derry, 1838–1948' in Gerard O'Brien (ed), *Derry and Londonderry: History and Society* (Dublin: Geography Publications, 1999), p. 545; Eva O Cathaoir, 'The Poor Law in County Wicklow' in Ken Hannigan and William Nolan, *Wicklow: History and Society* (Dublin: Geography Publications, 1994), pp. 535–6; *Tuam Herald*, 12 January 1850; *Limerick Reporter and Tipperary Vindicator*, 2 August 1850; O'Mahony, *Famine in Cork City,* p. 100.

15. *Eighth Report from the Select Committee on Poor Laws*, p. 25, q. 6293.

16. *Nation*, 2 October 1852; Pat Conaghan, *The Great Famine in South-West Donegal* (Killybegs: Bygone Enterprises, 1997), p. 174.

17. O'Mahony, *Famine in Cork City*, p. 100.

18. *Ninth Report of the Select Committee on Poor |Laws (Ireland)*, HC 1849 (259), xv, pp 77–8, q. 8259.

19. McLoughlin, 'Superfluous and unwanted deadweight', p. 77.

20. See Gerard Moran, *Sending Out Ireland's Poor: Assisted Emigration to North America in the Nineteenth Century* (Dublin: Four Courts Press, 2004), p. 133.

21. *Galway Vindicator*, 24 June 1854. In many cases the guardians provide the funding for clothes so that the children could travel.

22. *Tuam Herald*, 25 October 1851.

23. *Third Report from the Select Committee on Poor Laws (Ireland) Act*, HC 1849 (931), xv, p. 61, q. 1502.

24. Anna Clark, 'Orphans and the poor law: rage against the machine' in Virginia Crossman and Peter Gray (eds), *Poverty and Welfare in Ireland, 1838–1948* (Dublin: Irish Academic Press, 2011), p. 97.

25. *Clare Journal,* 2 November 1848.

26. Ibid., 15 June 1850.

27. Tom Nolan, 'The Lismore Poor Law Union and the famine' in Des Cowman and Donal Barry (eds), *The Famine in Waterford, 1845–50* (Dublin: Geography Publications, 1995), p. 114.

28. *Galway Vindicator*, 13 May 1854.

29. Kilrush Poor Law Union Minutes, dated 30 September 1849 in *Kilrush Union Minute Books,* p. 325.

30. *Mayo Telegraph*, 9 October 1850.

31. Ibid., 29 January 1851.

32. *Third Report of Select Committee on Poor Laws*, pp. 123–4, q. 2449.

33. Dympna McLoughlin, 'Workhouses and female paupers, 1840–70' in Maria Luddy and Cliona Murphy (eds), *Women Surviving: Studies in Irish Women's History in the Nineteenth and Twentieth Centuries* (Dublin: Attic Press, 1990), p. 122.

34. Burke, *The People and the Poor Law,* p. 191.

35. *Galway Vindicator*, 13 July 1853.

36. The concept of 'settlement' was an integral part of the English and Welsh, and the Scottish, Poor Laws. In the former, the Poor Removal Act of 1846 governed the returns to Ireland during the Famine years.

37. *Limerick and Clare Examiner*, 21 October 1848.

38. *Nation*, 16 September 1854. The Act of Settlement was not amended until 1861 when a five-year residency provision was applied.

39. *Limerick Reporter*, 13 February 1849.

40. *Nation*, 22 July 1848.

41. *Tuam Herald*, 25 March 1854; *Limerick Reporter and Tipperary Vindicator*, 25 July 1854.

42. *Limerick Reporter and Tipperary Vindicator*, 2 August 1850; 3 December 1852.

43. *Nation*, 16 October 1850.

44. *Third Report of the Select Committee of Poor Laws*, p. 84, q. 1953.

45. O'Mahony, *Famine in Cork City*, p. 75; *Limerick Reporter,* 9 June 1848; *Nation*, 30 March 1850.

46. Ibid., 4 March 1848; West Clare Historical Society/Fas Community Response Project, *Ennistymon Union: Minutes of Board of Guardians, 1839–50*, meeting of 10 January 1850 (Ennistymon, 1992), book 8, p. 21.

47. *Limerick Reporter and Tipperary Vindicator*, 7 January 1851; *Nation*, 2 March 1850.

48. *Mayo Telegraph*, 13 February 1850.

49. *Tuam Herald*, 17 February 1855.

50. *Nation*, 13 July 1850; *Western News*, 19 June 1852.

51. *Nation,* 2 March 1850.

52. *Eighth Report from the Select Committee on Poor Laws*, p. 52, q. 6663.

53. *Sligo Champion*, 8 January 1850; *Fourth Report from the Select Committee of the House of Lords appointed to inquire into operations of the Irish Poor Law, and the expediency of making any amendment to its enactment*, HC 1849, (365) xvi, p. 742, qs 7668–9.

54. *Tuam Herald*, 30 March 1850.

55. Philomena Gorey, 'Childhood ophthalmia in Irish workhouses, 1845–61' in Anne MacLellan and Alice Manager (eds), Growing Pains: *Childhood Illness in Ireland, 1750–1950* (Kildare: Irish Academic Press, 2013), pp. 71–2.

56. Ibid., p. 83.

57. *Limerick Reporter and Clare Examiner*, 18 June 1850; *Nation*, 22 January 1848.

58. O'Connor, *The Workhouses of Ireland*, p. 147.

59. *Clare Journal*, 31 August 1848.

60. Clark, 'Orphans and the poor law,' p. 100.

61. Burke, *The People and the Poor Law,* p. 229.

62. *Nation*, 19 January 1850.

63. *Sligo Journal*, 16 April 1847.

64. *Galway Vindicator,* 22 November 1851.

65. O'Mahony, *Famine in Cork City,* pp. 108–13.

66. *Nation,* 30 March 1850.

67. *Copies or Extracts of Correspondence relating to the state of Union Workhouses in Ireland,* HC 1847, (776), lv, p. 11.

68. *Mayo Telegraph*, 7 May 1851.

69. Ibid., 21, 28, 4 June 1851.

70. Ibid., 7 May 1851.

71. Burke, *The People and the Poor Law*, pp. 92–3.

72. Gerard Moran, *The Mayo Evictions of 1860: Fr Patrick Lavelle and the 'War' in Partry* (Dublin: History Press, 2007), pp. 23–5.

73. Minutes of the Galway Poor Law Guardians, 23 May 1850 (Galway County Library, Galway Poor Law Minute book, August 1849-March 1850).

74. Minutes of the Mountbellew Poor Law Guardians, dated 5 March 1853 (GCL, Mountbellew Poor Law Minute Book.

75. *Tuam Herald*, 14 September 1850; *Nation,* 17 August 1850. On the question of riots in the workhouses see Gerard Moran, 'Disorderly conduction: riots and insubordination in the workhouses during the Great Famine' in John Cunningham and Niall O Ciosan (eds), *Culture and Society in Ireland since 1750: Essays in Honour of Gearoid O Tuathaigh* (Dublin: Lilliput Press, 2015), pp. 160–80.

76. *Galway Mercury*, 2 November 1850; *Tuam Herald*, 15 July 1854.

77. *Report from the Select Committee on the Poor Law (Ireland); together with the proceedings of the committee, minutes of evidence and appendix*, HC 1861 (408), x, pp. 89–91, qs 1706–78. This opinion was also confirmed by Mrs Woodlock, manager of the St Joseph's Industrial School in Dublin, see Burke, *The People and the Poor Law*, pp. 223–4.

78. *Galway Vindicator*, 11 May 1850, 27 May 1854; O'Mahony *Famine in Cork City,* p. 60; *Western Star*, 14 December 1850; Tom and Teresa Wickham, 'The workhouse opens, pt ii' in *Journal of the Taghmon Historical Society*, no. 6 (2005), pp. 81–2.

79. Rev. Peadar Livingstone, 'Castleblaney Poor Law Union: the early years, 1839–49' in the *Clogher Record*, v (2) (1964), pp. 239–41; *Tuam Herald*, 6 November 1852.

80. *Nation*, 18 May 1850.

81. Moran, *Sending Out Ireland's Poor*, p. 126; O'Mahony, *Famine in Cork City*, pp. 139–40.

82. *Clare Journal*, 11 December 1848; Rita Byrne, 'The workhouse in Waterford city, 1847–9' in Des Cowman and Donald Brady (eds), *Teacht na bPratai Dubha: Famine in Waterford*, 1845–1850 (Dublin: Geography Publication, 1995), p. 136.

83. Reprinted in *Mayo Telegraph*, 25 April 1849.

84. Burke, *The People and the Poor Law,* p. 199.

85. *Tipperary Vindicator*, 9 September 1848.

86. *Nation,* 8 December 1849; *Sligo Journal*, 5 October 1849.

87. Anna Clark, 'Wild workhouse girls and the liberal imperial state in mid nineteenth-century Ireland' in the *Journal of Social History*, 39:2 (2005), p. 399.

88. Quoted in O'Mahony, *Famine in Cork City,* p. 144.

89. *Tuam Herald*, 25 May 1850.

CHAPTER THREE

GRIM SCARS OF THE GREAT HUNGER

Orphaned and abandoned children in the workhouses during the 1850s and 1860s

Simon Gallaher

Children suffered greatly during the Great Hunger in Ireland between 1845 and 1852. The young, particularly vulnerable to the physical ravages of starvation and infectious disease, accounted for almost half of the estimated one million famine-induced fatalities.[1] Children were vulnerable also to the emotional traumas of dislocation from their homes through eviction and the disintegration of their families as a consequence of the death or emigration of parents and siblings. Families driven to seek relief within the workhouse faced the prospect of forced separation of parents from their children who were often sent to overcrowded, unsanitary and distant auxiliary accommodations. The number of children held within workhouses continued to rise until 1852 when the end of the crisis enabled families to leave. Yet, for many workhouse children, the passing of famine conditions did not mark an end to the impact of the Great Hunger upon them. A large number were orphaned, abandoned, or without a traceable relative and had little capacity to leave these institutions until they were old enough to find work to support themselves outside. This residual population of orphaned and deserted children in the workhouse during the 1850s is described by Joseph Robins as one of the "grimmest scars" of the Great Hunger.[2]

A scar is an effective analogy. Famines are traumatic events, which leave lingering and sometimes visible physiological and psychological marks upon those individuals affected by them. Melinda Grimsley-Smith argues that if an analysis of the impact of famine is limited to the immediate event, we lose sight of the ways in which "sudden and chronic nutritional deprivation, coupled with intense psychological trauma, devastates human bodies and minds not just while they are starving, but for decades afterward."[3] Historians have begun to investigate the impact of the Great Hunger on the physical and mental health of workhouse children. Jonny Geber's bioarchaeological study of Famine victims in Kilkenny Union workhouse reveals that many child survivors were stunted in growth and displayed dental defects as permanent reminders of the catastrophe.[4] Psychological scars are more difficult to uncover. Mel Cousins suggests that behavioral problems and insubordination exhibited by young women in the South Dublin Union workhouse between 1857 and 1862 corresponded with the "coming-of-age" of children who were admitted during the Great Famine.[5] Although these long-term consequences of famine have been acknowledged, however, little attention has been directed to the identities and experiences of the thousands of children left as a demographic scar.

The extent to which the ideologies and policies of the Poor Law changed in response to the needs of a large juvenile population has rarely been considered in detail. As workhouse children's wards took on the appearance of orphanages, the question of child welfare transformed from one of financial burden into one of social responsibility. The North Dublin Union schoolmaster, John Taylor, argued that as "nearly all the children in workhouses are virtually orphans," Poor Law authorities had a responsibility to "stand in loco parentis" toward them for whom, "every dictate of humanity and wise economy demands that immediate and thorough provision should be made."[6] During the 1850s, children were often the most discussed subject in the workhouse boardroom. Liz Thomas has shown that workhouse architecture was altered in a "physical manifestation" of the changing ideological positions of children and childhood.[7] Newly designed dormitories and schoolrooms placed renewed emphasis on the segregation of children from adults and reflected officials' concerns about the perceived dangers of moral contamination. Greater attention was directed toward institutional methods of education and industrial training. These changes left their own scars, however, in the form of the physical and psychological damage to child health caused by institutionalization. This paper examines these ideological changes and the grim scars that were left upon the multitudes of children left orphaned and abandoned in the workhouses of Ireland during and after the Great Hunger.

The Poor Law after the Great Hunger

The 1850s was a decade of recovery across Ireland, particularly in southern and western Poor Law unions where pressure upon the relief system during the crisis had left several unions bankrupt. The Poor Law Commissioners and local boards of guardians hoped for a rapid return to the principles and administrative norms of the original Poor Law legislation of 1838. The provision of outdoor relief, as permitted by the amended Poor Law of 1847, was viewed with concern. During the Great Hunger, workhouse overcrowding and high mortality rates had revealed the limitations of an entirely indoor relief system at a time of crisis. Boards of guardians were empowered under the Poor Law Extension Act of 1847 to offer outdoor relief in the form of food when their workhouse was either full or the site of infection. Families deemed deserving enough, such as those with a sick or injured head of household as well as widows with two or more legitimate children, qualified for outdoor relief even if a workhouse was not full. Many guardians, however, viewed even this limited measure of outdoor relief as a "new and hazardous experiment," as it diluted the workhouse test and undermined the ideological principles of deterrence and less eligibility whereby poor relief was to be made less attractive than independent labor.[8] Consequently, outdoor relief was withdrawn as soon as pressure upon a workhouse abated. As a proportion of the total number of persons in receipt of relief, those on outdoor relief declined from 71.6 percent to 1.9 percent between 1848 and 1852. In 1852, the Poor Law commissioners, who argued that outdoor relief was expensive, liable to abuse, and demoralizing for the poor, reported that "the transition from out-door to in-door relief may be said to be complete throughout Ireland."[9] For destitute children and families in need of poor relief during the 1850s, the workhouse was the only available option.

The historiography of the Irish Poor Law has been primarily focused upon its "horrendous failure" during the Great Hunger which has shaped a distorted impression of a system that operated and evolved until the 1920s.[10] In recent studies, attention has been directed toward the provision and consumption of poor relief in post-Famine Ireland. A key finding of these studies has been the extensive regional and local variation that characterized post-Famine poor relief. Distinctive welfare regimes have been identified in the northern, southern and western regions of the country: northern Poor Law unions were characterized as providing below-average rates of relief despite average levels of rateable wealth; southern boards of guardians provided higher levels of relief funded by above-average valuations, while the peripheral western unions were extremely poor and provided the lowest levels of relief.[11] Analysis of the admission and discharge registers of individual workhouses has revealed that local economic and social conditions were important factors in the administrative policies of boards of guardians and that the workhouse was used in a myriad of ways by a broad spectrum of the destitute poor.[12]

The Great Hunger affected every region of Ireland but subsided earliest in the north-east and latest in the southwest. After the crisis, there was a period of marked economic recovery. Population loss caused by Famine-induced mortality and emigration contributed to "the material improvement in the rate of wages" and an "increased constancy of employment of agricultural labourers and their families" by the mid-1850s.[13] Despite the economic recovery, it took almost a decade for the number of workhouse inmates to reflect what might be termed "normal" post-Famine destitution. In 1860, the Poor Law commissioners judged that they could not "anticipate any further annual decrease of pauperism from the cause which has for many years past influenced it—namely the continued subsidence of the effect of the famine." Henceforth, they expected that any changes in the workhouse population would be "solely dependent on the favourable or adverse character of the respective years."[14]

Blight and distress returned in the autumn of 1860 but, given higher wages and reduced reliance upon the potato among the laboring classes, as well as the smaller population, the Poor Law commissioners noted that when compared with 1845, "one cannot but wonder at the present comparative state of confidence in Ireland."[15] But economic recovery was not experienced by all. Edward Senior, a Poor Law inspector, warned that the consolidation of smallholdings and their alteration from tillage to pasture had left a large proportion of the population, particularly in the west, "with no certain means of livelihood."[16] Denis O'Connor, the Cork workhouse medical officer, noted that "a person observing the state of this country in 1855, as compared with its condition in the previous ten years, might imagine he had awoke from a horrid dream." But O'Connor added that there had been little change in the workhouses, "for they still contained within them all those whom the famine had disabled, like the wounded after a battle."[17]

Famine Orphans and Abandoned Children

At the end of the Great Hunger, children were overrepresented within the workhouse population. In the 1851 census, children under 15 years of age accounted for 35 percent of the whole population (a reduction from 40.5 percent in 1841), whereas in the workhouses children of that age represented 52.9 percent of inmates and 6.5 percent of all children in Ireland.[18] Officials anticipated "that for some few years to come the number of these children, relative to the whole mass of the destitute, is not likely to undergo any material decrease."[19] Workhouse population statistics indicate that it took almost 10 years for this overrepresentation to subside. Figure 1 illustrates changes in the average daily number of workhouse inmates over the first two post-Famine decades and details the proportion represented by each pauper category: children aged under 15 years, able-bodied adults, the aged and infirm, and hospital patients. In 1852, the average number of workhouse inmates was 166,821. The average number of inmates then declined to its lowest level of 40,380 in 1859 before it increased to 57,910 by 1863 due to renewed distress before following a gradual downward trend which continued until the twentieth century. The number of children declined from 75,961 (45.5 percent of all inmates) in 1852 to 11,511 (28.5 percent) in 1859. Until 1856, children declined at a slower rate than able-bodied inmates and it took slightly longer for the juvenile population to fall to its lowest level of 11,216 (27.2 percent) in 1860. The number of able-bodied adults, in which women consistently outnumbered men by around three to one, declined from 52,251 (31.3 percent) in 1852 to 7.764 (19.2 percent) in 1859. The number of aged and infirm inmates and hospital patients was reduced also but their proportions increased respectively from 7.3 to 15.7 percent and from 15.9 to 34.8 percent between 1852 and 1859. These population changes were reflected in the changing role of the workhouse as the principal causes of destitution shifted from famine related distress to old age and sickness. In 1853, the Poor Law Commissioners, who permitted Boards of Guardians to open their workhouses to the non-destitute sick poor, observed that "the Workhouses of Ireland are assuming, especially in large towns, the character of hospitals".[20] It is likely that a significant proportion of such patients were children but the exact number was not defined.

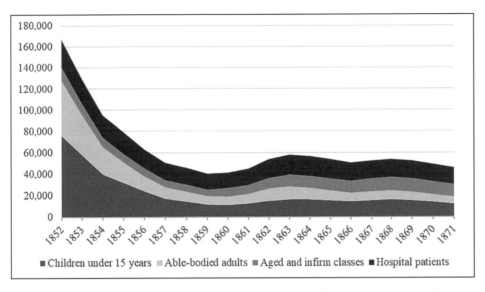

Figure 1: The average daily number of persons in the workhouse population, 1852–71

The scale of the demographic scar left by the Great Hunger is indicated through statistical analysis of children who were in the workhouse without their parents. Changes in the number of such children followed the general trends of the national average statistics. Between March and September 1851, the number of parentless children relieved in the workhouse was 87,697. Parentless children declined each subsequent year until a low of 9,634 children in March-September 1860 after which they increased by several thousand during the early 1860s and declined again thereafter. As shown in Figure 2, however, this pattern changes when children without their parents are measured as a proportion of the total number of children. In 1851, 39 percent of workhouse children were without their parents. This proportion then increased to a peak of 52.8 percent in 1856 before declining to a low of 23 percent in 1862. Parentless children fluctuated between 24 and 30.3 percent for the remainder of the decade and fell below 20 percent only by 1886. Yet the proportion represented by children orphaned or abandoned during the Great Hunger is unclear within these statistics as the measurement included those who lost parents in the succeeding years and children sent into the workhouse for hospital treatment unaccompanied.

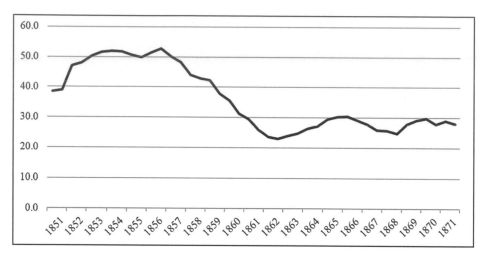

Figure 2: Children without their parents as a proportion (%) of the total number of children in receipt of indoor relief, 1851–71

Other evidence points to the large number and long-term residency of Famine orphans as the chief cause for the overrepresentation and delayed reduction of the number of children in the workhouse. The admission and discharge registers of the Ballymoney workhouse in County Antrim, for example, reveal that between October 1850 and September 1851, of the 41.4 percent of children admitted without their parents, 51.7 percent were orphans and 27.7 percent were deserted. By 1860–61, however, only 13.8 percent of children were unaccompanied of whom the majority were of imprisoned parents or were sick.[21] While visiting the Enniskillen workhouse in County Fermanagh in 1853, Sir John Forbes reported that over two-thirds of the children were orphans. According to Forbes, the number of children had decreased since 1850 but that, "the proportional decrease … is much less than that of the adults, a circumstance easily to be explained by the orphaned condition of so large a proportion of them preventing their removal from the house."[22] Additionally, many boards of guardians, particularly in Ulster, restricted the admission of more orphaned and deserted children into their workhouses after the Famine. In 1850, the Belfast Guardians refused to take in deserted infants "as other and better provision by law has been made for the relief of such children," namely parish overseers of deserted children.[23] Similarly, the Antrim Guardians did not accept deserted children "until they are two or three years old."[24] Guardians justified these decisions by arguing that their workhouse nurseries were overcrowded already and that the institutional environment was detrimental to infant health. In 1851, the Newry Guardians refused the admission of two infants without their mothers as "the proper care of these seriously adds to the master's difficulties, and he is less suited for the health of an infant than them ... it is in fact almost certain death."[25] These sources provide context for observations by Poor Law officials and social commentators that almost all the children in the workhouses of the 1850s were orphans who "remain there as in their fixed home."[26] Considering the longer length of stay of orphans as compared to children with parents, and that Figure 3 illustrates the proportion of the total number removed within a year, it is probable that a large majority of children in many workhouses on an average day during the 1850s were orphans of the Great Hunger.

Few sources provide details on the identities and personal experiences of workhouse children and it is easy for the historian to lose sight of the individual within statistical analysis. The statements provided by orphaned and abandoned girls from the North Dublin Union workhouse are rare testimonies by children who had lost their families during the Great Hunger. In 1859, seven girls were selected for transfer to a nearby industrial school for training as domestic servants. According to the school managers, "These girls were not selected for the strangeness of their history, or as quite extraordinary examples of desertion and utter friendlessness. They were taken, almost at random, from a class of nearly *three hundred*."[27] The testimonies of five of the girls are listed below:

> 1. "Age between fourteen and fifteen. Has been *nine* years in the Workhouse; is an orphan. Heard that her mother died long ago, and that her father also died soon after he came to the Union, with his two children. Does not

remember to have ever seen her father. No one has ever come to enquire for them since. The little sister is still in the Union. Has no acquaintance whatsoever outside."

2. "Age between fourteen and fifteen. Has been *fourteen* years in the Workhouse; is an orphan. Knows nothing of her father and mother; never heard how she came to the Union. Has no acquaintance any where."

3. "Age about sixteen. Has been *fourteen* years in the Workhouse; is motherless and knows nothing of her father; thinks he may be alive; heard that he went to America long ago. Has an aunt in Dublin, but cannot tell where she lives. Has heard nothing of these relatives for some time."

4. "Age sixteen. Has been *ten* years in the Workhouse. Is motherless; cannot tell whether her father is alive. Was brought to the Union by her mother, who died there soon after; does not remember her. Thinks she has brothers in Kilkenny, but knows nothing about them. Has no relative in the Union, is not acquainted with any one outside."

5. "Age sixteen. Has been *nine* years in the Workhouse; is an orphan; her father, a soldier, died ten years ago, and his widow about a year after went to the Union with five children ... where, after lingering in very bad health for four years, she died. Two of her brothers are in situation, she cannot tell where; another brother, and a sister, remain in the Union."[28]

The accounts above indicate the permanency of orphaned or deserted children's confinement within the workhouse. They also highlight how little these children knew or remembered about their parents and family circumstances. Such ignorance also suggests a lack of accurate record keeping by Poor Law officials at the time of admission. For James Kavanagh, the National Education inspector of workhouse schools, the "weakening and disruption of those social and family ties, the strength of which heretofore formed so remarkable a feature in the Irish home and heart" was "one of the worst results of the famine."[29] In many cases, officials were unsure whether a child was orphaned or deserted. In 1853, of the 50,129 workhouse children aged 9–14 years, 16,306 were orphans, 17,730 had lost one parent, and 10,656 were deserted.[30] The distinctions between these categories were blurred and became conflated as public commentary increasingly stereotyped all work-house children under the term "orphan" and effectively discounted any exis-tent familial relationships; an assumption that has been perpetuated within much of the historiography on child welfare in Britain and Ireland.[31]

The Poor Law commissioners suspected that among children admitted during the Famine "a larger portion of them are entered as orphans than really are so."[32] Geber suggests that parents did so to secure relief for their children as they feared guardians would consider the family undeserving due to the presence of able-bodied adults.[33] A "large number" were believed to have been left by parents who had emigrated to Britain, Canada or the United States and had planned on sending remittances back to pay for their children's passages.[34] In 1853, remittances sent by relatives in America, Australia and Britain amounted to £2,333 9s. 3d., which enabled 996 children and 1,605 adults to emigrate.[35] Dympna McLoughlin argues that parents used workhouses as "a safe place" to leave young or ill children who may not have survived an arduous ocean crossing or would have hindered their parents' search for employment.[36] Temporary abandonment was the result of parental despera-tion and was a difficult and emotional decision. O'Connor, the Cork medical officer, recounted that "it was most touching to see one of these poor men hanging over a sick child in hospital, whom he represented to be his nephew, but whom the affectionate embrace, the close whispering lest the conversa-tion should betray them, the sobs and tears of both when parting, showed to be in a closer degree of relationship."[37] Many families had no reunion as "often this was their last meeting in this world; for children then went out of life like bubbles bursting on the stream."[38] Even when remittances were sent back months or years later, frequently addressed to the workhouse chaplain, there was no guarantee that the child would be sent out. When officials received a remittance letter for a child, "it sometimes required several days' search before its identity could be established, amidst the multitude of the same name; or, as sometimes happened, the child having altogether forgotten its own surname, and the fact of its having any surviving parent."[39] Children who were successfully identified were usually sent by the guardians in the company of other emigrant pauper families or under the charge of the captain of the vessel. The children were provided with a new suit of clothing onto which the name and address of their parent was stitched: "a singular piece of goods, priceless to one individual, valueless to all the world beside."[40]

Boards of guardians attempted to locate and prosecute parents who left their children in the workhouse but did not emigrate from Ireland. There is a degree of ambiguity in the interpretation of such cases of abandonment. Some parents left their children on a temporary basis to facilitate travel for seasonal employment. McLoughlin suggests that many boards of guardians allowed parents to leave children on an agreed temporary basis. By allowing a parent to find work, and conveniently recording their children as orphaned or deserted, the guardians avoided the expense of supporting an entire family upon the poor rate.[41] Poor Law authorities generally took the view, however, that such children were "absolutely and wholly abandoned" by parents who "feel relieved of a weighty burden."[42] During and after the Famine, the Belfast Guardians issued numerous warrants and rewards for the arrest of fathers for desertion. By February 1851, there were so many children without their parents that the guardians ordered the master to make inquiries on whether any had fathers who were employed outside.[43] The North Dublin Union's relieving officer made similar investigations in June 1851 as "it might satisfy these boys as there are many from the country who are anxious as they say to go home."[44] Letters were sent to relatives, friends and parish priests based upon information provided by the boys. In September 1852, the relieving officer reported that one boy was taken by his stepmother while another was sent to his uncle.[45] Only a few such inquiries were successful, however, which prompted the guardians to propose a more direct approach whereby the "relieving officer take the deserted children down to the neighbourhood ...

and endeavour to get the child to point out its former residence."[46] Guardians recognized that most children would not be removed by a relative and instead sought other means to remove these potentially long-term burdens.

Hiring-out and Pauper Education

Economic recovery in the immediate aftermath of the Great Hunger encouraged a sense of optimism within public commentary. Nonetheless, there were concerns about a shortage of labor caused by the loss of population during the crisis and its continued decline through emigration. The mass of orphaned and deserted children in the workhouses, maintained by the ratepaying public, was increasingly viewed as a solution to this problem by employers, authorities, and the wider public. The Society for the Promotion of Irish Manufacture and Industry provided spinning looms and textile material to several workhouses for use by both pauper adults and children.[47] It was hoped that workhouses would become self sufficient through the production, sale and export of manufactured goods and that paupers would learn industrial skills for future employment. The *Freeman's Journal* hoped that "the workhouses could be made training schools all over Ireland, and be converted into the agent for rebuilding up the country" and expected that "enterprising men here and there would start manufactories seeing that they could get disciplined labour at a low rate."[48] Likewise, in the agricultural sector, the *Belfast Mercury* predicted that from the workhouses "a large body of young people will be coming forth, very soon, with new ideas, good habits, and qualifications which will make of them a higher order of peasantry than Ireland has ever yet known."[49] This was a remarkable shift in public perceptions of the workhouse when it is considered that, only several years previously, these institutions had been the overcrowded sites of infectious disease, mass mortality and family disintegration.

Boards of guardians were often the chief promoters of the hiring-out of children to factories and farms. They believed it was the surest means to reduce the poor rates and provide children the opportunity to become self-supporting adults. At a meeting of the Board of Irish Manufacturers and Industry in February 1851, the guardians of the South Dublin Union exhibited a selection of textile products, which had been manufactured by children in their workhouse. The items included embroidery work, lace mittens and stockings, window curtains, shoes, and other clothing, which were "handed round and were really beautiful." One guardian explained that, "Now those things were made by children of nine, ten, and twelve years of age" and he asked the audience "will it be tolerated that hundreds of thousands of such children shall be kept idle and rotting in the poorhouses of Ireland?"[50] Ulster manufacturers were quick to apply for workhouse children from all parts of Ireland. In December 1852, a Belfast textile company sent a circular to all boards of guardians "stating they have employment for 300 or 500 weaving boys should the Irish unions have that number to supply the demands."[51] The wages offered to the boys were 4*d*. per day in their first month, which progressed to 5*d*. per day in their second month and 10*d*. per day by their seventh month. Such arrangements appeared as mutually beneficial for both boards of guardians and employers, but they were criticized by the Poor Law commissioners and some workhouse officials for amounting to little more than exploitation of vulnerable children.

The oversupply of workhouse children and the eagerness of guardians to reduce the rates meant that employers had little cause to hire children on more generous terms of employment. Children were employed on low or non-existent wages and often on short-term contracts of six months or less in which the child was hired out in May and sent back to the workhouse in November. Employers neglected the care of children and offered little industrial training while boards of guardians, who considered their responsibilities for a child as largely finished upon its employment, provided little supervision over them. A workhouse teacher described hiring-out practices as "a species of slavery" as children who refused an employment contract were discharged from the workhouse.[52] The Belfast Board of Guardians introduced some safeguards in the form of a ban on the hiring of children under 13 years of age and a requirement for employers to provide a certificate of character signed by a clergyman, but these were made after instances of neglect or abuse had already occurred.[53]

In 1853, the Poor Law commissioners communicated to boards of guardians their disapproval of the hiring-out system. They stated that the practice "of procuring labour at convenient seasons, and letting the servant return at intervals ... until again wanted, may appear to be beneficial to the employers" but should not be "a benefit enjoyed by them at the expense of a public fund."[54] Instead, they suggested that children should remain in the workhouse school and receive a course of industrial training until "the age at which it may be practicable for them to obtain engagements likely to be permanent."[55] Workhouse officials who had responsibility over the teaching and welfare of children occasionally criticized their own board of guardians for hiring out young children. In 1857, the Presbyterian chaplain of the Antrim Union complained that children were hired out from 8 years of age. He stated that "this is an evil I have long deplored" and asked, "if they do not receive education before leaving where will they receive it?"[56] Yet despite condemnation from poor relief authorities and increasingly from the wider public, the practice of hiring-out children at a young age on short-term underpaid and exploitative contracts was subject to little reform and persisted into the early 20th century.

The increasing preference to provide pauper children with greater literacy and industrial education reflected an ideological shift away from a view of orphaned or abandoned children as primarily a financial burden toward one which perceived them as children of the state and a social responsibility. This shift in ideology was facilitated by a reduction in the number of children by the mid-1850s. During the Great Hunger, the workhouse schools were described as "schools only in name."[57] Overcrowding, the prevalence of disease among children, and their removal to auxiliary accommodations meant that education was "deemed altogether a secondary duty" and workhouse teachers "were more required to relieve want and preserve discipline, than to teach."[58] After the Famine, an increasing majority of boards of guardians associated their schools to the National Education system which had been established in 1831. Under this system, workhouse schools qualified for a free supply of books while National Education inspectors were empowered to examine the literacy standards of both children and teachers. In a special inspection in 1854, James Kavanagh found that the abilities of workhouse children in reading, writing and arithmetic were far below the standard of laboring class children in ordinary National Schools.[59] Kavanagh blamed the parsimonious policies of boards of guardians, which had resulted in the inadequate number and inferior qualifications of workhouse teachers. The Poor Law Commissioners refuted these findings and argued that workhouse teachers experienced "peculiar disadvantages" as many children were of vagrant parents whose habits of frequently leaving and returning with their children negated any progress previously made by the child or teacher.[60] According to Kavanagh however, only 3 per cent of orphans who had been "inmates for years" could write "tolerably fair," while many could not read words of one syllable, and some did not know the alphabet.[61] Although inspector reports suggest that literacy standards and teacher qualifications had improved by the 1860s, a disconnect formed between National Education inspectors who placed emphasis upon literary education and Poor Law authorities who considered industrial training as more appropriate for pauper children.

By the mid-1850s, stone-breaking and capstan mills were increasingly replaced with what officials considered productive industrial training. The most extensive provisions for industrial training were in urban workhouses where larger numbers of resident children facilitated better economies of scale. The industrial curriculum was gendered with boys instructed in trades such as carpentry, shoemaking, textile weaving or baking, while girls were limited to household duties including laundry work, cooking, scrubbing floors, cleaning dormitories and looking after infants. Some boards of guardians acquired fields adjacent to their workhouses on which boys were educated in agriculture and produced vegetables for consumption by the inmates. The Poor Law commissioners claimed that industrial training rather than literary education had enabled 112,053 children aged 12–15 years, and 92,200 adolescents aged 16–18 years, to leave the workhouses to permanent employment in Ireland or abroad between 1849 and 1854.[62] Despite public concern at the hiring-out of children at a young age from the workhouse school, there was widespread belief in the irrelevance of prolonged literary education for what were considered the narrow future prospects of a pauper child. Archbishop Paul Cullen informed a parliamentary committee that "those children are destined to have a shovel or a spade" and if they were not trained for such occupations "any literary education supplied to them is of little value, and will only render them more unhappy."[63] But rather than the content of Poor Law education, the environment in which it was provided was much more detrimental to the health of pauper children, many of whom left the workhouses with visible and permanent scars upon body and mind.

Institutionalization

Children confined within the workhouse environment for extended periods of time suffered physical and psychological damage to their health. A monotonous and inadequate diet combined with overcrowded dormitories and a lack of exercise facilitated the spread of infectious diseases associated with nutritional deficiencies. Between 1849 and 1871, 198,572 children contracted ophthalmia within the workhouse, an eye disease caused by a deficiency of vitamin A which in many cases resulted in partial or total loss of sight. Poor nutrition and neglect by workhouse officers were blamed also for the prevalence of scrofula and other skin diseases in almost every workhouse.

Upon inspection of the Bailieborough workhouse school in 1854, Kavanagh observed: "Girls not at all clean; boys and girls in the very lowest bodily condition; skin livid and purple; children looking thin, old, and miserable."[64] An investigation by John Arnott into the children's dietary of the Cork workhouse provoked a national scandal in 1859 when he claimed that poor diet and neglect had caused an annual child mortality rate of 18 percent.[65] Welfare reformers asserted that, instead of educating a new generation of independent laborers, the Poor Law had maimed thousands of children and made them paupers for life.

Frequent observations were made on the psychological problems of workhouse children. Children who had "the 'poor-house look,' by which visitors so easily distinguished them" were described as listless, sullen, dull and mechanical.[66] Geber argues that the loss of parents during the Great Hunger may have been a contributing factor to the behavioral and emotional dysfunction displayed by many workhouse children during the 1850s.[67] Teenage girls who had grown up in the workhouse were noted by officials as particularly difficult, short-tempered and easily roused to violence over either real or perceived grievances as typified by girls in the South Dublin workhouse who rioted in response to the withdrawal of offers of emigration.[68] Employers of hired-out children similarly noted that they were uncaring and indifferent, but quick to anger. The most common observation was that pauper children exhibited no individualism. Public opinion hardened against such children for their perceived otherness. In 1861, the North Dublin workhouse master reported that fewer employers applied for pauper children as servants since "they have got such a bad account of them outside."[69] The stereotype of the innocent orphan had morphed into one of an institutionalized and damaged childhood. Social commentators made repeated calls for the adoption of a system of boarding-out with local small-holding families for orphaned and abandoned children. This was considered by reformers as the best method to raise children under domestic and parental influences. The Poor Law commissioners resisted these changes however, and reaffirmed the institutional model of care. They argued that the workhouse school "differs in no respect materially from the boarding school to which parents in a better class of life send their children from home."[70] Despite changes in the family circumstances of children admitted to the workhouse during the 1860s, authorities were slow to reform either the ideology or infrastructure of their institutional policies developed in the aftermath of the Great Hunger.

Conclusion

The tens of thousands of children in the workhouses of Ireland who had been orphaned or abandoned during the Great Hunger were indeed one of the "grimmest scars" of the disaster.[71] The experiences of those children who remained confined within these institutions for years, or in some cases for over a decade, highlight the necessity of considering the impact of the Famine upon children in a longer timeframe. While the rest of Ireland began to recover and move on during the 1850s, these children were effectively left in the same position as when they were first admitted. Viewed in economic terms as both a financial burden and a national labor resource, such children were vulnerable to exploitative child labor practices. As the number of workhouse inmates declined and attitudes shifted toward pauper education, Poor Law authorities considered themselves as *in loco parentis* to these children of the state. Yet the policies and ideology that shaped the provision of education and industrial training during this decade created an institutionalized environment, which inflicted physical and psychological scars upon workhouse children for the remainder of the century.

NOTES

1. Phelim P. Boyle and Cormac Ó Gráda, 'Fertility trends, excess mortality, and the Great Irish Famine, *Demography*, 23 (1986), pp. 543–62.

2. Joseph Robins, *The Lost Children: a study of charity children in Ireland, 1700–1900* (Dublin: Institute of Public Administration, 1980), p. 192.

3. Melinda Grimsley-Smith, 'Revisiting a "demographic freak": Irish asylums and hidden hunger', *Social History of Medicine*, 25 (2012), p. 307.

4. Jonny Geber, *Victims of Ireland's Great Famine: the bioarchaeology of mass burials at Kilkenny Union Workhouse* (Gainesville, 2015), pp. 76–8.

5. Mel Cousins, 'Collective action and the Poor Law: the political mobilisation of the Irish poor, 1851–78' in William Sheehan and Maura Cronin (eds), *Riotous assemblies: rebels, riots and revolts in Ireland* (Cork, 2011), p. 116.

6. John Taylor, *Amalgamation of unions, and pauper and National education in Ireland* (Dublin, 1857), p. 185.

7. Liz Thomas, 'The evolving moral and physical geometry of childhood in Ulster workhouses, 1838–55', *Childhood in the Past*, 6 (2013), p. 22.

8. Alexander Thom, *Statistics of Ireland, from Thom's Irish almanac and official directory for 1849* (Dublin, 1849), pp. 142–3.

9. *Fifth annual report of the commissioners for administering the laws for relief of the poor in Ireland*, [1530], H.C. 1852, xxvi, 547, pp. 4–5.

10. Peter Gray, *The making of the Irish Poor Law, 1815–43* (Manchester, 2009), p. 333.

11. Mel Cousins, *Poor relief in Ireland, 1851–1914* (Oxford, 2011), pp. 33–43.

12. Olwen Purdue, 'Poor relief in the north of Ireland, 1850–1921' in Virginia Crossman and Peter Gray (eds), *Poverty and welfare in Ireland, 1838–1948* (Dublin, 2011), pp. 23–36; Donnacha Seán Lucey, 'Poor relief in the west of Ireland, 1861–1911' in Crossman and Gray, *Poverty and welfare*, pp. 37–52; Georgina Laragy, 'Poor relief in the south of Ireland, 1850–1921' in Crossman and Gray, *Poverty and welfare*, pp. 53–66; Virginia Crossman, *Poverty and the Poor Law in Ireland, 1850–1914* (Liverpool, 2013).

13. *Ninth annual report of the commissioners for administering the laws for relief of the poor in Ireland* [2105], H.C. 1856, xxviii, 415, pp. 10–11.

14. *Thirteenth annual report of the commissioners for administering the laws for relief of the poor in Ireland* [2654], H.C. 1860, xxxvii, 327, p. 4.

15. *Fourteenth annual report of the commissioners for administering the laws for relief of the poor in Ireland* [2803], H.C. 1861, xxviii, 305, pp. 4–5.

16. *Report from the select committee on criminal and destitute children* [674], H.C. 1852–53, xxiii, 567, p. 394.

17. Denis C. O'Connor, *Seventeen years' experience of workhouse life: with suggestions for reforming the poor-law and its administration* (Dublin, 1861), pp. 51–2.

18. Jane Barnes, *Irish industrial schools, 1868–1908: origins and development* (Dublin, 1989), pp. 11–14.

19. *The twentieth report of the Commissioners of National Education in Ireland* [1834], H.C. 1854, xxx, 1, p. 633.

20. *Sixth annual report of the commissioners for administering the laws for relief of the poor in Ireland* [1645], H.C. 1852–53, 1, 159, pp. 4–5.

21. Ballymoney Board of Guardians indoor admission and discharge register, July 1849 – June 1861 (Public Record Office of Northern Ireland (hereafter P.R.O.N.I.) BG/5/G/2).

22. John Forbes, *Memorandums of a tour in Ireland* (London, 1853), p. 96.

23. Belfast Board of Guardians Minute Book, October 1850 (P.R.O.N.I., BG/7/A/10).

24. Antrim Board of Guardians Minute Book, May 1856 (P.R.O.N.I., BG/1/A/5).

25. Newry Board of Guardians Minute Book, October 1851 (P.R.O.N.I., BG/2/A/7).

26. *Twentieth report*, p. 639.

27. Anon., 'St. Joseph's Industrial Institute with special reference to its intern class of workhouse orphans', *The Irish Quarterly Review*, 8 (1859), pp. 4–5.

28. Ibid., pp. 2–4.

29. *Twentieth report*, p. 634.

30. Barnes, p. 9.

31. Lydia Murdoch, *Imagined orphans: poor families, child welfare, and contested citizenship in London* (New Brunswick, 2006), pp. 69–73.

32. *Report from the select committee on criminal and destitute children*, p. 347.

33. Geber, *Victims*, p. 158.

34. *Report from the select committee on criminal and destitute children*, p. 353.

35. *Seventh annual report of the commissioners for the relief of the poor in Ireland* [1785], H.C. 1854, xxix, 531, p. 7.

36. Dympna McLoughlin, 'Superfluous and unwanted deadweight: the emigration of nineteenth-century pauper women' in Patrick O'Sullivan (ed.), *Irish women and Irish migration* (London, 1995), pp. 76–7.

37. O'Connor, p. 48.

38. Ibid.

39. Ibid.

40. Ibid.

41. Dympna McLoughlin, 'Workhouses and Irish female paupers, 1840–70' in Maria Luddy and Clíona Murphy (eds), *Women surviving* (Dublin, 1989), pp. 132–6.

42. *Twentieth report*, p. 635; Taylor, p. 186.

43. Belfast Board of Guardians Minute Book, February 1851 (P.R.O.N.I. BG/7/A/10).

44. North Dublin Board of Guardians Minute Book, June 1851 (National Archives of Ireland (hereafter N.A.I.) BG/78/A/17).

45. North Dublin Board of Guardians Minute Book, September 1852 (N.A.I. BG/78/A/19).

46. Ibid.., September 1862 (N.A.I. BG/78/A/40).

47. *Freeman's Journal*, 12 February 1852.

48. Ibid., 21 February 1851.

49. *Belfast Mercury*, 16 October 1852.

50. *Freeman's Journal*, 21 February 1851.

51. North Dublin Board of Guardians Minute Book, December 1852 (N.A.I. BG/78/A/19).

52. Taylor, p. 167.

53. Belfast Board of Guardians Minute Book, November 1850 (P.R.O.N.I. BG/7/A/10).

54. *Sixth annual report*, p. 82.

55. Ibid.

56. Antrim Board of Guardians Minute Book, January 1857 (P.R.O.N.I. BG/1/A/6).

57. *Twentieth report*, p. 627.

58. Ibid.; Taylor, p. 165.

59. *Twentieth report*, pp. 644–8.

60. *Eighth annual report of the commissioners for administering the laws for relief of the poor in Ireland* [1845], H.C. 1854–55, xxiv, 523, p. 37.

61. *Twentieth report*, pp. 644–6.

62. *Eighth annual report*, pp. 15–16.

63. *Report from the select committee appointed to inquire into the administration of the relief of the poor in Ireland* [408], H.C., x, 647, p. 197.

64. *Twentieth report*, p. 660.

65. John Arnott, *The investigation into the condition of the children in the Cork workhouses, with an analysis of the evidence* (Cork, 1859), pp. i-xii.

66. Anon., p. 6.

67. Jonny Geber, 'Mortality among institutionalised children during the Great Famine in Ireland: bioarchaeological contextualisation of non-adult mortality rates in the Kilkenny Union workhouse, 1846–1851', *Continuity and Change*, 31 (2016), p. 120.

68. Anna Clark, 'Wild workhouse girls and the liberal imperial state in mid-nineteenth century Ireland', *Journal of Social History*, 39 (2005), pp. 389–409.

69. *Report from the select committee appointed to inquire into the administration of the relief of the poor in Ireland*, p. 235.

70. *Twenty-fourth annual report of the commissioners for administering the laws for relief of the poor in Ireland* [C 361], H.C. 1871, xxviii, 1, p. 13.

71. Robins, p. 192.

CHAPTER FOUR

"WRETCHED IN THE EXTREME"

Investigating child experiences of the Great Hunger through bioarchaeology

Jonny Geber

Bioarchaeology—the study of human remains from archaeological contexts—is a multidisciplinary science. Based on the notion that the human body adapts and responds to living conditions, quality of life and disease, the archaeological skeleton allows for studies of cultural effects of social change in the past.[1] Bioarchaeology studies earlier living conditions at both population and individual levels, and has the unique ability to recognize all individuals across the social strata, including that of people who, in general, never wrote their own accounts of their lives; namely, the children, the illiterate and the poor. Skeletal remains of children are, therefore, uniquely placed for gaining insights into childhood experiences in past societies, and particularly those from impoverished, marginalized and socially deprived sections of the community. By determining the age-at-death from the skeletal remains, it is also possible to assess age-related morbidities on a detailed level.[2] Additionally, the analysis of the human remains does not only give insights into life experiences of those who did not survive but also reveals a different perspective on how society and the workhouse system cared for the sick and the dying child inmates during the height of the Famine.[3] This chapter describes how workhouse children in Kilkenny City experienced the Famine. The study is based primarily on the bioarchaeological analysis of human remains that were discovered in mass burial pits during an archaeological excavation adjacent to the former institution in the mid–2000s. Further valuable insights, however, are given when the findings of these skeletal observations are interpreted and discussed within their wider historical context, which relates not only to poverty and famine, but also the experience of institutionalization.

In early February 1843, less than a year after it first opened, the Kilkenny Union Workhouse housed a total of 354 child inmates within its walls.[4] In late May 1851, that number had increased over five times to a massive 1,909 children.[5] It is clear that one of the most noticeable social changes that occurred in Kilkenny during the period of the Great Famine was the, more or less, forced institutionalization of its poorest and most vulnerable members of society, of which children were particularly affected. Despite that fact, the recollections and shared memories of the workhouse experience, which would have involved many local families, was never passed down through the generations. Eventually, most of the local knowledge and awareness of the history of the workhouse and, indeed, the Famine itself, in the city was ultimately lost. Many of those hundreds of children who would have spent their most formative years in the workhouse between 1845 and 1852 are likely to have been deeply affected on a psychological level. This outcome would not only have been a consequence of experiencing the horrors of the Famine itself but also resulted from other aspects of psychosocial stress relating to institutionalization within the workhouse system.[6]

An estimated 2,194 children died in the Kilkenny workhouse between 1846 and 1851, and they comprised just over 53 percent of all recorded deaths in the institution for that period.[7] Mass mortality during the Famine had resulted in overcrowding of the city cemeteries, and by August 1847 the Guardians of the Kilkenny Union had no other choice than to allow for intramural burials within the boundary walls of the workhouse and fever hospital (which functioned as an auxiliary to the workhouse infirmary).[8] These overflow cemeteries, which were in use until at least March 1851, were never consecrated and never marked on any maps. The local awareness of these burial grounds was lost until 2005 when mass burials adjacent to the former workhouse were discovered during an archaeological evaluation of the area.[9] An archaeological excavation of the burial ground took place between January and June 2006, during which 63 mass burials containing the skeletal remains of a minimum of 970 individuals were found.[10] A total of 522 children—303 of whom were less than 5 years old at the time of death—were present among these. (Figure 1.)[11]

Figure 1. Photograph of one of the burial pits (F114) from the Kilkenny mass burial ground, taken from a north-east direction during the archaeological excavation in February 2006. This burial pit contained the remains of 25 individuals of which 20 were children aged less than 15 years. Credit. Margaret Gowen & Co. Ltd.

The archaeological discovery of the mass burials and the subsequent bioarchaeological analysis of the human remains has enabled a direct investigative link to how people experienced the Famine on both an individual and communal level. The surviving historical records pertaining to the Kilkenny Poor Law Union are limited to minute books from the weekly meetings of the Board of Guardians, surviving correspondence with the Poor Law Commissioners, and contemporaneous newspaper articles from the local press. Insights into how the Famine and workhouse institutions were experienced by the inmates themselves are very limited. And this is particularly true for the children. (Figure 1.)

"Debility of constitution": the condition of the infant children

The nursery of the Kilkenny Union Workhouse was located within the central axis building of the complex, behind the dining hall/chapel, at the female section of the institution facing the courtyard at the corner to the infirmary block. This small room, which measured only 10×14 feet (c. 3.5×4.3m) in size, is unlikely to have been the only space where infants were cared for, and sections of the female accommodation block are likely to have been allocated to women who were still nursing their children.[12] The minute books from the weekly meetings of the Board of Guardians frequently address the poor care of the infant children. Reports from the medical officers stated that several mothers provided inadequate care to their children and that this mistreatment had resulted in a "debility of constitution" of many infant children.[13] Even before the Famine, in early March 1843, a two-month-old infant girl had died from starvation in the house allegedly due to neglect that was blamed on her mother.[14] Concerns by the guardians and medical officers also were raised for foundlings and other infants who were cared for by other women. Allegedly, some female inmates in the workhouse who were assigned the care of infants other than their own expressed a complete indifference to these children. As an attempt to remedy this, by recommendation from the medical officers, the board put forward the suggestion to pay these women one shilling a week, hoping that a salary would ensure an improved behavior on their part.[15] The proposal was, however, quickly rejected by the Poor Law Commissioners, who, in reply to the board, referenced the Poor Law and the necessity of making sure that the workhouse did not turn into a foundling hospital.[16] It was nevertheless a fact that the workhouse took care of several foundlings. A lack of wet-nurses and inadequate care left foundlings exhibiting a "precarious state of health" even by as early as October 1842, and the medical officers expressed particular concerns about the slim chances for them to survive the impending winter.[17]

The mass burial ground at the Kilkenny workhouse contained a minimum of 161 children belonging to the infant age class (0–2 years old), of whom 32 were neonates. Based on the specific age-at-death distribution of these new-borns, about 84 percent ($n = 26$) of these are likely to have primarily died due to endogenous factors that would have related to the poor health of their mothers during the gestation period.[18] Even those children who survived the first 28 weeks were severely affected by the poor health that was experienced by their mothers, and an estimated 91 percent (32/35) of children less than 2 years of age suffered from growth retardation that is likely to derive from intrauterine conditions.[19] One of these infants (DCCXCI) was within a burial pit with 20 other individuals located in the middle of the burial ground. The child had been interred in a coffin, carefully shrouded with the arms along the sides of the body, and with the head slightly facing toward the left of the body. (Figure 2.) The status of the dental eruption and mineralisation suggested that this child was between 12 and 13 months old at the time of death. The relative size of the bones in the skeleton, however, was more similar to the expected size of an infant aged about 6 months in a modern population.[20]

The aforementioned child also displayed further indicators of physiological stress, such as subtle porotic lesions at the roof of the eye sockets (orbits), the temples of the skull, as well as periosteal inflammation (new bone formation) on the shafts of the thigh (femora) and leg bones (tibiae). These skeletal lesions were active at the time of death, and the manifestation and distribution of the pathological changes are suggesting that scurvy (Vitamin C deficiency) is the most likely cause of these.[21] Scurvy is a severely debilitating and painful disease, and when lesions appear in the skeleton, the pain would have been excruciating. The osseous lesions on the bones are the result of micro-trauma at muscle attachment sites; deprivation of Vitamin C in the human body impairs the collagen formation in connective tissues, which start to break down as a result.

Figure 2. In-situ photograph of skeleton DCCXCI—a 12–13-month-old infant—taken during the archaeological excavation of the Famine burial ground at the Kilkenny Union Workhouse in 2006. The skeleton exhibited signs of growth retardation and several pathological changes indicative of Vitamin C deficiency. Credit: Margaret Gowen & Co. Ltd.

Scurvy in infants is rarely reported upon in clinical literature today, as it is an easy to remedy Vitamin C deficiency. However, the symptoms of a case diagnosed by a physician in California in 1904 gives a very vivid account of what this infant, and many other small children in Ireland during the Famine, most likely experienced in the weeks leading up to his/her death:

> Case No. 2. Seen in consultation in Alameda, February 3, 1904; a male infant, aged 13 months. This baby, so the mother said, cried violently whenever his legs were moved, as in putting on his shoes and stockings or changing his napkin; and had done so for eight to ten weeks before I saw him. He had gradually grown worse in this regard, so that now he would no longer sit up and could not lie in any position for any length of time without crying from pain. The mother knew of no cause, and the baby had been treated for a long time for rheumatism. He screamed violently when his legs were examined; both were found swollen from the knees down, markedly about the ankles and feet. The baby was found to have four teeth—two upper and two lower incisors; the gums about these were much swollen, so that the teeth were nearly hidden, were dark in color and bled when touched.[22]

The description of this early twentieth-century clinical case of infantile scurvy provides some insight into the reality of the Great Famine on many of its youngest victims. As potatoes have a very high content of Vitamin C, scurvy during the Famine was a direct consequence of the blight.[23] Access to the workhouse would, however, for many have meant relief from scurvy, as the workhouse diet provided some Vitamin C (e.g., from the milk rations). Recovery from scurvy is also evidenced by the palaeopathological record, as skeletal changes due to scurvy can only appear once some Vitamin C is reintroduced to the diet.[24] About 60 percent (n = 312) of all children (n = 522) in the mass burial ground exhibited lesions indicative of scurvy, and it does suggest that their health somewhat improved once they gained access to the institution.[25] But for many of the infant children, it may have been too late. Other than having an adverse effect on the adaptive immune system, and therefore impairing the body's ability to combat infectious diseases, scurvy may have made it too painful for the smallest children to feed. In early 1848, the Kilkenny Union medical officers expressed concerns over the fact that they had frequently seen mothers trying to feed their infant children with gruel rather than through breastfeeding. The reason for this may have been a desperate attempt by the mothers to feed their children, who may not have been able to suckle on the breast due to pain.[26]

Institutional stress, trauma and disease

In his book, *The lost children: a study of charity children in Ireland, 1700–1900*, Joseph Robins highlighted the general fact that, due to the manner in which febrile diseases struck the impoverished Irish population during the Famine, adults would often be affected and suffered premature deaths before the children. Ultimately, this meant that a countless number of children would have been forced to attempt to survive the Famine as orphans.[27] It is unknown how many orphans were receiving indoor relief in the Kilkenny workhouse during the Famine period, but they are frequently mentioned— along with foundlings—in both the minute books and contemporaneous local newspaper reports. But even children who entered the workhouse with their parents would have experienced a sense of loneliness and aban- donment due to the segregation policy of the institution. According to the workhouse rules, children over the age of 2 years were brought into the boys' or girls' wards of the house, and male and female inmates were to be kept isolated from each other at all times. This parental separation is likely to have caused further psychosocial stress to the children, which in turn may have influenced the mortality risk of the youngest ones in particular. The archival records contain very few references to children that belonged to the 2- to 5-year age class, but the skeletons from the mass burial ground at the workhouse reveal that this age group had seen the highest mortality rates during the height of the Famine.

In collation, the age-at-death profile of the non-adults from the Kilkenny mass burials exhibit a noticeable peak in mortality occurring around the age of 3 years. That would have been the age shortly after when they had been separated from their mothers if they had entered the institution together. Paediatricians and psychologists have recognized mortality risks and poor health as a consequence of maternal/parental deprivation in small children since at least the 1940s, which relates to psychosocial stress affecting the auto-immune system.[28] Unbeknownst to the workhouse physicians, the guardians and Poor Law commissioners at the time, this separation between mother and children within the workhouse system may very well have been a substantial factor that contributed to the high child mortality rates in these institutions before, during and after the Famine.[29] An entry in the minute books from late July 1851 reveal that parents were allowed to see their children once a week, and then only by appointment.[30] This directive was somewhat in contrast to the workhouse rules according to the Poor Law, which stated that mothers to children aged between 2 and 7 years were to be permitted access to them "at all reasonable times."[31] In Kilkenny, these "reasonable times" may have been restricted because many children were housed in auxiliary rented accommo-dation premises at various locations throughout the city during the Famine.

The standard of these auxiliaries was much inferior, and the workhouse physicians expressed concerns that this was the cause of the high rates of disease among the children. One of the dormitories of a rented house on Patrick Street in the middle of the city, where "children of tender age" slept, had no windows, and the rented auxiliary at St. Francis' was reportedly infested with rats.[32] Children in these premises also were suffering from ophthalmia,[33] which the medical officer was convinced was caused by the icy cold, damp flags of the floors.[34] By mid-November 1851, these children were reportedly "wretched in the extreme" and exhibited signs of poor blood circulation. Nearly 250 children were completely barefoot, and the Board purchased clogs and stockings for them.[35] Ill health due to poor housing conditions had, however, been a reality for the child inmates for a long time. About four years earlier, in early March 1848, many of the boys in an auxiliary converted from an old brewery building in the middle of the city were suffering from "itch" (typhus), and the board ordered the thorough cleansing of the wards, beds and children's clothing.[36] The majority of the children in these rented premises are likely to have belonged to the slightly older age categories, of between 5 and 9 years. According to the minute books, an estimated 588 children from that class died in the Kilkenny workhouse during the Famine.[37] In the intramural mass burial ground, however, "only" a total of 124 skeletons of children from this age group were discovered. One of these children (DLXXVIII), aged approximately 5 years at the time of death, did not exhibit any skeletal evidence of disease. The relative size of the long bones in the skeleton did, however, reveal an estimated living stature of only c. 95 cm (37 in), which was about 12 cm (5 in) shorter than the average 5-year-old in Ireland in the late 1980s.[38] The child was interred in a mass burial pit together with nine other children and five adults. (Figure 3.)

The skeleton of this child is in many ways representative of those interred in the Kilkenny workhouse Famine burial ground. The short stature of this individual is a reflection of both poverty and living conditions for children who grew up in Ireland during this period, but also for children in general during the 19th century. In comparative terms, the height of the workhouse children in Kilkenny—with the exception of the infants—is more or less the same reported from analyses of skeletons of children from all social classes in archaeologically excavated cemeteries in England.[39] At first glance, the lack of any visible skeletal manifestations of disease in the remains may suggest good health. However, the opposite is likely to be the case. This is based on the concept of the so-called "osteological paradox," which has been debated within the palaeopathological discipline ever since it was first published in 1992.[40] The main premise of the theory argues that the prevalence of disease in archaeological skeletal samples is a poor reflection of the true occurrence of disease, as the lack of pathological changes in a skeleton may simply mean that an individual was too weak to survive long enough for pathological changes to manifest on bone. This is particularly relevant when interpreting skeletal health from individuals who died as a consequence of famine, as infectious so-called "famine diseases" such as cholera, typhus and typhoid fever results in relatively rapid deaths in a population that is severely weakened by malnutrition and starvation.[41] The lack of pathological changes in the skeleton is therefore not necessarily an indication of lack of disease, but rather of a rapid mortality rate that occurred before osseous changes due to infections and other pathological conditions occurred.

Figure 3. Skeleton DLXXVIII, the remains of a five-year-old child, severely affected by growth retardation, as found during the archaeological excavation. This skeleton exhibited no pathological changes, which in a famine context most likely meant that the child died fairly quickly after having been affected by a disease. Credit: Margaret Gowen & Co Ltd.

Children of the Famine

Scholars have scarcely considered the experiences of the Irish Famine from the perspective of the child to date, and this despite the well-known fact that a majority of those who died as a consequence of starvation and disease would have been children. The human remains from the Kilkenny workhouse mass burials enable a physical insight into aspects of the human experience of the Famine that is not obtainable from historical records and folklore alone. The bones and teeth of the child skeletons exhibit both subtle and substantial marks of disease, malnutrition and trauma, and the manner in which they were buried has exposed how they were cared for in death.[42] Even the distress experienced by the infants (and their mothers) is discernible from the bioarchaeological record. But to be able to interpret these skeletal markers of stress and disease accurately, it is essential to consider their cultural and socio-historical context. The surviving archival accounts from the Kilkenny Union workhouse are sparse in specific references to individual children, and the skeletal analysis of the remains in the mass burials is, therefore, a valuable supplement for assessing the individuality of the Famine child experience. The archival records from before and after the Famine do, however, provide insights into how children reacted to their environment in the workhouse, which the skeletal analysis cannot obtain. For instance, in late August 1845, six boys had attempted to escape the institution by climbing over the boundary wall but were caught and reprimanded.[43] Another possible form of "protest" occurred in late May 1856 when several boys burnt boards and books with lucifer matches, and broke 44 window panes, in the school room. Their punishment was flogging, and hard labor and some boys were denied their milk ration.[44]

Both the bioarchaeological and historical sources reveal that children evidently suffered from institutionalization. On the other hand, both sources also give witness to how the workhouse as an establishment did attempt, regardless of the draconian regulations governing the provision of relief, to provide them with the best care possible under the circumstances. The Kilkenny Union Workhouse provided shelter, health care and food (albeit, meager rations) during the most desperate of times, and the guardians displayed responsibility toward the children, which not only referred to their health care but also their education.[45] The latter was intended to give them a chance to escape poverty in their adult lives, and included training in needlework and domestic duties for the girls, and shoemaking, weaving and agricultural work for the boys. In early October 1851, the guardians could announce to the Poor Law commissioners that "nine boys had gone out from the workhouse within nine months after having received instructions," and that they were now supporting themselves.[46] Older children, near the age of 15 years, were, by proportion, relatively few in the mass burial ground. This fact is probably not only a reflection of a decreased mortality risk for this particular age group but also a reflection of the admission policy of the workhouse institution. The Poor Law classified a 15-year-old inmate as an adult, and an adolescent of relatively good health, even if an orphan, would most likely have been considered able-bodied and refused entry.[47] It may have been that many children were forced to leave the workhouse when they reached the age of 15 years, although it has not been possible to confirm this from the historical records.

It is clear that children were genuinely cared for and, considering the circumstances, relatively well treated in the institution. Even though the guardians and the medical officers would have had the best intentions for the children in mind, psychosocial stress and the health risks induced by the overcrowded conditions of the workhouse institution and emotional deprivation drastically reduced the chance of survival and, for over 2,000 children, the Kilkenny workhouse was to become a place of death. The intramural mass burial ground contained only about a quarter of all these children, and the bioarchaeological analysis of their skeletal remains reveals osteobiographical life stories that are sometimes as shocking as they are emotive. (Figure 4.) These life stories are unique for each skeleton, just as the Famine experience would have been for the children who endured it. While the archival records relating to the inmates in Kilkenny workhouse is limited mainly to statistical accounts, the skeletons reveal a unique individuality of each victim interred in the mass burial ground. The bioarchaeology of the Kilkenny Union Workhouse has enabled a new way to tell the story of the children in mid-19th-century Ireland, who, until very recently, were the forgotten victims of the Great Irish Famine.

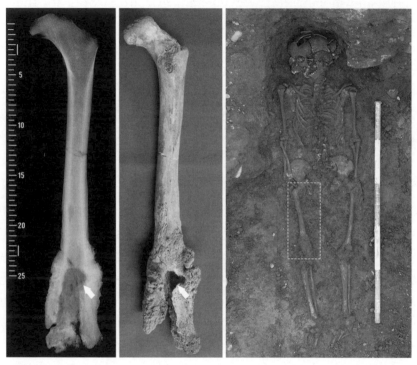

Figure 4. The skeleton (DCLIX) of a 12–13-year-old child (right), affected with severe chronic infection (osteomyelitis) of the distal end of the left thigh bone (femur) (left: radiograph (100Ð120); right: photograph, both posterior-anterior view). The infection is mostly bacterial, can occur due to trauma, open wounds, etc., or spread via the blood (haematogenous osteomyelitis) to the marrow space of the bone. It generates considerable bone build-up, and also pus which may break through an opening through the bone (cloaca) and skin; in this case, the cloaca (arrow) is located at the lower portion of the back of the right thigh, just above the knee. Other than pain, this child is likely to have suffered inflammation and muscle spasms in the affected area, high fever and chills. This child did also exhibit lesions indicative of Vitamin C deficiency, which would have substantially increased the experienced level of physical agony. Credit: Jonny Geber and Margaret Gowen & Co. Ltd.

NOTES

1. See Clark Spencer Larsen, *Bioarchaeology: Interpreting behavior from the human skeleton* (Cambridge, 2015).

2. For generic literature on osteological methodologies and palaeopathological analyses, see Margaret Cox and Simon Mays (eds.), *Human osteology in archaeology and forensic science* (Cambridge, 2000); Donald R. Brothwell, *Digging up bones: The excavation, treatment and study of human remains* (Ithaca, 1981); Tim D. White and Pieter A. Folkens, *The human bone manual* (Amsterdam, 2005).

3. See Lorna Tilley and Alecia A. Schrenk (eds), *New developments in the bioarchaeology of care: further case studies and expanded theory* (Basel, 2017).

4. *Kilkenny Moderator*, 11 February 1843.

5. Minutes of the Board of Guardians, Kilkenny Union, 29 May 1851, Kilkenny County Library Local Studies (hereafter KCLLS) 17/10K.

6. See Robert B. McCall, "The consequences of early institutionalization: can institutions be improved? – should they?" in *Child and Adolescent Mental Health*, vol. 18 (2013), 193–201; Kim MacLean, "The impact of institutionalization on child development" in *Development and Psychopathology*, vol. 15 (2003), pp. 853–884.

7. The number of child deaths during the Famine period (here defined as between October 1846 and September 1851) has been estimated from surviving archival records (Minutes of the Board of Guardians, Kilkenny Union, KCLLS 12/7K–17/10K) and contemporaneous newspaper articles (*The Kilkenny Journal* and *Kilkenny Moderator*), see Jonny Geber, "Mortality among institutionalized children during the Great Famine in Ireland: bioarchaeological contextualization of non-adult mortality rates in the Kilkenny Union Workhouse, 1846–1851" in *Continuity and Change*, vol. 31 (2016), pp. 101–126.

8. Jonny Geber, *Victims of Ireland's Great Famine: the bioarchaeology of mass burials at Kilkenny Union Workhouse* (Gainesville, 2015), pp. 44–51; Geber, 'Burying the Famine dead: Kilkenny Union Workhouse' in John Crowley, William J. Smyth and Mike Murphy (eds), *Atlas of the Great Irish Famine, 1845–52* (Cork, 2012), pp. 341–348.

9. Cóilín Ó Drisceoil, 'Archaeological assessment of workhouse burial site, MacDonagh Junction Development, Kilkenny' (Unpublished report, Kilkenny Archaeology, Kilkenny, 2005).

10. See Brenda O'Meara, 'A preliminary account of recent excavations adjacent to Kilkenny Union Workhouse' in *Old Kilkenny Review*, vol. 58 (2006), pp.154–162;

Geber, *Victims of Ireland's Great Famine*. After the osteological and palaeopathological analysis of the human remains, the skeletons were reinterred in a purpose-built crypt at the Famine Memorial Garden on Hebron Road in Kilkenny City, in May 2010.

11. Geber, 'Mortality among institutionalised children,' passim.

12. The allocated space for the nursery is marked on the original architectural plan of the Kilkenny Union Workhouse (see Workhouse Drawing Collection, 1839–1929, Irish Architectural Archive 0085/138), although the use of particular rooms and spaces in the workhouse is likely to have changed throughout its use (see Liz Thomas, "The evolving moral and physical geometry of childhood in Ulster workhouses, 1838–55" in *Childhood in the Past: An International Journal*, vol. 6 (2013), pp. 22–51.

13. Minutes Kilkenny Union, 27 January 1848, KCLLS 13/8K.

14. Ibid., 9 March 1843, KCLLS 6/2K.

15. Ibid., 27 October 1842, KCLLS 6/2K.

16. Ibid., 9 November 1842, KCLLS 6/2K.

17. Ibid., 27 October 1842, KCLLS 6/2K.

18. Geber, "Mortality among institutionalised children," p. 111.

19. Jonny Geber, "Skeletal manifestations of stress in child victims of the Great Irish Famine (1845–1852): prevalence of enamel hypoplasia, Harris lines, and growth retardation" in *American Journal of Physical Anthropology*, vol. 155 (2014), pp. 149–161.

20. The greatest length (GL) of the right femur in this individual measured 112mm. For comparison with a modern population sample, see Marion M. Maresh, 'Measurements from roentgenograms, heart size, long bone lengths, bone, muscle and fat widths, skeletal maturation' in Robert W. McCammon (ed.), *Human growth and development* (Springfield, 1970), pp. 155–200.

21. Megan Brickley and Rachel Ives, *The bioarchaeology of metabolic bone disease* (Amsterdam, 2008), pp. 41–74.

22. William Fitch Cheney, 'Scurvy in infants' in *California State Journal of Medicine*, vol. 2 (1904), pp. 179–180.

23. E. Margaret Crawford, 'Scurvy in the Ireland during the Great Famine' in *Social History of Medicine*, vol. 1 (1988), pp. 281–300.

24. Jonny Geber and Eileen Murphy, 'Scurvy in the Great Irish Famine: Evidence of Vitamin C deficiency from a mid–19th century skeletal population' in *American Journal of Physical Anthropology*, vol. 148 (2012), pp. 512–524.

25. Ibid.

26. Jonny Geber, 'Children in a ragged state': seeking a biocultural narrative of a workhouse childhood in Ireland during the Great Famine (1845–1852)' in *Childhood in the Past: An international journal*, vol. 9 (2016), pp. 120–138.

27. Joseph Robins, *The lost children: a study of charity children in Ireland, 1700–1900* (Dublin, 1980), pp. 178–179.

28. Geber, 'Mortality among institutionalised children,' passim.

29. See William Neilson Hancock, "The mortality of children in workhouses in Ireland" in *Journal of the Statistical and Social Enquiry Society of Ireland*, vol. 20 (1862), pp. 193–198.

30. Minutes Kilkenny Union, 31 July 1851, KCLLS 17/10K.

31. *Second annual report of the commissioners for administering the laws for relief of the poor in Ireland*, 1849, appendix a, no. III, p. 63.

32. *The Kilkenny Journal*, 14 March 1849; 2 March 1850.

33. Ophthalmia, also referred to as "famine blindness," was frequently diagnosed during the Great Famine in Ireland, but it was a clinical misdiagnosis which is a reflection of the understanding of disease of the time, see Liam Kennedy, Paul S. Ell, E. Margaret Crawford and Leslie A. Clarkson, *Mapping the Great Irish Famine: a survey of the famine decades* (Dublin, 1999), p. 110. The condition people suffered was most likely xerophthalmia, which is caused by Vitamin A deficiency and results in eye dryness and ultimately un-repairable damage to the cornea of the eye if not treated in time.

34. Minutes, Kilkenny Union, 25 September 1851, KCLLS 17/10K.

35. Ibid., 13 November 1851, KCCLLS 17/10K.

36. Ibid., 2 March 1848, KCCLLS 13/8K.

37. Jonny Geber, 'Mortality among institutionalised children,' passim.

38. Living stature was estimated from the greatest length of the right humerus (145.52 mm) using the following method: Shelley L. Smith, "Stature estimation of 3–10-year-old children from long bone lengths" in *Journal of Forensic Science*, vol. 52 (2007), pp. 538–546. There is currently only one published clinical growth standard available for the Irish population, for the ages 5–18.5 years: Hilary M.C.V. Hoey, James M. Tanner and Leslie A. Cox, "Clinical growth standards for Irish children" in *Acta Paediatrica Scandinavia*, Suppl., vol. 338, pp. 2–31.

39. Geber, 'Children in a ragged state,' passim.

40. See James W. Wood, George R. Milner, Henry C. Harpending and Kenneth M. Weiss, 'The osteological paradox: problems of inferring prehistoric health from skeletal samples' in *Current Anthropology*, vol. 33, pp. 343–370.

41. Donald J. Ortner, *Identification of pathological conditions in human skeletal remains* (Amsterdam, 2003), p. 115.

42. Jonny Geber, 'Interring the "deserving" child: The archaeology of the deaths and burials of children at the Kilkenny Union Workhouse during the Great Famine in Ireland, 1845–52' in Eileen Murphy and Mélie Le Roy (eds.), *Children, death and burial: archaeological discourses* (Oxford, 2017), pp. 249–262.

43. Minutes Kilkenny Union, 21 August 1845, KCLLS 9/5K.

44. Ibid., 29 May 1856, KCLLS 22/14K.

45. Geber, 'Children in a ragged state,' passim.

46. Minutes Kilkenny Union, 9 October 1851, KCCLLS 17/10K.

47. *The Kilkenny Journal*, 22 June 1844.

Orphaned in Canada

CHAPTER FIVE

RETHINKING THE IRISH FAMINE ORPHANS OF QUEBEC, 1847-1848[1]

Mark G. McGowan

"Molly Johnson." The heavily French-accented voice of a man echoed throughout the dark cavernous room. A young priest with a parchment list in his hand steps into the foreground, calls the name, as a train of ill-clad, motley looking children queue into the room. The lament of violin music is heard in the background. The scene of this Canadian *Heritage Minute*, produced in the early 1990s, addresses the French-Canadian adoption of hundreds of Irish children, orphans of the Great Irish Famine of the late 1840s.[2] The picture of well-dressed French-Canadian families, as directed by their priests, accepting Irish children into their homes has become near iconic in the Canadian collective imagination of the coming of more than 120,000 Irish Famine refugees to Canada in 1847 and 1848. The image of the French-Canadian largesse was immortalized by John Francis Maguire in his monumental *The Irish in America* (1880) when he wrote "Half-naked squalid, covered with vermin generated by hunger, fever, and the foulness of the ship's hold, perhaps with germs of the plague lurking in their vitiated blood, these helpless innocents of every age—from the infant taken from the bosom of its dead mother to the child who could barely tell the name of its parents—were gathered under the fostering protection of the Church."[3] The memorial Celtic Cross at Grosse Île speaks about the valiant efforts of French-Canadians to assist the starving Irish children. Even prior to the erection of the cross and the writings of Maguire, the motif of the great orphan rescue was alive in words used by the local bishop to accuse the Irish in Montreal of ingratitude. During a squabble over the parish boundaries of St. Patrick's Church, Bishop Ignace Bourget reminded Father Patrick Dowd, Thomas D'Arcy McGee and others, that they should remember the great kindness demonstrated by French-Canadians to the destitute Irish orphans of the Famine.[4] Thus one of the most memorialized, representative and impactful moments of the Great Irish Famine on Canada, has been the charity extended by French-Canadians to orphaned children.

In this study, a University of Toronto research team endeavored to dig deeply into routinely generated records to assess just what actually happened to the Irish Famine orphans of 1847 to 1848. In the process of examining the lives of 619 Famine orphans, at Quebec City, and a number of other Irish "foundlings" discovered along the way, the team cultivated new questions regarding the nature of adoption in this period, the manner in which Irish children were accepted into French-Canadian families, the persistence of the Irish surnames of the orphans—a feature of the story highlighted throughout its telling and in the *Heritage Minute* itself—and the characteristic mobility of these orphans, which were akin to general demographic movements among immigrants in this era.[5] In the process, this preliminary study suggests that the mass "adoption" of Irish orphans by French-Canadian families was not as it first appears. Although there is still much work to be done, it is clear at this early stage of research that first, adoption is not an appropriate term to be used in the context of this story; secondly, that children were essentially in a semi-indentured service to the families in which they were placed; thirdly, that siblings were separated from one another and sometimes at great distances; and fourthly, many orphans were keen on leaving their placements as soon as possible in order to secure independence or reunite with extended family members elsewhere in British North America and the United States. In fact, the findings of this study suggest that the most famous of the Famine orphan stories, that of Daniel Tighe of Lissanuffy, Roscommon, and later of Lotbinière, Quebec, was atypical of the orphan experience. Few orphans were embraced by their placement families and few appear to have inherited property as a result of the placement.

The Passage of 1847-48

The passage of Irish Famine refugees on board the so-called "coffin ships" from the United Kingdom to North America has become a well-known feature of Famine narratives. In 1846 and 1847, fares were cheaper to British North America than to American ports, where standards for landing passengers were higher, as were the fines for captains who were in violation of those standards. The ships were certainly less than optimal for passengers since they were primarily designed for the transportation of timber and other cargo in the North Atlantic triangle of trade. Irish and other migrants were simply used as human ballast for what would have been empty ships upon their return to North America. Passengers were crammed below decks in makeshift bunk areas, often with inadequate food and water, and susceptible to numerous bacterial infections often stemming from poor sanitary facilities. Under such cramped and fetid conditions, disease spread. Diarrhea, dysentery and typhus (also known as ships fever) struck at the young and the old, killing thousands at sea and in the makeshift quarantine stations set up near their eventual ports of call. It is not surprising that under such conditions so many orphaned children required attention once they landed in the New World.

The Famine would prove to be the high watermark for Irish mass migration to British North America, a region that had already witnessed the arrival of about 450,000 Irish since the end of the Napoleonic wars.[6] In 1847 alone, 109,000 passengers set out for Canada, New Brunswick, and Nova Scotia. The port of Halifax, Nova Scotia, one of Britain's key naval installations in the North Atlantic, admitted around 2,000 migrants that year largely because the Lieutenant Governor, Sir John Harvey, warned the Colonial Office that there was no work to be had in Nova Scotia and eastern sections of the province were suffering the effects of a devastating potato blight as well.[7] Close to 17,000 migrants landed in New Brunswick at either the Mirimichi region or in the port of Saint John, which had well-established maritime trade links with Derry and Cork. It is estimated that at least 90,000 migrants set out for the interior Canadian port city of Quebec, which was a gateway to the United Province of Canada, and for many migrants a mere jumping off point to the interior of the United States of America. In Black '47 alone, over 400 ships landed at Quebec. Migrants intending to land at the city proper had to first clear the quarantine station of Grosse Île, a small island in the Gulf of Saint Lawrence about 35 kilometers northeast of Quebec. Here, the sick and dying would be removed from the ships and placed in lazarettos staffed by an overworked medical team. Over 5,000 Irish migrants were buried on Grosse Île in a mass grave in Black '47. One of the indelible images surviving from the "summer of sorrow" at Grosse Île was the staggering number of Irish orphan children. The data from all ports indicated that these orphans could be classed in three ways: children left completely parentless as a result of the voyage and quarantine; children with a single parent who could no longer manage them and left them with local religious groups or charities for further care; and, finally, families in which both parents could not manage to care for their children, either in the short term or the long term, and elected to leave them at the orphan asylums, or simply abandoned them.[8]

Quebec was not alone among British North American cities in having to cope with the influx of hundreds of Irish Famine orphans in 1847 and 1848. Several hundred children without families were gathered at Saint John, New Brunswick and then dispensed to farm families elsewhere in the province.[9]

Similarly, the number of orphans staying in the fever sheds of Point St. Charles in Montreal became so high that Bishop Bourget enlisted the services of both the Soeurs de Charité de Montreal (Grey Sisters) and the Sisters of Providence to shelter and arrange for the placement of Irish children.[10] From 11 July 1847 to 18 August 1848, 221 children were sent to St. Jerome's Asylum run by the Sisters of Providence. Of that number, 103 died, 105 remained in the orphanage, while 13 were placed with parents or protectors.[11] Farther up the St. Lawrence River, at Kingston, Canada West, the Catholic church was also visible on the front lines of famine relief, as the Sisters Hospitallers of St. Joseph, admitted over 100 orphans to their new Hotel Dieu hospital facility.[12] Elsewhere in the "upper province," the priests of the diocese of Toronto, arranged for orphans to be contracted out to "upstanding" Catholic farmers in the hinterlands of the province's commercial center, once again placing over 100 Irish boys and girls in steady jobs, with shelter, and a monthly wage.[13] The scope of relief of these Irish orphans, primarily by the Catholic Church, west of Saint John, is much too extensive for adequate treatment here. This having been said, the Quebec orphans, as the best known of these unfortunates of Black '47, may offer researchers insight on how to research and challenge assumptions about Famine orphans elsewhere. Situated in the principal *entrepôt* to Irish migration in the central British provinces, the treatment and dispersal of the Quebec City Irish orphans may provide insights into the definition of orphan, the concept of legal adoption in pre-Confederation Canada, and the role of the Catholic Church as guardian of the faith of these young refugees.

The current research on the Quebec orphans has some solid historiographical foundations upon which to build. Jason King's exceptionally fine essay "Remembering Famine Orphans: The Transmission of Famine Memory between Ireland and Quebec," published in 2012 has offered insightful analysis on how John Francis Maguire and others helped to shape the orphan story and indirectly offers a caveat to any researcher who might take these constructions of the orphan story at face value.[14] The current work does not replicate King's observations, other than to tease out, through the use of routinely generated records—census data, parish registers, the Drouin list and the manuscripts generated by religious orders—to get behind the historical realities of the orphan stories. Much of this quantitative study was facilitated by the work of the late Marianna O'Gallagher, who compiled a list of 619 orphans from the registers of Grosse Île and the Dames de Charité of Quebec City, who initially received the children from the quarantine station. The "O'Gallagher List" (as to which it will be referred) was a comprehensive ledger, committed primarily by the Dames, including the names of each child, date received, parents' names, county of origin, age, ship from which they disembarked and, whenever possible, the name of the adopter and the place of relocation. The entire list was reprinted, for easy use, in O'Gallagher's *Grosse Île: Gateway to Canada, 1832–1937*, ergo the origin of the reference to the name of the list.[15] A third important foundation has been a little-known Master's thesis written by Marie-Claude Belley at Université Laval in 2003. Belley carefully examines the 619 orphans on the O'Gallagher list, but includes additional names derived from ecclesial and civil sources. Her data set was 702, but the names of the additional 83 children were not appended to the thesis, so the current research is grounded solely in data pulled from the O'Gallagher list.[16] Belley offered some preliminary analysis of her data set and has set some broad parameters for future research, including a comparative study, between the Quebec orphans, and the list appended to Peter D. Murphy's *Poor Ignorant Children*, which chronicles the plight of Irish orphans in the same period in Saint John, New Brunswick. The current study takes up the challenge posed by Belley nearly 15 years ago, and envisions Quebec's orphans as the first in a comparative study including the published and unpublished data from the four other British North American centres.

Research Methods

The five-member team consisting of a principal investigator and four student researchers used the O'Gallagher List as its foundation. Each student team member was assigned about 130 names and the principal investigator focused on orphans exclusively from County Roscommon. The latter analysis of Roscommon orphans would form part of the larger University of Toronto study on mapping the locations and lives of the 1,490 migrants from the county who were "assisted" off the Strokestown Estate of Major Denis Mahon in 1847.[17] It was also coincidental that orphans from Roscommon accounted for the highest number of orphans from any single county, among the 360 orphans who had a county recorded beside their name on the list. After those declared dead were removed from the data sets, the researchers proceeded methodically to search orphan names through a variety of sources, the Canadian Census, beginning in 1851–52 and continuing to 1921, the Census of the United States, beginning in 1850, the databases at Ancestry.ca, FamilySearch.com, and parish registers and records for British North America. There were eight categories that would measure a match: 1) surname; 2) given name; 3) Irish birth; 4) "adoptive family"; 5) approximate age; 6) timing based on age and birthplace of children (for later censuses); 7) location of place of settlement; and 8) religion. The latter category (#8) was problematic when using the American census, since religion is not recorded. Four color-coded categories were created: green (6–8 matches), blue (4–5 matches); orange (less than 4); yellow (did not find). The team met weekly to discuss their findings and every month a new color-coded master list was created, based on the revisions and additions up to that point. The research project lasted just over three months, and provided a relatively clean data set of names and location, upon which a historical narrative might be constructed, and the prevailing ideas about "orphan adoption" tested.

Orphans and French Canada

In general, the analysis of the O'Gallagher List shows a number of interesting patterns in terms of county origins and in terms of primary placement, or in the words used by contemporaries, location of the adoptions. Of the 360 orphans who could be identified by county, Roscommon led all counties with 52 orphans or just over 14 percent of the total in this subset. County Tipperary followed with 33, or just over 9 percent; Clare had 26 orphans at 7.2 percent of the total, while Fermanagh and Laois had 20 each or about 5.6 percent, respectively (See Table 1).

Table 1: Counties of Origin of Irish Famine "Orphans" at Quebec, 1847–1848
N=619

County	Number	Percentage	County	Number	Percentage
Roscommon	52	8.4	Meath	7	1.1
Tipperary	33	5.3	Limerick	7	1.1
Clare	26	4.2	Louth	6	0.9
Fermanagh	20	3.2	Armagh	4	0.6
Queen's	20	3.2	Antrim	3	0.5
Leitrim	20	3.2	Donegal	3	0.5
Mayo	18	2.9	Derry	3	0.5
Kildare	17	2.7	Monaghan	3	0.5
Tyrone	16	2.6	Waterford	2	0.3
Kilkenny	16	2.6	Carlow	2	0.3
Sligo	13	2.1	Kerry	2	0.3
Galway	11	1.8	King's	1	0.2
Wicklow	11	1.8	Longford	1	0.2
Cork	11	1.8			
Westmeath	11	1.8	Non-Irish	5	0.8
Cavan	10	1.6	Unknown	259	41.8
Wexford	7	1.1	Total	619	100.0

Source: Marianna O'Gallagher, *Grosse Île: Gateway to Canada, 1832–1937* (Ste-Foy: Carraig Books, 1984), Appendices. Note neither Dublin nor Down were represented. Non-Irish consisted of two orphans from both England and Scotland and one from Quebec.

The first caution is the high numbers of Roscommon orphans, particularly for a county which generally was remarked as having lower levels of migration to British North America in the period than other counties. The numbers of orphans are likely inflated because of the concentration of Major Denis Mahon's 1,490 assisted migrants on just four ships destined for Quebec: The *Virginius, Erin's Queen, John Munn,* and *Naomi.* The *Virginius* and the *Naomi* were notorious for the high rates of deaths at sea and in quarantine and certainly deserved the colloquial moniker of "coffin ship."[18] The fact that the *Virginius* was filled exclusively with Roscommon migrants and the vast majority of passengers on the *Naomi* were also from Roscommon, helps to explain why the numbers of Roscommon orphans appear inflated, when compared to general migration figures for the county among the arrivals in British North America in the sailing season of 1847.

It was noted also that the aggregate analysis of the O'Gallagher list reveals that, in Canada East, there were four significant geographic clusters where orphans were sent and placed (See Table 2). The largest number of orphans was placed in the Quebec City area, both in the city itself, the suburbs and the county. This cluster also included Quebec City's neighboring counties of Portneuf and Montmorency. The second largest cluster was located in the frontier area of Rimouski, about 300 kilometers to the northeast of Quebec City, on the south shore of the St. Lawrence River. The third area of significance was the agricultural county of Lotbinière, located west of Quebec City, on the south shore of the St. Lawrence, across the river from the city of Trois Rivières. The fourth cluster was found adjacent to Lotbinière in the town and county of Nicolet. There also were smaller groups of children who were sent to families in the United States and Upper Canada. Often the destination of the orphans was determined by family ties, particularly those orphans who had relatives who settled prior to the Famine in the Canadian interior, or the United States tidewater ports, or the opening frontier in western New York and Ohio valleys. In the four principal cluster areas in Canada East (Quebec), however, the chief agent of placement was the Roman

Catholic Church, which included in its ranks over 80 percent of the population of Canada East (now Quebec). The Archbishop of Quebec City, Joseph Signay, mandated that Catholic families take in these children and his priests voluntarily brought back orphans to their home parishes, not coincidently in Rimouski, Lotbinière, Nicolet and St-Grégoire.[19] Priests would accompany the children on the steamer *St. George* from Grosse Île to the Marine Hospital at Saint-Roch.[20] From there, the healthy children would be transferred to the orphanage founded by the Charitable Ladies of Quebec, which was later assumed, in 1849, by the Grey Sisters from Montreal. At that time, the Church in Quebec City had no non-cloistered order of women religious to undertake such a task, therefore the Souers de Grises answered the call. Father Charles-Felix Cazeau, secretary to Archbishop Signay, coordinated the Church's effort,[21] and he may very well have been the model for the priest crying "Molly Johnson" in the vignette. Thus, as the *Heritage Minute* observes quite accurately, the Church became a key player in the allocation of these children to: "welcoming families."

Table 2A: Placement Locations of the Orphans of 1847–1848
N=406

Location	Number	Percentage
Quebec City & Region	107	25.5
Rimouski & Area	57	13.6
Nicolet & St. Grégoire	56	13.3
Lotbinière & Region	25	6.0
United States of America	22	5.2
Upper Canada	19	4.5
Montreal & Region	5	1.2
Other Placement Areas	129	30.7
Total	420	100.00

Source: Marianna O'Gallagher, *Grosse Île: Gateway to Canada, 1832–1937* (Ste-Foy: Carraig Books, 1984), Appendices. Many of the "other" placement areas involved less than three children per place.

Table 2B: Placement of Orphan Children as Located on the "Green list"

N=77

Location	Number	Percentage
Rimouski & Area	24	31.2
Quebec & Area	20	26.3
Nicolet & St. Grégoire	16	21.1
Upper Canada	9	11.8
Montreal & Area	5	6.6
Lotbinière	2	2.6
United States of America	1	1.3
Total	77	100.00

Source: Marianna O'Gallagher, *Grosse Île: Gateway to Canada, 1832-1937* (Ste-Foy: Carraig Books, 1984), Appendices. The one foundling was not included in the count since she did not appear on the O'Gallagher List.

The inclusion of the name of the adopter on the O'Gallagher List was an excellent means to track down orphans whose Irish names were likely misspelled and misunderstood by the French Canadian adults who recorded names from the children, and who themselves would have spoken in a heavily accented English. Another discovery of note was that children were not placed exclusively in French-Canadian homes. About 375 adopters were identified in the list of 619, and of these 118 or 33.1 percent were actually Irish in origin and 16 others, or 4.5 percent had English or Scottish surnames. The remaining 222 individuals (or 62.2 percent) were identifiably French-Canadian by their surname. Only one person could not be identified ethnically by the spelling of the surname. Therefore, the process of placement was not exclusive to French-Canadians, but Irish families, particularly in the Quebec City area volunteered to accept at least one or more Irish orphans into their homes. In the other three cluster areas—Lotbinière, Nicolet and Rimouski—the overwhelming number of placements was in French-Canadian Catholic homes. In the case of the latter, the orphan children did retain their Irish names.

The team's discoveries compare favourably to the overall picture for the "619." Over the course of its digging, the team eliminated some 448 names of orphans (or just over 72 percent of the total) who either died in the Orphan's Home in Quebec or for whom no trace could be found in either the Canadian or American censuses or in the extensive databases made available for genealogists online. Seventy-seven children (or 12.4 percent) were positively identified and fit nicely into the green category, while 94 (15.2 percent) orphans were included on the blue list and warrant further investigation. In sum, the team was able to locate almost 28 percent of the orphans at least as far as the first census counts, and two additional foundlings, simply other Irish children detected within the census while searching for our lists, were added to the green list. One suspects that they may have been part of Belley's larger data set of 702.

The areas in which children on the green list were found generally corresponded to the clusters identified more generally in an analysis of the entire O'Gallagher List (See Table 2B). The highest concentrations were in the Quebec City area and in Rimouski, and some orphans were tracked for several decades, including a small minority who intermarried with local French-Canadian men or women. The majority of orphans located on the green list were female and all were Roman Catholic, making further tracking of them through Catholic parish registers possible. It should also be noted that the majority of the 78 orphans (77 plus one foundling) on the green list were not listed as family members, with many serving as day laborers on farms, domestic servants in the cities and towns, and some just labelled as "none" for occupation. The green list also included Irish names as potential adopters, including John Kelly, who ran a tavern in Fraserville, near Rimouski, employed four orphans, none of whom were listed as a family member in the census of 1851–52.[22] It would appear those children placed in Irish circumstances were treated similarly to those orphans placed in French-Canadian businesses and farms. They were valued for their work, particularly when families were in need of teens and pre-teens to labor, because the family's children were in infancy. While certain general patterns of orphan placement appear, individual stories help unpack orphan experience more vividly.

One should not be surprised to find that these children were used for little more than indentured labor on French-Canadian farms and Irish-Canadian businesses. When any romantic notions conjured up by the *Heritage Minute* regarding adoption and the preservation of culture by keeping one's Irish name are removed, one is left with the stark reality of being a child in mid-19th century British North America. In Upper Canada, for instance, Veronica Strong-Boag comments that apprenticeships "were the only legislative provision for poor or orphaned children from 1799 to 1851."[23] In the Maritime Provinces, children could be auctioned off to serve on farms or other local businesses. As Bettina Bradbury reports on 19th-century Montreal, children were expected to work in order to support their impoverished working-class families.[24] Given the practical attitudes toward children and labor that prevailed in the colonies in the period, the revelation that Irish orphans were put to work in their new home was simply part of the expectations placed on children in 19th-century Canada.

Moreover, the concept of legal adoption was not enshrined in Canadian legal code in the 1840s. Irish orphan children who appeared in the census were overwhelmingly listed as not being family members, in the columns allocated to identifying their relationship to the family. In 1873, the province of New Brunswick, at which point was one of the founding provinces of the Dominion of Canada, was the first Canadian jurisdiction to create the category of legal adoption.[25] In the 1840s, the *Droit Civile* of Quebec did not anticipate legal adoption, nor did the revised *Code of 1866*, on the eve of Canadian Confederation. There were provisions made for the legal transfer of property to heirs, which in some cases might be *de facto* orphans, as was the case of Daniel Tighe, but no legal adoption. In the case of Tighe, the

Coulombe family in which he and his sister were placed, was childless, so Francis Coulombe contracted a notary to transfer title to the family farm to the indentured Irish boy.[26] Thus, while the term *de facto* adoption might be suitable for identifying the Irish orphans in their new domestic situation, the term legal adoption would be an anachronism.[27]

Finally, it should also be noted that one ought to be careful in using the word orphan, which often denotes a child who has experienced the death of both parents. The case of the Irish orphans adds several layers of complexity to the definition of orphan which could also describe a child abandoned by both living parents to "better" care provided by the Church's orphanages, or those left in an institution by a surviving parent, who did not have the means to care for the children after the death of a spouse and with precarious employment opportunities in the colonies. The Mahoney family may serve as an illustration of this complexity. Patrick Mahoney, and his six daughters departed Coolmean, County Clare, in 1848, boarded the *Governor* bound for Quebec. His wife, Honora Kelly, had died during "Black '47" at the age of 40. Upon landing at Grosse Île, in May, Mahoney lost his second youngest daughter, Ellen, aged 4. This left the remaining five siblings and Mahoney in mourning and nearly destitute in Quebec City. Keeping his eldest daughter Elizabeth, aged 13, with him, Patrick delivered his four other daughters Bridget, aged 11, Mary, 10,[28] Catherine, 6, and Nancy Ann, 4, to the orphanage run by the Grey Sisters. Each of these four sisters, in turn, were placed with French-Canadian farm families in the Rimouski area, both Mary and Nancy with the family of Antoine Larouche, and the two other girls with the Mavinon and Pineau families.[29] The Mahoney experience confirms that the placement of orphans did not universally exclude the possibility that families would be split up. Curiously, the 1851 census indicates that Patrick Mahoney and eldest daughter Elizabeth did not abandon the girls, but travelled to Rimouski as well and took up residence with farmer Hubert Levesque and his wife Genevieve Ruest. Both were listed as non-family members and Patrick was working on the farm, although later records would identify his original vocation as a merchant.[30] Thus, although separated by residences, the "orphans" and their father remained in close proximity to one another in the frontier area of Rimouski. The records of the Catholic parish of St. Germain de Rimouski for 1858 reveal that Catherine Mahoney married Joseph Pineau, a relative of her "placement father." And her sister Elizabeth married Joseph St Pierre, a neighboring farmer. These marital unions confirm the commonly held assumptions that some Irish orphan children did remain in their placement areas and assimilated with the local French-Canadian Catholic population. It should be noted that in later censuses, Elizabeth St. Pierre always identified English as her first language. Patrick Mahoney relocated to Quebec City, where he died in 1871, at the Hotel Dieu, listed as a laborer.[31]

The Mahoneys were only one group of Irish children settled in Rimouski, one of the most remote locations for the mass placement of orphans having arrived at Quebec City. Rimouski provides a good laboratory in which to study orphan placement because the census records for 1851–52 are complete as are the registers for the Catholic parish of St. Germain. Lotbinière County, another area of heavy placement, is frustrating to study because of the fragmentary nature of the census data for huge swaths of the county. What the research team has discovered in Rimouski and surrounding area has been seen in various forms in the Nicolet area, Quebec City region, and in the sections of Lotbinière for which information is available. The current research is grounded on a data set of 24 children (See Table 3), which, in itself, constitutes the largest regional subset in our green data set of 78 children and our blue data list of 94 children.[32] Thus the Rimouski subset is not insignificant in terms of the total number of orphans identified in this study, particularly within the context of the green list data set.

Table 3: Irish Orphans Placed at Rimouski, 1847–1848
N=25*

Name	Age	Father	Mother	County	Placement	Religion	Ship	Status
Francis Brady	10	Andy Brady	Margaret McGauran	Fermanagh	NA	RC	Superior	NF
Peter Cavagan	10	Peter Cavagan	Mary Clarme	NA	Pierre Langis	RC	NA	NF
Catherine Connor	8	Patrick Connor	Bridget Sweeny	Mayo	Alex Rivard	RC	Marchioness of Breadalbane	NF
Mary Dempsey	9	Bryan Dempsey	Mary Queen	Kildare	Marie Grace	RC	Lady Campbell	NF
Patrick Hynes	12	James Hynes	Mary Hines	Mayo	Luc St. Laurent	RC	Rankin	Family
Honora Kane	13	John Kane	Bridget McInanly	Mayo	George Lizotte	RC	Sarah	NF
Timothy Kane	11	John Kane	Bridget McInanly	Mayo	Hiliare St. Laurent	RC	Sarah	NF
Ellen Leahy	11	Jacob Leahy	Ellen Heffernan	Tipperary	Pouliot Pilote	RC	NA	NF
James McGill	8	NA	NA	NA	Jean B. Beaulieu	RC	NA	NF
John McManus	11	Hugh McManus	Catherine Skey	Tyrone	Mr. Spencer	RC	NA	NF
Patrick McManus	8	Hugh McManus	Catherine Skey	Tyrone	Mr. Kelly	RC	NA	NF
Thomas Boyle	?	Thady Boyle	Peggy Jennings	NA	Thomas Parent	RC	NA	NF
Honora Joice	18	John Joice	Sealy Joice	Galway	Dr. Poulin	RC	St. John	NF
Mary Joice	16	John Joice	Sealy Joice	Galway	Henri Martin	RC	St. John	NF
Catherine Mahoney	7	Patrick Mahoney	Honora Kelly	Clare	Etienne Pineau	RC	Governor	NF
Mary Mahoney	13	Patrick Mahoney	Honora Kelly	Clare	Anton Larouche	RC	Governor	NF
Patrick Shalloo	6	Patrick Shalloo	Ellen Hanarahan	Clare	Narcisse Banville	RC	Governor	NF
Anne Conray	14	Bernard Conray	Catherine Scott	Roscommon	Thomas Durette	RC	Georgiana	NF

Name	Age	Father	Mother	County	Placement	Religion	Ship	Status
George Cox	9	Martin Cox	Mary Maloney	Roscommon	Andre Gauvreau	RC	Virginius	NF
Mary Cox	7	Martin Cox	Mary Maloney	Roscommon	Andre Gauvreau	RC	Virginius	NF
Michael Hanley	12	Edward Hanley	Mary Egan	Roscommon	Germain Langis	RC	Virginius	NF
Bridget Holden	14	Henry Holden	Bridget Mahan	Roscommon	Auguste Lavoie	RC	Naomi	NF
Henry Holden	9	Henry Holden	Bridget Mahan	Roscommon	August Lavoie	RC	Naomi	NF
John Dalton	5	William Dalton	Onah Tierney	Roscommon	Pierre Coté	RC	Erin's Queen	NF
Catherine Prior*	9	Thomas Prior	Margaret McGinnis	Leitrim	Barth. Lemieux	RC	Superior	NF

Source: O'Gallagher List; Census of 1851–1852, Canada East, District of Rimouski. Note* that included are the 24 orphans from the "O'Gallagher List" and one foundling.

A Profile of Irish Orphans in Rimouski, Canada East

The county of Rimouski is located about 300 kilometers north east of Quebec City, with its northern boundary forming part of the southern shore of the St. Lawrence River, as it widens into the Gulf of St. Lawrence. It is primarily hilly terrain, an extension of the Appalachian mountain chain, punctuated by lakes and rivers which ultimately empty into the St. Lawrence.[33] Given its potential as home base for fishermen and with the promise of some agriculture on the coastal plain and in the river valleys the French Crown ceded this remote seigneury to Renée Lepage de Sainte Claire in 1688. The village, later to become the town of Rimouski, was founded in 1696 and soon became the primary center of seigneurial life,[34] although its name remains controversial in terms of its origins: some say it is derived from the Mi'kmaq *animouski*, "the place where dogs live," or "dog river," or from the Malecite *lemouskeg*, "the place where dogs live."[35] Regardless of its etymology, Rimouski would become a place of Irish orphan settlement, as dozens of orphans were transported to the seigneury in 1847 and 1848 to live among the Rimouskois. Because of its remote location, poor road connections with older seigneuries to the west, and perceived limited economic opportunities, Rimouski witnessed very slow population growth. In 1790, over a century after its founding, Rimouski had only 333 inhabitants. Over the next 30 years, and with increased agricultural settlement, the population reached 1,963. At the time of the arrival of the Famine orphans, the region had a growing population of over 3,600, about three quarters of whom were farmers.[36] The rise in population was certainly facilitated by the completion, in the late 1830s, of the King's Road from the village of Trois Pistoles, west of Rimouski. Ironically, when the Irish children arrived in the region, local farmers were facing their own food crisis: local harvests had been poor and there were critical food shortages in the region. The other, perhaps pleasant irony for the Irish children was that they would likely meet other Celtic settlers in Rimouski; a group of Scottish migrants had already settled in the Parish of St. Germain.[37]

As was the case in other areas that had received orphans during the Famine, the Roman Catholic Church in Rimouski had been instrumental in orphan placement. The Church had been a presence in the region since 1793, when the Diocese of Quebec established the first chapel for missionary priests.[38] When Famine migrants overwhelmed Grosse Île in 1847, Archbishop Joseph Signay of Quebec recruited priests from across the diocese to assist with the overwhelmingly Catholic refugee population on the island. Antoine LeBel, the vicar or associate pastor of St. Germain de Rimouski parish, and a native of nearby Kamouraska, served on the island for eight days between 3 August and 10 August 1847. He witnessed the human devastation first hand, burying at least 123 migrants during his short sojourn on the island. His encounters with the Irish also included the conversion and marriage of two sailors who wished to be wed to two young Catholic passengers from county Longford.[39] The short time left an indelible impression on the 31–year-old priest. With the assistance of Father Felix Cazeau, Signay's secretary, LeBel pledged himself to honor the archbishop's intention that Catholic families in the diocese take in the orphaned Irish children. LeBel himself took 30 Irish children to Rimouski, and reported to Cazeau that he would return to Quebec for more to be placed among his parishioners.[40] This was not quite the dramatic commissioning of the "adoptions" as depicted in the *Heritage Minute*, but a long journey by wagon and foot from the orphanage at Quebec to the final destination nearly 300 kilometers away. Within the year, LeBel's superior at St. Germain, Father Thomas-Ferruce Picard-Destroismaisons reported to the archbishop that the Irish children were adapting well to their new surroundings, while keeping their Irish surnames although converting their Christian names to a French equivalent.[41] He added that many were learning French with some success, thus confirming the story of another orphan, Thomas Quinn, who became a priest of the Diocese of Nicolet and lost his English entirely after his placement.

While local historians estimate that as many as 60 Irish children were placed in Rimouski,[42] the O'Gallagher List indicates that 57 children, or 13.6 percent of the 406 traceable locations on the list, were relocated to Rimouski. (See Table 2A). Of these 57 children, only 24 were traceable to the 1851–52 census. Admittedly, at least four years elapsed between the placement of the Irish children and the taking of the census, which actually was completed in 1852. Much can happen in this short time to account for the number of missing orphans at the time of the census. Children on the cusp of adulthood could have easily left their placements, seeking friends and relatives in other parts of British North America or the United States. Some may have left for other districts adjacent to Rimouski. Some may have died, although if they had done so their deaths occurred outside of the parish, since the records of St. Germain do not record any burials of Irish children during these intervening years. Nevertheless, the "disappearance" of these children from the public record, so soon after placement, casts considerable doubt on even their "de facto" adoption by French-Canadian farmers. It would appear life on the frontiers of the future province of Quebec was merely a way station for these Irish children, as they eyed independence and betterment elsewhere.

For the 24 children who stayed there were many life trajectories. The children had few common county ties except the seven children from Mahon's estate in County Roscommon. There were four from each of Clare and Mayo, and the rest hailed from Fermanagh, Tipperary, Tyrone, Galway, Kildare and Leitrim.[43] From disparate parts of south and west Ireland, these children were now bound by the trauma of the Famine, loss of family, and transportation to a remote and seemingly wild place where few people spoke their language. All of the children were placed in French-Canadian Catholic homes, with the exception of the welcome given by some Anglo families to the few children placed in Rivière de Loup. Of the 24 children, only one was listed as a family member on the census (See Table 3),[44] confirming that there was no adoption per se, but a living arrangement in which Irish orphans would help supplement the family workforce on the farm. Irish girls would assist French-Canadian women with domestic and farm chores and the caring for little children. Boys would work in the barns and fields. The census confirms that eight boys were listed as "journalier" or day workers or laborers, one child was permitted to go to school, one was listed as a servant, and one as a farmer. At least seven of the children were identified as having no occupation and three children were unidentified in terms of their work status. What is clear from the census, however, that in a fashion not atypical within 19th century family life, these orphan children were expected to work.

As has been made evident in the case of the Mahoney orphans, siblings did not universally have the benefit of being placed together in the same home. In this small sample from Rimouski, at least five pairs of siblings were placed in the same home, but others like the Mahoneys or the Shalloo brothers were not. Like the Mahoneys, Thomas and Patrick Shalloo were from Coolmean, County Clare and arrived at Grosse Île in 1848. The elder Shalloo, Thomas (aged 13) was placed with a Major Joseph Samson in Point Levis, across the river from Quebec City, while his brother Patrick, who was only 6, was taken to the farm of Narcisse Banville at Rimouski. The historical record leaves no trace if they ever met again. Honora and Timothy Kane, 13 and 11 years respectively, were a little more fortunate. After their journey from Newport, County Mayo, Father LeBel took the children to Rimouski, but placed them in different families. Honora was placed in the home of the town blacksmith, George Lizotte, while her younger brother, now listed officially as Thadee, worked as a farm laborer for Hilaire St. Laurent and his family. In addition to his work for the St. Laurents, Tim was permitted to attend local school, which would have been conducted in French.[45] Finally, John and Patrick McManus, 11 and 8 respectively, from County Tyrone, both ended up in Rivière de Loup, a town to the south west of Rimouski on the south shore of the St. Lawrence; they were among the few Irish children in the region placed in a non-Francophone environment; John lived with the Spenser family and worked as a labourer, by 1861 he was still living in Rivière de Loup and working as a barkeeper and was married to Elizabeth, a women five years his senior; his younger brother, Patrick, had been placed with the Kelly family who kept an inn in the town; another Irish orphan, Jane Harvey, who is not counted among the 619 on the "O'Gallagher List", appears to be living in the Inn as well, as does a 15-year-old orphan, Cornelius O'Keefe. One suspects that Mr. O'Kelly took the opportunity to "employ" some Irish orphans as workers in his hotel. With the exception of the McManus brothers, most of the orphans identified in the census of 1851–52, are not recorded in the local census 10 years later, a testament to immigrant mobility and children coming of age and seeking independence.

Reasons for the orphan disappearance from Rimouski in the official records after 1851 are many. Honora and Mary Joice, were not long together; at 18 and 16 respectively, they were close to marrying age; Honora was placed with Dr. Poulin in Rimouski, but appears to have left for Quebec City before 1851; her sister, Mary, had been placed with Henry Martin and his family in Rimouski, but had moved to Chambly, near Montreal to work as a servant by 1851. These young women probably represented a segment of the orphan population, who when coming of age, sought marriage, gainful employment, and less of a frontier environment to call home. Elizabeth Mahoney's life path took a different course. In 1858, she married Joseph St. Pierre, a farmer in Rimouski at St. Germain Parish, and one of the families who had taken in one of the Mahoney sisters. Elizabeth and Joseph had 10 children; Joseph died in 1911; the St. Pierre's, by 1871, are in the Saguenay region north of the St. Lawrence, and then Chicoutimi, where more abundant acreage was being opened for rural settlement.[46] Mary Dempsey's story is also different, perhaps unique in the sample. A native of Boldkell, County Kildare, she and her four sisters arrived at Grosse Île in June 1847, on board the *Lady Campbell*. Two sisters Anne, 6, and Bridget, 4, died in the orphanage at Quebec, and subsequently Mary, aged 9, and her sisters Hannah, 11, and Elizabeth, 10, were placed in three separate Rimouski families: Rivard, L'Allemand, and Grace. Although her sisters disappear from the records after placement, Mary, listed in the census as Mary Damphery, in 1851, is living with a new family— Jean-Baptist Fiola, his wife and two children. Mary stays in Rimouski, never marries, and dies at the age of 20, on 23 July 1858, from unrecorded causes. She was buried in the parish cemetery.[47]

Among the unsung Mahon orphans who could be traced, there was George and Mary Cox, 9 and 7, who were part of the 1490 assisted immigrants from the Mahon Estate, in County Roscommon, Bumblin Townland, and had survived passage on the notorious ship "Virginius"; parents Mary and Martin had not survived the voyage or quarantine; the children were placed with the Gauvreau family in St. Luce, in Rimouski County; Marie remained with the Gauvreaus, while George worked as a day laborer on the neighboring farm of Eusebe Lavoie. There is almost no documentation about them after 1851. Similarly, Bridget and Henry Holden, aged 14 and 9, were orphaned after Grosse Île, their parents, Henry and Bridget, do not appear on the Grosse Île registers as having died at sea or in quarantine. They were from Strokestown and had sailed on the *Naomi*, a ship with a reputation only second to the *Virginius*, they were both taken by Auguste Lavoie, *dit* Samson, a farmer in

Rimouski; they are listed as Olden, which meant they were very hard to find; neither were considered members of the family. In 1851 Henry was listed as a *journallier*—or day worker on the farm. The Holdens were among the few orphaned siblings who were actually placed in the same home.

The fate of the Irish orphans placed at Rimouski may enlighten researchers to broader themes, challenges, and the fate of most of the "adopted" Irish orphans in the Quebec cohort. First, they were very difficult to track down in the official records, and what fragments do exist challenge the prevailing motifs as exemplified in the *Heritage Minute*. Invisible in most routinely generated records after 1851, the Irish orphans appeared to be as mobile as the other immigrants to British North America in that era. Secondly, it is no small wonder why the Irish children retained their names. They were not truly adopted in the sense that would be considered a legal option today. The Lower Canadian *Civil Code* made few references to adoption, and few provisions for it, except in the case of inheritance. This continued to be the case under the revised Civil Code of Lower Canada framed in 1866. It appears clear, that in most of the cases of "adoption" there was no intention by the families concerned—French-Canadian or Irish—to adopt the children in their care. The 1851–1852 census is clear that most were registered as non-family members. The word "placement," therefore, would be a better term to describe their collective predicament than the more popularly accepted notion of "adoption." Thirdly, what is certain is that the children were put to work, which was probably the intention all along—extra hands to help on the farm or in the tavern, or extra hands to help with the young children in their placement families, or in a crass expression cheap labor. Daniel Tighe, the lad from Lissanuffy, Roscommon, placed with Francis and Marie Coulombe in Lotbinière, appeared to be an exception. His childless patrons looked to him to inherit the land. Most of his childhood friends from Lissanuffy and Irish orphans from other townlands and counties were not so fortunate. Thus, as this microstudy has suggested, the story of the Quebec Irish Famine orphans is not easily reduced with integrity to a one-minute sound bite.

NOTES

1. I am indebted to the work of my four senior undergraduate research assistants from the University of Toronto: Meghan Drascic-Gaudio, Conor Finan, Britany Powell, and Michaela Vukas. Their work on the data set of 619 orphans on the O'Gallagher List was invaluable to this study. Michaela, Meghan and Conor also travelled to the Great Hunger Institute at Quinnipiac University to help me present the findings. All errors and omissions in this paper are clearly of my doing, not theirs.

2. Historica Canada, "Irish orphans," Heritage Minute #16, DVD, 1991, re-launched 2012.

3. John Francis McGuire, *The Irish in America* (New York: D. and J. Sadlier, 1880), p. 138.

4. David A. Wilson, *Thomas D'Arcy McGee: Volume 2, The Extreme Moderate, 1857–1868* (Montreal and Kingston: McGill-Queen's University Press, 2011), pp. 301–3.

5. The mobility of migrants to the Canadas is evidenced in David Gagan, *Hopeful Travelers: Families Land and Social Change in Mid-Victorian Peel County, Canada West* (Toronto: University of Toronto Press, 1981) and Michael Katz, *The People of Hamilton, Canada West: Family and Class in a Mid-Nineteenth-Century City* (Cambridge: Harvard University Press, 1975).

6. Cecil Houston and William Smyth, *Irish Emigration to Canada: Patterns, Links, and Letters* (Toronto: University of Toronto Press, 1990), pp. 20–25.

7. Mark G. McGowan, "A tale of two famines: famine memory in Nova Scotia, Canada," in Patrick Fitzgerald, Christine Kinealy and Gerard Moran, eds., *Irish Hunger and Migration: Myth, Memory, and Memorialization* (Hamden: Quinnipiac University Press, 2015), pp. 57–68.

8. Marianna O'Gallagher, *Grosse Ile: Gateway to Canada, 1832–1937* (Ste-Foy: Carraig Books, 1984), Appendices.

9. Peter D. Murphy, *Poor Ignorant Children: Irish Famine Orphans in Saint John, New Brunswick* (Halifax: D'Arcy McGee Chair of Irish Studies, St. Mary's University, 1999).

10. Jason King, "Remembering Famine Orphans: the transmission of famine memory between Ireland and Quebec," in Christian Noack, Lindsay Janssen & Vincent Comerford, eds., *Holodomor and Gorta Mor: Histories, Memories, and Representations of Famine in Ukraine and Ireland* (London: Anthem Press, 2012), pp. 115–40.

11. Marianna O'Gallagher, "The orphans of Grosse Ile and the adoption of Irish Famine orphans, 1847–1848," in Patrick Sullivan, ed., *The Meaning of the Famine* (Leicester: Leicester University Press, 1997), p. 102.

12. Nancy McMahon, "Les Religieuses Hospitalieres de St-Joseph and the Typhus Epidemic, Kingston, 1847–1848," in Canadian Catholic Historical Association, *Historical Studies*, 58 (1991), pp. 41–55.

13. Mark G. McGowan, *Death or Canada: The Irish Famine Migration to Toronto, 1847* (Toronto: Novalis, 2009), pp. 95–6.

14. King, "Remembering Famine Orphans," pp. 115–40.

15. O'Gallagher, *Grosse Ile: Gateway to Canada*, Appendices.

16. Marie-Claude Belley, "Un exemple de prise en charge de l'enfance dependente au milieu de XIXe siècle: Les orphelins Irlandais á Quebec en 1847 et 1848 (Unpublished Master's Thesis, Laval University, 2003).

17. Mark G. McGowan, "Migration, mobility, and murder: assisted immigration from the Mahon estate, Strokestown, County Roscommon, Ireland, 1847" *Breac* (online Journal of Irish Studies, Notre Dame University, 2017).

18. Ciarán Reilly, *Strokestown and the Great Irish Famine* (Dublin: Four Courts Press, 2014), pp. 71–73.

19. Marianna O'Gallagher, "Children of the Famine," *The Beaver* (February–March, 2008), pp. 50–56.

20. Belley, p. 62.

21. O'Gallagher, "The orphans of Grosse Ile," pp. 104–5.

22. United Province of Canada, Canada East, *Census of 1851–1852*, District 2, Rimouski, Village de Fraserville, p. 33 [17], John Kelly, line 35.

23. Veronica Strong-Boag, *Finding Families, Finding Ourselves: English Canada Encounters Adoption from the Nineteenth Century to the 1990s* (Toronto: Oxford University Press, 2006), p. 18.

24. Bettina Bradbury, "The Fragmented Family: family strategies in the face of death, illness, and poverty, Montreal, 1860–1885," in Joy Parr ed., *Childhood and Family in Canadian History* (Toronto: McClelland and Stewart, 1982), pp. 109–11.

25. Margaret E. Hughes, "Adoption in Canada," in D. Mendes da Costa, QC, ed., *Studies in Canadian Family Law*, vol.1 (Toronto: Butterworth, 1972), p. 105.

26. O'Gallagher, "Children of the Famine," p. 56.

27. Hughes, "Adoption in Canada," 104; Dominique Goubau et Claire O'Neill, "L'Adoption, L'Eglise et l'Etat : les origines tumultueuses d'une institution légale," *Les Cahiers de Droit*, 38, no. 4 (decembre 1997), p. 771.

28. My thanks to my research assistant Britany Powell for discovering Mary and Catherine Mahoney.

29. *Census of 1851–1852*, Canada East, District 14 of Rimouski, p. 131 identifies Elizabeth Mahoney, 17, living with the Levesque family as a non-family member; Patrick Mahoney, age 47, is also included as a resident. The *Register of Baptisms, Marriages and Deaths* for the parish of St. Germain de Rimouski, page 247, identifies the marriage of Catherine Mahoney to Joseph Pineau, 25 October 1858.

30. Ibid.

31. Drouin List, *Register of St.Patrick's, Quebec*, John Patrick Mahoney, laborer, deceased 14 May 1871, at Hotel Dieu.

32. The 170 children in the green and blue data sets constitute about 28 percent of the O'Gallagher List.

33. Jean Larrivée, "Une Ville en Pline nature," in Jeannot Bourdages, et al. *Rimouski Depuis Ses Origines* (Rimouski: Société d'histoire du Bas Saint-Laurent, 2006), pp. 3–4.

34. Sylvain Gosselin, "Les terretoires et ses premiers occupants," in Bourdages, pp. 21–22.

35. Ibid., p. 27.

36. *Census of 1851–1852* indicated that 3,653 were in the district, most of whom were rural dwellers. See also, Paul Larocque, "Un Region de Peuplement (1790–1855)," in Bourdages, pp. 95–112.

37. Larocque, pp. 114–117.

38. Ibid., 100. The parish is erected in the 1820s and named after St. Germain d'Auxerre, the patron of Paris. Coincidentally, the father of the first seigneur was Germain Lepage. Gabriel Langlois, *Dossier Sur La Paroisse de Saint-Germain de Rimouski (histoire religieuse) 1701–1987* (Rimouski: Centre Pastorale, 1988), pp. 12, 55–56.

39. Marianna O'Gallagher and Rose Masson Dompierre, *Eyewitness: Grosse Isle, 1847* (Ste-Foy: Carraig Books, 1995), p. 253 and pp. 262–4.

40. LeBel to Cazeau, 18 April 1848 as cited in Larocque, pp. 116–7.

41. Ibid., p. 117. For more on Father Destroismaisons see Langlois, p. 151.

42. Jacques Watts, "L'emigration britannique de 1847–1848," *L'Estuaire*, 21 (juin 1998), pp. 21–3.

43. The census indicates: Roscommon 7; Mayo 4; Clare 4; Fermanagh, Tipperary, Tyrone, Galway and Leitrim each with one, and three unknown.

44. Twenty-three were listed as non-family members and one was included in the family count. Family membership is indicated by sex in four columns on the second page of each return—a page that has not been used carefully by historians in assessing the issue of orphans and legal adoption.

45. All case studies are derived from the data in the *Census of 1851–1852*, Canada East, District of Rimouski.

46. The entire genealogy is re-created in ancestry.com with some minor errors in transcription by the family.ancestry.ca/family-tree/person/tree/53223284/person /13473817770/facts?ssrc=.

47. "Mary Dempsey," *Register of Baptisms, Marriages and Burials*, St-Germain de Rimouski Parish, 23 July 1858, p. 236.

CHAPTER SIX

FINDING A VOICE

Irish Famine orphan Robert Walsh's search for his younger sister

Jason King

Ten years after he was left an orphan (aged 7) on Grosse Île, Quebec, in 1847, Robert Walsh wrote a letter hoping to find his baby sister who had been left behind in Famine Ireland. Both of his parents and younger brother had died after crossing the Atlantic in the island's fever sheds; Robert and his elder sisters, Mary and Anne, survived. The three children were escorted from Grosse Île in July of that year by the Reverends Bernard O'Reilly and Jean Harper to the small French town of Saint-Grégoire, where Robert was taken in by Joseph Parr and Marie Aubry, and his sisters by neighbouring families.[1] He was so traumatized by his experience that he "lost the power of speech through fright or starvation."[2] Unlike most Famine orphans, Walsh was given a good education and entered the nearby seminary in Nicolet in 1854. Not only did he recover his voice, but he rose through the ranks of the clergy as a seminarian (1854–59) and student at St. Michael's College in Toronto (1863–64; now the University of Toronto), was ordained in 1864 and became professor of "Belle-Lettres" in Nicolet thereafter.[3] Nevertheless, he was profoundly influenced by the loss of his family and younger sister. "My sister, my dear sister, if she exists," he wrote in 1857, "when she would learn that she has a brother and sisters in Canada who are thinking of her she would write to them ... We will see then we are not alone in the world, and it is this thought that will give us courage to endure our separation here."[4] In 1871–72, Walsh realized the "cherished dream of his life"[5] and returned to his native Ireland, but was distraught to discover no trace of her and died soon thereafter at the age of 33. This chapter recounts Walsh's search for his sister. It provides a case study of the traumatic effects of the Famine migration that marked even its most resilient survivors long after they had left the coffin ships. As an orphaned child of the Great Hunger, Walsh lost and regained his voice, but he never found the consolation of lasting kinship in his native land.

The story of Robert Walsh was first recounted by John Francis Maguire, the founder and editor of the *Cork Examiner*, in *The Irish in America* (1868). Maguire's book is based on his tour of the United States and British North America in 1866 when he interviewed many Famine emigrants. His tour was inspired by his desire to find evidence that the Irish fared better abroad than under British rule at home. Maguire never met Walsh, nor does he mention him by name. Yet he could only be the Famine orphan in Maguire's narrative who "grew up a youth of extraordinary promise, and... became a priest," having "entered the College of St. Michael, near Toronto, to learn the language of his parents, of which he had lost all remembrance."[6] As Maguire recalls at length:

> A decent couple had sailed in one of the ships, bringing with them two girls and a boy, the elder of the former being about thirteen, the boy not more than seven or eight. The father died first, the mother next. As the affrighted children knelt by their dying mother..., she invoked a blessing upon him and his weeping sisters. Thus the pious mother died in the fever-shed of Grosse Île. The children were taken care of, and sent to the same district, so as not to be separated from each other. The boy was received into the home of a French Canadian; his sisters were adopted by another family in the neighbourhood. For two weeks the boy never uttered a word, never smiled, never appeared conscious of the presence of those around him, or of the

attention lavished on him by his generous protectors, who had almost come to believe that they had adopted a little mute, or that he had momentarily lost the power of speech through fright or starvation. But at the end of the fortnight he relieved them of their fears by uttering some words of, to them, an unknown language; and from that moment the spell, wrought, as it were, by the cold hand of his dying mother, passed from the spirit of the boy, and he thenceforth clung with the fondness of youth to his second parents. The Irish orphan soon spoke the language of his new home, though he never lost the memory of the fever-sheds and the awful death-bed, or of his weeping sisters ... Of his Irish name, which he was able to retain, he is very proud; and though his tongue is more that of a French Canadian, his feelings and sympathies are with the people and the country of his birth.[7]

In finding his voice and then becoming a priest, the Famine orphan's ordination represents the posthumous fulfilment of a maternal pledge. "The spirit of the boy" epitomizes an ideal of adaptability and linguistic facility as well as a remarkable story of escape from adversity. The formative experience "of the fever sheds and the awful death beds" takes on the qualities of a fable in Maguire's prose.

This story of Robert Walsh helps define the cultural memory and myth of the Famine orphans. As noted elsewhere, this cultural memory combines three core motifs: firstly, the posthumous fulfilment of the maternal pledge to maintain the orphans' Catholic identity, secondly, the children's procession from the fever sheds under the care of a priest into nearby communities, and thirdly, the retention of their Irish surnames after their adoption into French-Canadian families.[8] Maguire's *The Irish in America* provided the conduit through which the memory of the Famine orphans was popularized, both in an Irish and North American context. The importance of Maguire's text lies both in the fact that he came to Quebec City and Montreal in 1866 to converse with Famine emigrants and those who ministered to them in 1847, and that it found a mass readership on both sides of the Atlantic. Because he was editor of the *Cork Examiner*, the paper reported in detail on Maguire's travels and reprinted the numerous reviews his book received. In *The Irish in America*, he repeatedly emphasized the spectacle of the dying Irish mother bequeathing her children to the care of Catholic clergy who presided over their adoption into French-Canadian households. As the Irish beneficiaries of French-Canadian compassion, the orphans appeared to be, in a cultural sense, immaculately conceived, effortlessly integrated into French-Canadian society without the anxieties of assimilation or of losing their Irish identity. They were summoned to memory as reminders of the instinctive good will that the French and Irish should have felt toward one another in the decades after 1847 when they increasingly came into conflict.[9] Communal tensions and ethnic rivalries were set aside by the symbol of the Famine orphans. Indeed, their memory was often compensatory for the varying degrees of tension that existed between Irish Catholics and French-Canadians in the latter nineteenth century.

This myth of the Famine orphans has been largely dispelled in Mark McGowan's chapter in this volume. As he reveals, census records indicate that the vast majority were not adopted or regarded as members of the family, and were more akin to indentured servants than lovingly embraced by "second parents." As an Irish orphan who did have "attention lavished on him by his generous protectors," Walsh was the exception and not the rule.[10] He was taken in to a loving family and given a better education than most French-Canadian children could hope to receive. Nevertheless, Maguire's account of the Walsh siblings' evacuation from Grosse Île when "the children were taken care of, and sent to the same district, so as not to be separated from each other" is corroborated in the "Emigration Agent Returns of Emigrant Orphans, 1847"[11] and the Saint-Grégoire orphan register.[12] These records indicate that Robert, Mary and Anne Walsh were taken from the island under the care of the Reverends Bernard O'Reilly and Jean Harper of Saint-Grégoire on 14 July 1847. Their family had sailed from Cork on the *Avon*, which arrived at Grosse Île on 13 July, after 54 days at sea, where it was detained in quarantine until 26 July.[13] It was one of the worst of the coffin ships, with a death toll of 246, including 136 at sea, 26 on board ship at Grosse Île, and 84 in the island's fever sheds, including Walsh's parents and younger brother. Rev. Bernard O'Reilly testified about his experience entering the hold of the *Avon* before Montreal's Board of Health on 23 July. He claimed that "I only visited two ships, the *Avon* and the *Triton*... We administered the last rites of religion to about two hundred on board these two ships, and many others were in a state of great debility." Each vessel had "scarcely a single truly healthy person on board."[14] O'Reilly added that emigrants from Ireland:

So long as they are sent away from the ports of Great Britain and Ireland crammed up by hundreds in the hold of a ship, without air, food, or the necessary means of procuring cleanliness and ventilation, as on board the *Avon* and the *Triton*, they must die by hundreds; disease must seize on the strongest frames and soon consume them.[15]

Among the children rescued from the hold of the *Avon* were the three Walsh children. O'Reilly had a profoundly moving experience while escorting these Irish orphans from Grosse Île to the towns of Trois Rivières and Saint-Grégoire, between Quebec City and Montreal.[16] On 18 July 1847, he presided with Father Jean Harper over their mass adoptions into French-Canadian families. As described in a letter by Father Thomas Cook, "Messrs Harper and O'Reilly went through here this morning, in great spirits. Charitable people everywhere are arguing over who is to have the orphans whom they have brought from Quebec."[17] Their procession also was reported in *The Gazette* and *The Pilot*, both of which noted that "in less than an hour [they] found worthy *habitants* with either small families, or who had no children, to adopt these poor little destitute orphans, and to secure for them the comforts of a home, and the care of parents, under [their] immediate eye." According to the *Pilot*, such adoptions attest to "the humane and Christian dispositions of our [French-] Canadian brethren" in spite "of the calumny which imputes to them hostility to the Irish race."[18]

O'Reilly still vividly recalled these mass adoptions 40 years later in *The Mirror of True Womanhood; A Book of Instruction for Women in the World* (first published in 1877, and then reprinted in 16 editions by 1883). He claims to "remember returning from quarantine, in the second week of July, with the Rev. John Harper," after having:

> spent a fortnight among the fever-sheds, and [having] had, at the urgent request of their parishioners, brought home with them a large number of orphans... We had been delayed..., and on our arrival about midnight at Three Rivers, we found a crowd of eager and excited women, mothers of families all of them, waiting and watching for us... It was a spectacle worthy of the admiration of angels, which was beheld that sultry midnight in July, these farmers' wives, weeping every one of them with that holy emotion which the sweetest charity creates, pressing around their pastor and choosing, when they could, in the uncertain light, the child that pleased them best, or accepting joyously and folding in a motherly embrace the little orphan allotted to them.[19]

His reminiscences attest that the Famine orphans' myth does have some foundation. Many were embraced by their French-Canadian new mothers who had waited so steadfastly to receive them. O'Reilly also recalls crossing the St. Lawrence River with Rev. Jean Harper and the children in their care, to find:

> the entire population of St. Grégoire, and every available mode of conveyance waiting for us; and so we proceeded some two or three miles to the beautiful parish church, where priests and people knelt in devout thanksgiving,—the priests grateful for their preservation from the plague, the people thanking God for the precious boon charity had bestowed on them. They did not rest contented with this, however: hundreds of other orphans were sought after subsequently and added to the happiness, and—let us hope—the prosperity of this excellent people. Not one of these stranger-children but became in every sense the child of the home into which it was received.[20]

Among these "stranger-children" who became part of their new families were Robert, Anne and Mary Walsh. Unlike many, they were genuinely welcomed and made to feel that they belonged in their new home.

Robert Walsh, courtesy of the Archives du Séminaire de Nicolet.

Nevertheless, as he grew older, Walsh's most earnest desire was to find his living relations and younger sister in Ireland. In 1857, when he was still a seminarian, he drafted two versions of a letter in halting English and in French addressed only to "Reverend Sir" ("Révérend Monsieur"), an unnamed Irish bishop, seeking assistance in tracing his Irish family. In Walsh's own words:

> In the horrendous emigration of 1847, my father, David Walsh, and my mother, Honora O'Donnell resolved to go with their family to [the new world] where they had relatives. They had five children; but they left in Ireland with relatives or acquaintances a little girl, aged roughly five to six months, if I remember well. She could have been more or less, for I then was but seven years old and had experienced a long voyage so my misfortunes

made me lose the exact memory of these things. My oldest sister was ten and called Mary, the youngest was eight and is called Anny; I had a younger brother called Patrick; I think he was only four years old.

We all arrived in Quebec on the St. Lawrence at the end of June or begin- ning of July 1847. There, my father, my mother, and my brother Patrick died. They were sick of the typhus which caused so much devastation in this year in Canada. We were three, my two sisters and me, without any support in a foreign country. Providence alone remained for us. Also, He did not forsake us. We were helped by a Catholic priest who was very good to us and ensured that we were adopted into a French-Canadian family and provided with an excellent education. My two sisters are teaching in a good school and receive sufficient wages for their needs. As for me, I am now studying in a Canadian college and I will finish my studies within two years. Also, I am not more than ten or fifteen miles distant from my sisters so that we can write easily and even see each other sometimes, espe- cially during the two months of holidays we are given in the fine season of summer that we spend together.[21]

In his letter, Walsh goes on to request information about his younger sister who had been left behind in Ireland after the family emigrated. He contends that:

The purpose of the present letter is then to inform your greatness the particular account of these things in order that you can be moved to take an interest in the fate of these three orphans, to search and discover if they still have any relations left in Ireland. For a decade we have learned nothing of them, and we are like those who have no relatives or acquaintances. I hope that you will do all that is in your power to find some people, if any, who will be dear to us. We were of Kilkenny, if I am right, and there must still be some of our relations there.

My father was the intendant of the Lord Montgomery who lived very near Kilkenny then I believe. It was he who conveyed labourers in the lord's service. I was then an infant and I remember that I would go sometimes with my mother and sisters and the lord to a magnificent orchard near his estate. How I love to recall these memories which are for me like a fair dream! Yes, I had a father, a mother, and now they are no more. If only I learned one day that we have relations who think of us, who know the details of our misfortune, and who would write to me, then I would be a little comforted; for they also have learned nothing of us for ten years. They would be glad to know something of us. My sister, my dear sister, if she exists, when she would learn that she has a brother and sisters in Canada who are thinking of her she would write to them, although she does not know them! Oh! how much these words would mean in our hearts! We will see then we are not alone in the world, and it is this thought that will give us courage to endure our separation here.[22]

In closing his letter, Walsh requests that the unnamed Irish bishop help him in tracing his father's former employer and landlord, Lord Montgomery, and in rediscovering his extended family. He believed that Lord Montgomery's letter of reference would help him locate his living relations in Ireland. Walsh also apologizes for having "forgotten my native tongue in Canada." In his own words:

I hope that your Lordship will take into consideration my questions and that you will do all that charity permits on this occasion. I will be in your debt if you may discover some of my relations and let me know of them soon.

I still have something else to ask of you if you will permit me, on what I have said lately. It is that, as I said, my father was a steward of Lord Montgomery, and also that his Lordship had given him a letter of recommendation. I think that if he was still living, he would be glad to know the fate that has befallen his old friend. So then, if you had the noble goodness to tell him of that, if you can, I will remember always with gratitude your charity towards me.

There is the task I am endeavouring to impose on you; you will find me certainly impudent, but I think that you will praise at least my purpose.

You will excuse my English composition because I have forgotten my native tongue in Canada.

It is with the greatest respect that I am your fellow countryman and your son in Jesus Christ.

Robert Walsh[23]

Unfortunately, there is no record of the reply Walsh received to his entreaty, but it was sufficiently encouraging for him to embark on his own voyage to Ireland in 1871. He was sorely disappointed, however, to discover no trace of his younger sister or where his family had lived. The story of his search is recounted in the history of Nicolet seminary:

In 1871–72, he was able to realize the dearest dream of his life, that of seeing his native country, Ireland, to which he was devoted. He was very fond of his adoptive homeland, and the memory of his long suffering brought tears and often patriotic sentiments. He had seen his parents, with hundreds of others, expire on the far shore, where misery, famine, persecution had violently thrown them. In his tenderest years, he had experienced the cruel separation from everyone who was dear to him. In the midst of his long journeys back to such a painful past, he had always harbored the hope that one day, by returning to the land of his ancestors, he might find relatives who were very anxious to know the fate of his family. So it was with a lively sense of anticipation that he left, in 1871, for a trip overseas, with his friend M. Proulx, then director of the Seminary, expecting to realize his sweet hope of meeting there his own flesh and blood, his kindred whose hearts beat in unison with his own. Cruel disappointment! Not a parent [did he find], not even a friend who remembered his family and the place where she [his sister] lived; there remained no memory, no vestige of what he had so long and so eagerly desired to find. Mr. Walsh, therefore, had only the consolation of seeing his native country again, without even recognizing the places where he experienced the joys of his first years, while admiring the beauties of his dear Ireland, and then groaning over the misfortunes which drove a million inhabitants to foreign lands where they could find hospitality and solace. It was for his sensitive soul and his patriotic heart a great trial; he preserved a memory full of bitterness, regrets which saddened the few days he lived after his return.[24]

Indeed, Walsh was so distraught to discover no trace of his sister that he passed away soon after he returned to Canada on 31 January 1873, at the age of 33. "He was seized with a serious illness, a fatal consequence of the typhus he had been infected with when he arrived in the country in 1847, when his parents died of this plague at Grosse Île."[25] He had lost his resilience and succumbed to complications of typhus from which he had not fully recovered. Walsh never found that "little comfort" of lasting kinship in Ireland. His profound desire to rediscover his infant sister as proof that "we are not alone in the world" had come to nothing.

Ultimately, his tragedy was to return to the wrong part of the country. Walsh's itinerary in Ireland can be reconstructed from a letter that he wrote in London to Fr. J.A. Irénée Douville on 6 July 1871.[26] In it, he notes that his visit with Nicolet seminary director M. Proulx began well when they were invited to dine with Cardinal Paul Cullen in Dublin. Shortly thereafter, they parted company and Proulx travelled to Killarney, Walsh to Kilkenny, expecting to finally meet his blood relations. As recounted in his letter:

> I saw the family that was said to be mine, but I knew right away that they were not related to my parents. From house to house, from village to village, from parish to parish, I have travelled a good part of county Kilkenny, without finding the least trace of those who are dear to me. In one day, I travelled to twenty places, returning to my inn at one o'clock in the morning. It is easy to believe that my heart was broken. Having come back, after a twenty-five year absence, to my country, and not to find the place of my birth, no evidence of my flesh and blood! I received only sympathy from the clergy, the people, everyone I told my sad story to, and corresponded with. I have searched everywhere. I accepted this sympathy, as you would think, and after all these unexpected setbacks, I left Kilkenny to join Mr. Proulx in Killarney, via Waterford.[27]

Walsh travelled extensively through the villages and parishes of Kilkenny but found no trace of his sister and family. Having come back, after twenty-five years, he encountered only setbacks. Despite his endeavors, he had become a stranger in the place of his birth. "Unfortunately, I have not succeeded in my efforts to find my family," Walsh wrote to Thomas Caron from London on 6 July 1871.[28] The very memory of his flesh and blood had seemingly disappeared from the community in which he was born. He found no kinship ties to console him at the end of his journey. Walsh left Kilkenny with only his "sad story" and feeling of bitterness, sadness and regret.

Walsh failed because he could not locate the estate of Lord Montgomery. The National Library of Ireland's digitization of Catholic parish registers has made it possible now to complete his search. The crucial error that Walsh had made in trying to rediscover his lost sister was his supposition that: "We were of Kilkenny, if I am right." In fact, he was not correct. Walsh's father was never "the intendant of the Lord Montgomery who lived very near Kilkenny" because there were no resident Montgomery landlords in the county. Rather, the Lord Montgomery in question was the Reverend William Quinn Montgomery (c.1801–69), of Killee Castle, or Killee House, near Mitchelstown in County Cork. "It was probably during his lifetime, or possibly a little earlier," notes Bill Power, "that the Georgian style family house was built at Killee. It commands pleasant views of the neighbourhood and is undoubtedly the best surviving house of the Anglo-Irish gentry in the Mitchelstown area."[29] The "magnificent orchard" on the estate can be seen on an 1842 Ordnance Survey map.[30] Unlike Kilkenny Castle and the county's grand estates, Killee Castle is a modest country house and residence for the minor gentry, not a wealthy landed proprietor. As described in Samuel Lewis's *Topographical Dictionary of Ireland*: "Killee Castle, the residence of Montgomery, esq... is a vicarage in the diocese of Cloyne, and in the patronage of the Bishop" that consists mainly of "a large tract of bog."[31] The surrounding parish was particularly devastated by the Great Hunger, losing more than half its population between 1841 (229) and 1851 (95).[32] Yet "Killee" sounds sufficiently like "Kilkenny" to account for

Walsh's error. The little boy who lost his voice during the Famine voyage also misheard his place of origin.

More importantly, the discovery of Lord Montgomery's residence at Killee House in the Marshalstown civil parish of Cloyne Diocese made it possible to trace the baptismal certificates for Robert Walsh, his brother, Patrick, who died on Grosse Île, his two elder sisters, Mary and Anne, who survived the journey, and his missing "dear, dear sister" who had been left behind. As with all genealogical searches, there are some variations in the spellings of surnames and first names of the Walsh siblings. Robert's parents, David Walsh and Honora McDonald, were married in Buttevant, near Mitchelstown, on 7 February 1837.[33] Their eldest daughter Mary was baptized on 13 November 1837 in nearby Doneraile.[34] Anne Walsh was also born in Doneraile and baptized on 27 April 1839.[35] It was after her birth that the family moved to Mitchelstown where their eldest son was born. In fact, Robert was named William on his baptismal certificate—although the handwritten entry is for the most part illegible—which is dated 28 July 1840.[36] His younger brother, Patrick, who died on Grosse Île, was also baptized in Mitchelstown on St. Patrick's Day 1842, and was 5 years old at the time of his death.[37] Walsh's "dear, dear sister," whom he unsuccessfully tried to find in Kilkenny was baptized on 12 August 1846, less than a year before the family emigrated to Canada and she was left behind. She was named after her mother: Honora Walsh. Most importantly, her place of residence is recorded on her baptismal certificate.[38] It is Killee, where her father was the intendant of Lord Montgomery. If only her elder brother had travelled to Killee rather than Kilkenny when he made his return journey to Ireland, he almost certainly would have been reunited with her, or at least learned of her fate, in a small parish where everyone would have known his family origins and welcomed him home. He was tantalizingly close, but his tragedy was to mistake Killee for Kilkenny.

Walsh failed to find his younger sister, but there is every possibility that she survived the Famine and had children of her own. As of yet, she has not been traced on routinely generated records. The next stage in the search is to ascertain whether she has any living descendants who might, in Walsh's words, "think of him" and "know his misfortune" when made aware of his plight. More broadly, their story is that of countless children who disappeared and perished or were separated from their families during the Great Hunger and Irish Famine migration. The vast majority did not leave the slightest trace of their existence. Robert Walsh was the exception and not the rule. He embodied the myth of the Famine orphans. Unlike most orphaned children who were left bereft of their parents in 1847, he was escorted with his sisters from Grosse Île to be taken in by a loving family and given an excellent education. Yet he suffered profound psychological distress that marked even the most resilient of survivors of the Irish Famine migration. The little boy who lost and found his voice did become a priest. But he longed throughout his life for his younger sister who had been left behind, and his failure to find her hastened his early death. He yearned to belong in the place of his birth. The discovery of her baptismal certificate might seem a modest accomplishment. But make no mistake. It provides nothing less than proof of life. Robert Walsh did have a younger sister named Honora who was baptised in Killee House on 12 August 1846. This was his place of birth and she was his flesh and blood. He died disconsolate because he could not find her. To complete his search and discover documentary traces of their existence, proof of life for lost children from the Great Hunger is not simply a gesture of respect. It helps us fathom the magnitude of distress that separated families suffer during migration crises, both past and present. Indeed, it is more than an act of remembrance to trace the descendants of these lost children, to put a name and a face on the otherwise countless multitudes. It is an acknowledgement of a legacy of moral responsibility for child migrants that was forged during the Irish exodus of 1847 and continues to this day.

NOTES

1. Archives du Séminaire de Nicolet. Fonds d'archives Fabrique Saint-Grégoire, F356/A14/5.

2. John Francis Maguire, *The Irish in America* (Montreal and New York, 1866), p. 143.

3. J.A.Ir. Douville, *Histoire de Collège-Séminaire de Nicolet, 1803–1903*, vol. 2 (Montreal, 1903), p. 104. Translated by Jason King.

4. Archives du Séminaire de Nicolet, F091/B1/5/2 & F091/B1/5/3. Translated by Jason King.

5. Douville, p. 105.

6. Maguire, p. 143.

7. Ibid.

8. Jason King, "Remembering Famine Orphans: The Transmission of Famine Memory between Ireland and Québec," in Christian Noack, Lindsay Janssen and Vincent Comerford (eds), *Holodomor and Gorta Mór: Histories, Memories, and Representations of Famine in Ukraine and Ireland* (New York, 2012), pp. 115–144, 118.

9. Jason King, "L'historiographie irlando-québécoise: Conflits et conciliations entre Canadiens français et Irlandais," translated by Simon Jolivet, *Bulletin d'histoire politique du Québec*, vol. 18 (2010), pp 13–36.

10. Also see Jason King, "Une Voix d'Irlande: Integration, Migration, and Travelling Nationalism Between Famine Ireland and Quebec in the Long Nineteenth Century," in Ciarán Reilly (ed.), *The Famine Irish: Emigration and the Great Hunger* (Dublin, 2016), pp 193–208, for the remarkable and similar stories of Fathers Patrick and Thomas Quinn from Strokestown, Co. Roscommon.

11. "Emigration Agent Returns of Emigrant Orphans, 1847." Names of Orphan Children, 1847. Ottawa, Ontario, Canada: Library and Archives Canada, n.d. RG 4, C1, vol. 204, file 3036. Microfilm Reel H–2487.

12. Archives du Séminaire de Nicolet, Fonds d'archives Fabrique Saint-Grégoire, F356/A14/5.

13. Marianna O'Gallagher and Rose Masson Dompierre (eds), *Eyewitness: Grosse Île, 1847* (Sainte-Foy, Quebec, 1995), p. 349.

14. Ibid., pp. 194, 195.

15. Ibid.

16. Also see Jason King, "The Genealogy of *Famine Diary* in Ireland and Quebec: Ireland's Famine Migration in Historical Fiction, Historiography, and Memory," Éire-Ireland, vol. 47 (2012), pp. 45–69.

17. Ibid., 106.

18. *The Gazette*, 20 July 1847; *Pilot,* 22 July 1847.

19. Bernard O'Reilly, *The Mirror of True Womanhood; A Book of Instruction for Women in the World* (New York, 1877), p. 98.

20. Ibid.

21. Archives du Séminaire de Nicolet, F091/B1/5/2 & F091/B1/5/3. Translated by Jason King.

22. Ibid.

23. Ibid.

24. Douville, p. 105.

25. Ibid., p. 106.

26. Archives du Séminaire de Nicolet, Fonds J.A. Irénée Douville, F004/C4/11. Translated by Jason King.

27. Ibid.

28. Archives du Séminaire de Nicolet, Fonds Thomas Caron F132/C3/4, p. 69.

29. Bill Power, *Mitchelstown through Seven Centuries* (Fermoy, 1987), 24. Also see, Bill Power, *Another Side of Mitchelstown: A Street by Street & Townland by Townland history of the people, events & places associated with one of Ireland's best planned historic towns* (Mitchelstown, 2009), 233; Anna-Maria Hajba, *Historical Genealogical Architectural Notes on some Houses of Cork*, vol. 1 (Cork, 2002), p. 223; buildingsofireland.ie/niah/search.jsp?type=record&county=CO&regno=20901908, accessed 10 February 2018; http://landedestates.nuigalway.ie/LandedEstates/jsp/property-show.jsp?id=3354. accessed 10 February 2018.

30. maps.osi.ie/publicviewer/#V2,577249,612523,10,8, accessed 10 February 2018.

31. Samuel Lewis, *A Topographical Dictionary of Ireland*, vol. 1 (London, 1837), p. 345.

32. Bill Power, *Another Side of Mitchelstown,* p. 259.

33. National Library of Ireland. Catholic Parish Registers: registers.nli.ie/registers/vtls000632613#page/286/mode/1up, accessed 10 February 2018.

34. registers.nli.ie/registers/vtls000633250#page/14/mode/1up, accessed 10 February 2018.

35. registers.nli.ie/registers/vtls000633250#page/30/mode/1up, accessed 10 February 2018.

36. registers.nli.ie/registers/vtls000634792#page/81/mode/1up, accessed 10 February 2018.

37. registers.nli.ie/registers/vtls000634792#page/96/mode/1up, accessed 10 February 2018.

38. registers.nli.ie/registers/vtls000634793#page/16/mode/1up, accessed 10 February 2018.

CHAPTER SEVEN

NOT STANDING IDLY BY

Educating Famine orphans at the Emigrant Orphan Asylum in Saint John, New Brunswick, 1847 to 1849

Koral LaVorgna

...total idleness ("the root of all evil")[1]

When Alice Minette accepted the position at the Saint John Emigrant Orphan Asylum in 1847, she could not have anticipated that her teaching tenure would end abruptly, violating the terms of her contract. She might have understood, though, that the institution had been established in response to a crisis from the unprecedented and seemingly unrelenting arrival of distressed Irish immigrants. The number of immigrants who had landed at Saint John totaled 15,269 by 1 October 1847, an increase of more than 5,700 from 1846.[2] The port city was unprepared for an influx of immigration on this scale, especially given that the majority, who were diseased and destitute, urgently required care and assistance. The Famine immigrants strained the system of poor relief beyond its limits. Although accommodation at the quarantine station (Partridge Island), the emigrant hospital, and the almshouse were soon filled to overflowing, there was absolutely no provision or haven for the youngest casualties of the Famine: children.

Among the distressed immigrants of 1847 were countless children who would eventually lose one or both parents to disease or desertion. These parentless children could be found in every building or institution that served as temporary shelter, including the almost uninhabitable Emigrant Sheds, erected in quick order to house the distressed. Too many orphans had taken to life on the streets, begging from passersby or door to door. It was imperative to remove these "idle" children from such places to keep them healthy and safe from harm. However, there were no measures currently in place to provide refuge for the large number of Famine orphans. The Saint John Emigrant Orphan Asylum, which opened in October 1847, was the first institution of its kind, not only in Saint John but in the province.[3] Although local politicians and the Saint John elite supported its establishment, the provincial government ultimately considered the orphan asylum a temporary, emergency measure.

The orphan asylum commissioners created an institution which would not only rescue vulnerable children, but also would educate them. The asylum provided a free common school education based on the Infant School model, first popularized in England. Correcting "idleness" and instilling "proper" values and behavior, while teaching literacy, practical skills and an appreciation for individual industry were the paramount objectives of that educational scheme. The commissioners of the asylum hired Alice Minette, an inexperienced teacher of Irish Protestant extraction, to instruct the inmates at the school. Her abrupt dismissal less than two years later demands examination, and this study will delve into the nature and intent of the schooling provided at the Saint John Emigrant Orphan Asylum, while also exploring the reasons behind the closure of both the school and the orphanage.

During the first half of the 19th century, Saint John was a growing urban center, with a rapidly expanding commercial sector. A major port of entry, Saint John accepted an increasing number of British immigrants, especially in the decades after 1815. The 1832 Passenger Act instituted a head tax, and the monies collected were channeled into the Emigrant Fund. These funds were used to defray the costs associated with the care of indigent immigrants. The government provided aid and assistance for up to one year to "deserving immigrants."[4] As immigration increased, this busy and congested city had to contend with the consequent rise in social problems, including poverty, criminality and lunacy. According to the prevailing school of thought, these social problems could be contained and perhaps even cured within an institutional environment.[5] Institutional care for the poor was adopted in Saint John in 1801, with the establishment of the first almshouse in the province.[6]

The first poor house building was destroyed by fire in 1819, and was quickly replaced with a new facility in 1820, located a short distance east of the original site. The new building was designed to house 60 inmates, accommodations that would soon prove inadequate given the rise in local poverty, especially with the arrival of increasing numbers of distressed immigrants. In 1837, the Grand Jury representing the Saint John County Court of General Sessions visited the poor house and found upwards of 180 to 190 individuals crowded within the confines.[7] A great number of the inmates were sick, and even if the Keeper of the house wanted to separate them from the healthy, there was simply no room to do so. The Grand Jury suggested that it was time to erect a new poor house, and that the present building be converted to an infirmary. Although the city was in desperate need of a new and improved poor house, it would be another six years before a modern, commodious institution opened in the neighboring Simonds Parish. Until that time, additional accommodation was provided at the old cholera hospital, which also served as the lunatic asylum.[8]

Institutional care for the poor, the criminal and the insane helped "clean" up Saint John's streets by removing vagrant and idle adults. However, in this age of the asylum, such benevolent endeavors had yet to extend to children. The plight of destitute, deserted and orphaned children had come to the attention of the local elite, and in 1836 concerned citizenry organized the Saint John Orphan Benevolent Society.[9] Although the philanthropic group became incorporated and a fund started, the monies raised were not sufficient to support their efforts, and the plan to open an orphan asylum was abandoned at that time.[10] With child labor still in demand, poor and orphaned children were placed out as apprentices in both town and country. Others still were either confined to the almshouse or took to life on the streets. None of these options, though, adequately addressed the orphan problem. Children, perhaps more so than adults, could easily fall prey to wicked temptation and vice without proper care and guidance. The Grand Jury complained in December 1847 to the Saint John County Court of General Sessions that the "[w]harves are thronged by boys & girls who steal all that is portable without check or hindrance." The youth street culture was fueled by vice and immorality, whereby such vagrant children were "trained up to be our future robbers and burglars."[11] When caught, the thieving, drunken or vagrant youth were incarcerated for their crimes. The provincial penitentiary counted 305 youth from ages 12 to 18 among its inmates serving time for petty crimes between 1846 and 1857.[12] Most of the young boys who were imprisoned in 1857 were parentless and friendless, and therefore victims of idleness and suffering from a want of moral guidance. Although the need for an orphan asylum had long been recognized in Saint John, it was only because of the crisis of 1847 that the first child care institution was established.

Not only did the Famine Irish arrive in unprecedented numbers in 1847, but they were considered to be among the most distressed immigrants ever encountered. They were described as "the most miserable and helpless class of Irish Peasantry."[13] Benjamin Wolhaupter, Emigrant Agent and Poor Commissioner stationed at the provincial capital in Fredericton, complained that "they are the most helpless set of people I ever saw, and many appear to have been street beggars before they came to America, judging from their commencing immediately on their arrival."[14] Provincial Emigrant Agent Moses H. Perley reported in December 1847 that:

> The character of the emigration during the past year having been altogether different from any that has preceded it, no comparison can be drawn

between it, and that of any former year…a large proportion of the emigrants of this Season will require time and training to become even useful laborers.[15]

Lieutenant Governor Sir William Colebrooke despaired of the social problems arising from the overwhelming number of disadvantaged Famine immigrants. He wrote to Lord Earl Grey in London:

There is much vagrancy and mendacity amongst the adult emigrants, and which it has not been found practicable to arrest from the dearth of employment at this season; and the presence of so many idle people in the City has given occasion to much apprehension of disturbances.[16]

Colebrooke was gravely concerned about the immigrant children, especially those who were orphaned and abandoned. Having received reports regarding the number of vulnerable orphan children living among diseased and distressed adult immigrants in the almshouse, the Emigrant Sheds, the Emigrant Hospital, on Partridge Island and on the streets, the Lieutenant Governor was not standing idly by. In late September 1847, he ordered that an orphan asylum be outfitted for the immediate reception of these children. Colebrooke wanted to rescue them "from the fate that would otherwise have awaited them."[17] Thomas Frederick Elliot, Emigrant Agent at the Colonial Office concurred, stating that "to make some provision for the destitute children and orphans of this year was evidently indispensable."[18] Given the onset of winter, the matter was of some urgency, and it was quickly decided that the old poor house, converted to an infirmary in 1843, would suit their needs. In early October, Colebrooke appointed Saint John Almshouse Commissioners, Henry Chubb and William O. Smith, as commissioners of the Emigrant Orphan Asylum.

With a tight 10-day time-frame, the commissioners made arrangements to have the old poor house cleaned, fumigated and painted to transform it into an orphan asylum. The two-story building was fitted with beds, blankets and bedding, tables, benches, stoves and small wares including cups, plates, bowls and utensils. An Irish-Catholic married couple, James and Annie

Cunningham, were hired in short order as keeper and matron of the asylum. The foundation of the first child care institution aroused the interest of prominent local citizens. Colebrooke nominated a Committee of Ladies and Gentlemen to superintend operations at the asylum, and at least initially, a number of the ladies visited the institution on a weekly basis.[19]

When the Saint John Emigrant Orphan Asylum opened on 25 October 1847, 99 children were admitted.[20] More children were admitted with each passing week, and by the end of November, another 106 had entered the institution. Over the course of the two years that the asylum remained in operation, a total of 308 children were admitted to the institution, with boys representing 52.9 percent and girls 47 percent of the orphanage population. The children ranged from 1 to 22 years of age. Admission regulations at the Saint John asylum were not as rigid as at certain other 19th-century orphanages in British North America, accepting infants under 3 years of age and over 14 years. The asylum also admitted children whose parents were both still living.[21] Moreover, it had been organized to rescue not only immigrant but destitute children, and as such admitted locally born children, but their numbers were few. More than 90 percent of the children admitted to the Saint John Emigrant Orphan Asylum were casualties of the Famine, and almost all of these immigrant children had arrived during the crisis of 1847. More than half of the children admitted, or 53.4 percent, had at least one parent living, while nearly one in five had both parents still living. In cases where both parents were alive, they were either too sick or too destitute to care for their offspring. The full orphan, who had lost both parents, constituted 27.1 percent of all children ever admitted to the institution.[22] Very few of these children lost both parents on the transatlantic voyage; most succumbed to disease in the almshouse, emigrant sheds, at the quarantine station, or on the streets. Of the 82 children who lost both parents, eight of them had left Ireland as full orphans. Because most of these unfortunate children were adolescents, ranging in age from 11 to 17, it is entirely likely that their unaccompanied passage went uncontested.

Once admitted, the children were marched into the yard of the asylum to be cleaned and clothed. They shed their old clothes, which were placed in a pile and burned on the site. By this measure, it ensured that the children entered the institution "perfectly clean...without carrying any vermin with them."[23] Some clothing had been purchased with the monies allotted for the refitting and refurbishing of the old poor house, while the Ladies' Committee gathered at the Temperance Hall for the purpose of making additional clothing for the orphans.[24] Local citizens made small financial donations toward providing outer and winter wear for the orphans; enough cloaks, top-coats and bonnets had been donated for 100 children, but by late December 1847 the asylum was still in need of caps and mittens.[25]

The "well-ordered asylum" was regulated by routine,[26] and although a daily schedule probably existed at the institution, its actual operation is unknown.[27] When the school opened at the asylum in November 1847, instruction shaped the structure of daily life at the institution.[28] Colebrooke had insisted that both a School of Industry and an Infant School be established for the benefit of the children at the asylum. Both efforts were intended to teach children the habits of industry, encourage literacy and provide them with practical and employable skills. Soon after the asylum opened, a number of prominent ladies formed a School Committee and hired Alice Minette to conduct an Infant School.[29]

The Infant School model was imported from England to both British North America and the United States and served as a charity school. By the time the first Infant School was established in Saint John in 1834,[30] that mode of instruction was already falling out of favor in the United States. Infant schools catered to children between the ages of 2 an 8, sometimes even including children as young as 18 months. Critics of infant schools claimed that overstimulating the minds of the very young was detrimental to their mental health, possibly leading to lunacy in adulthood.[31] Given the success of the infant school in Saint John, the model was embraced by the Benevolent Society of Fredericton. The society induced Catherine Fayerweather,[32] who taught at the Infant School in Saint John, to open such a school in the provincial capital in 1841. The Benevolent Society focused its attention on rescuing poor children from neglect and unsavory influences, especially from wicked temptations that ran rampant on the streets. In essence, children were to be separated from adults to save or rescue them from idle and wanton ways. The formation of an infant school in Fredericton was intended to aid parents by engaging their children while they were at work, while also teaching them "habits of order and industry, and giving them early impressions of correct moral and religious principles."[33]

An infant school not only suited the moral objective of the orphan asylum by instilling "proper" values from a very early age, but it also fit the age demographic of the institution. One third of the inmates, who were between the ages of 11 and 14, were considered old enough to be apprenticed or "placed out." If these older children attended the school, it certainly was not for an extended period, as many were quickly released from the asylum when an apprenticeship placement became available. The removal of older children for placement as apprentices kept the age profile of the asylum very young—ideal for an infant school. More than half of the inmates ever admitted, or 57 percent, were under the age of 10. The proportion of "infants," or those under the age of 5, was recorded at 11.7 percent. Because both the Saint John and Fredericton infant schools included children as young as 2,[34] it is reasonable to expect that instruction at the orphan asylum began then too.

Teaching an infant school, given the sheer size and depressed circumstances of the children, was undoubtedly challenging and demanding. At 17 years of age, Minette was not that much older than the children under her charge. Her appointment to this position is rather curious given that she was both unlicensed and inexperienced. Her hiring marks a departure from the practice at the almshouse, in which married, middle-aged men of Irish birth who were licensed to teach were consistently selected during the late 1840s and into the 1850s to instruct the pauper children resident there.[35] Although Minette lived near the orphan asylum, proximity would not have been a factor, as teachers were known to travel great distances for school contracts. The answer quite possibly lies in a combination of gender and connections. It was a committee of ladies who ultimately chose to hire Minette, and women were generally preferred as teachers at infant schools given the tender age of the children. Minette's father, Robert C. Minette, an Irish Protestant who immigrated to Saint John in 1818, was the city surveyor, a position he held for 50 years. Minette Street, situated in nearby Carleton Parish, was named in honor of Robert. Given her father's prominence, it is entirely possible that Alice was either known by or mingled with the city's elite. It is also tempting to speculate that Alice Minette might have been familiar with the Irish language, which helped her to secure the position at the orphan asylum.[36]

Prominent ladies took an active interest in the infant school visiting frequently when the institution first opened. These women volunteered in the school, teaching a variety of lessons. The matron, Mrs Cunningham, helped in the classroom by teaching children how to sew.[37] As patroness of the orphan asylum, Lady Colebrooke was known to inspect the school periodically. Lady Colebrooke also patronized the Fredericton Infant School and supported that institution by paying the rent on the schoolhouse. That school, conducted by Catherine Fayerweather, was deemed rather progressive. Fayerweather taught the rudiments of a common school education with the assistance of monitors, while also placing considerable emphasis upon vocal music. The school inspector who examined the Fredericton Infant School in 1844 enjoyed the musical performance, and this portion of the instruction was "recreative and pleasing to the children."[38] Fayerweather's school was well-equipped with slates, a globe and the latest technical innovation: a blackboard. The blackboard was considered especially useful in delivering instruction to large numbers of pupils, as a means of focusing student attention on the teacher at the front of the room while also encouraging individual participation in the lessons. School inspectors and education reformers advocated its use, and by the mid–1840s, only 2.4 percent of New Brunswick schools had blackboards at their disposal.[39] The forward state of Catherine Fayerweather's Infant School might have been the result of Lady Colebrooke's patronage, in which her benevolence extended beyond simply covering the rent on the school-house. Should that have been the case, it is possible that the infant school at the Emigrant Orphan Asylum, also patronized by Lady Colebrooke, might have been similarly well-equipped.

A reporter from *The Morning News* who visited the orphan asylum in early December 1847 described the school then in operation. Minette had organized about 100 children into classes on the first floor of the building, and she conducted lessons in reading, writing and needlework. A number of the older boys, "who understood their letters," assisted in the classroom by serving as monitors.[40] According to the asylum's admittance ledger, there were 115 children between the ages of 2 and 10 resident at that time,[41] which accounted for two-thirds of the institution's population. If this were the group of students described by the reporter, then 60 percent were boys and 40 percent were girls. Three-quarters of these children had either one or both parents still living, while 23.2 percent were full orphans.

The reporter did not indicate how well-supplied the classroom was with instructional resources and textbooks. Fayerweather's infant school was rather well-outfitted for instruction, and even the Saint John Almshouse, which recorded in its financial statements how school funds were spent, counted slates, pencils, paper and spellers among its educational resources. Most parish or common schools in the province lacked an adequate supply of textbooks, and in November 1847, the New Brunswick government adopted the readers from the National Schools in Ireland.[42] Schools that could afford the expense were encouraged to purchase the Irish readers. Orphan Asylum Commissioner, Henry Chubb, who was not only a newspaper editor but a book dealer, was the Saint John agent supplying these Irish textbooks. Although there is no evidence to suggest that these readers were used at the orphanage, it is possible given Chubb's association with the asylum and his role as local supplier that indeed they were.

Minette was teaching her largest group of students when that newspaper report was made in December 1847. Although new children were admitted for the next six months, her classroom composition was ever-shifting and also on the decline with children being claimed by family, being placed out, or falling victim to mortality. Children were nearly as likely to be reunited with one or more family members as they were to be placed out, at 37.5 percent and 40.1 percent respectively. Admittance to the orphan asylum represented in many cases only a temporary disruption in the family. About two-thirds of the children who entered the institution were accompanied by one or more siblings. These siblings constituted their own family unit while in the asylum, and although there was no overt policy related to keeping relatives together, 42.6 percent of these sibling familial units remained intact during their stay. Nearly one-third of siblings were separated through placements or mortality. For the remainder of the sibling units, one or more siblings were placed, while a living parent claimed those children still resident in the asylum. Among the children who were placed out, nearly one in five were re-admitted to the asylum. Although no reasons were given for their return, clearly the placement was not satisfactory. Of the 22 who were re-admitted, 15 were girls, and of the three who were admitted *three* times, all of them were girls. Mary Carlton, who had first entered the asylum in November 1847 at age 15, was sent to live with a family in Saint John but returned within two months. She was next placed with a family at Long Reach, King's County, where she remained for about a month. It is most likely that Carlton ran away from the second placement, for in October 1848, she was found begging on the streets of Saint John by Commissioner William O. Smith, who brought her back to the asylum for the final time. Within a week of her return, Carlton's mother reclaimed her. These departures, and even the returns, necessarily changed the classroom composition on a frequent, if not a regular basis.

A few months after the school opened at the asylum, Colebrooke supplied the funds necessary to build a separate schoolhouse on the grounds of the orphan asylum. The building, which was constructed at a cost of £200, measured 80 feet by 20 feet and was divided into two "apartments."[43] The trouble and expense in providing a separate instructional facility suggests that the school was intended to continue, perhaps indefinitely. However, even as the new school was being completed, shifting priorities and changing sentiments would spell the ultimate demise of the orphan asylum and infant school scheme.

When the Saint John Orphan Emigrant Asylum first opened in October 1847, Provincial Emigrant Agent, Moses H. Perley, expected that the institution would be a permanent rather than a temporary measure.[44] The asylum's commissioners, Henry Chubb and William O. Smith, also desired that the institution would continue under Colebrooke's successor, Sir Edmund Head. However, these sentiments were evidently at odds with the new administration, especially once it appeared that the immigration crisis of 1847 had subsided. The number of immigrants, distressed or otherwise, had noticeably declined. By September 1848, the 4,020 immigrants[45] who had arrived displayed a very "different character" than those of 1847.[46] In May 1848, Provincial Secretary John Simcoe Saunders instructed the orphan asylum commissioners not to accept any new admissions to the institution. The number of orphans resident in the asylum had been on the decline since February 1848, with releases outnumbering admissions. Just a few days prior to the directive from the Provincial Secretary, the commissioners reported that only 108 children remained in the institution. The formerly indispensable institution was already beginning to outlive its usefulness. Trouble was also brewing at the infant school. That same month, May 1848, the School Committee petitioned Sir Edmund Head for additional funds to pay its teacher, Alice Minette, noting that they had been delinquent in remunerating her for past services. To this end, the committee suggested drawing from the Emigrant Fund, but if such a request were ever granted, there is no record of it.[47]

The zeal which had once attended the operations at the orphan asylum was quickly fading as 1848 drew to a close. In December 1848, the Grand Jury was rather alarmed to discover that the institution "seemed to exhibit a want of looking after. The children do not appear to be well fed, nor properly cared for."[48] It was a very different picture from the one painted just a year earlier in *The Morning News* where it was reported that: "The children are well fed and clothed. In the morning they have Indian or oatmeal, porridge, and molasses—soup for dinner—and plenty of good tea and bread for supper."[49]

The infant school continued at the asylum even as the number of children Minette taught dwindled considerably. The commissioners had largely adhered to the Provincial Secretary's directive that no new children be admitted to the institution, and over the course of the next year only 15 children were accepted. By May 1849, about 50 children remained at the institution. When the commissioners began to consider closing the school, they clearly did not share this opinion with Minette. Without warning, Commissioner Smith terminated her contract. By the terms of her employment, she was to have been given one month's notice should the committee wish to dispense with her services. She could not comprehend this abrupt action, especially since she believed that she gave no cause or provocation. She submitted a petition requesting compensation for the abrupt termination insisting that it violated the terms of her contract. In her petition, she promised that:

> [D]uring the period of her employment she has faithfully discharged its duties, the comparative improvement of the poor children will fully testify and for which she can confidently appeal to the Ladies & Gentlemen who have visited the School.[50]

After receiving Minette's petition complaining about the suddenness of her dismissal, the Provincial Secretary, James R. Partelow, forwarded it to Smith for consideration. It is uncertain whether this matter was ever settled in a manner that was satisfactory to the orphan asylum's only teacher—Alice Minette.

Beginning in June 1849, the asylum's commissioners ran notices in the *Morning News* advertising the availability of the young children resident at the institution for hire.[51] That same month, the Grand Jury was pleased to report that the orphan asylum was found greatly improved from its visit months earlier, noting that it "was found clean and orderly. The children healthy and apparently receiving every attention." The Grand Jury further suggested that the small number of children who remained in the institution be moved to the almshouse. The financial savings in closing the asylum, they argued, could be put towards "the engagement of a competent instructor for the whole number of pauper children which would be of manifest advantage to them."[52] This is a curious observation given that the infant school where Minette had been employed had been in operation just a month earlier. The intent behind the orders and suggestions issued was clear: close the orphan asylum.

On 8 November 1849, a full two years after its establishment, the Saint John Emigrant Orphan Asylum closed its doors. The remaining 23 children, 18 boys and five girls, were transferred to the almshouse. The majority of these last remaining children, or 20 of the 23, had resided at the asylum since the day it opened, 25 October 1847. More than half were between the ages of 5 and 10 when they entered the institution, making them too young to be placed out. In addition, more than half had lost both parents, and therefore had no family to reclaim them. It was a rather melancholy ending for such a promising and reportedly indispensable institution. Orphaned and destitute children were once again forced to embrace a life of "idleness," so deplored by contemporary social critics. Provision for friendless or parentless children in the port city was reinstated when crisis again struck with the cholera epidemic of 1854. St. Vincent's Roman Catholic Orphan Asylum and the Saint John Protestant Orphan Asylum, which both opened that year, remained in operation for several decades. In 1867, the Wiggins Male Orphan Institute was established specifically for the orphan sons of mariners.[53] Permanent institutional child care had finally arrived in the province.

The Saint John Emigrant Orphan Asylum, the first institution of its kind in the province, was established in response to crisis, and its closure two years later sent a clear message, at least in the minds of officials, that the immigration crisis was over. The institution had served its intended purpose: to rescue destitute and orphaned children from the dangers of idleness. The orphanage provided vulnerable children and youth with a refuge from the moral danger of the streets and the corrupting influence of any and all vice. In trying to teach these institutionalized children to shun idleness in favor of "habits of industry," the organizers and indeed the teacher, Alice Minette, were attempting to satisfy a more socially conscious objective than the customary tenets of a common school education. The organizers expected that the institutionalized children could be saved from negative influences and trained to appreciate moral and religious principles, while embracing hard work and personal industry. These lofty educational aims were intended to counter the code of misconduct which might have been learned on the streets of Saint John or from their native Ireland, rendering them not only respectable but hardworking. The enthusiasm for the school at the asylum, which inspired support from the local elite, the Orphan Asylum School Committee and Lady Colebrooke, suggests that, at least initially, these educational objectives were being satisfied. Even as interest in the asylum and its school began to wane, Minette's commitment to her classroom apparently did not. The school offered routine during a time of uncertainty, and even if Minette did not manage to inculcate them with "habits of industry," she had dispatched her duties to an ever-changing student body for 16 months, and that consistency alone was certainly beneficial to the children in her charge. While at school, there was no denying that the children were occupied by routine and industry rather than simply existing in "total idleness ('the root of all evil')."

NOTES

1. Saint John County Court of General Sessions, RS 156, 11 June 1836, Provincial Archives of New Brunswick (hereafter PANB). The Grand Jury presentment regarding inmates at the local jail, suggesting that it would be beneficial to have prisoners engaged in some form of labor or industry.

2. Colonial Office Correspondence, MC 416, CO 188/103, Frederick Rogers and Thomas Murdock to Herman Merivale, 8 December 1847, PANB.

3. James M. Whalen, 'New Brunswick Poor Law Policy in the Nineteenth Century,' (MA Thesis, University of New Brunswick, 1968), p. 32.

4. Ibid., pp. 15, 26–27.

5. David J. Rothman, *The Discovery of the Asylum: Social Order and Disorder in the New Republic* (Boston: Little, Brown and Company, 1971). See chapters 4 to 9.

6. James M. Whalen, 'Social Welfare in New Brunswick, 1784–1900,' *Acadiensis* 2, 1 (Autumn 1972), p. 57.

7. Saint John County Court of General Sessions, RS 156, 8 September 1837, p. 49, PANB.

8. James M. Whalen, 'The nineteenth-century almshouse system in Saint John,' *Histoire Sociale - Social History* 7 (April 1971), 7. For more on New Brunswick's Lunatic Asylum, see: Daniel Francis, 'The development of the lunatic asylum in the Maritime Provinces,' *Acadiensis* 6, 1 (Spring 1977), pp 23–38.

9. Whalen, 'New Brunswick Poor Law policy in the nineteenth century,' p. 34.

10. Provincial Secretary Correspondence, RS 13, John S. Saunders to Commissioners of the Almshouse, 22 December 1847, PANB. The Saint John Orphan Benevolent Society disbanded a few years after permanent orphanages were established following the cholera epidemic of 1854. Judith Fingard, "The relief of the unemployed poor in Saint John, Halifax, and St. John's, 1815–1860," *Acadiensis* 5, 1 (Autumn 1975), p. 37, see endnote 22.

11. Saint John County Court of General Sessions, RS 156, 18 December 1847, p. 430, PANB.

12. Patricia T. Rooke and R.L. Schnell, "Guttersnipes and charity children: nineteenth century child rescue in the Atlantic Provinces," in Patricia T. Rooke and R.L Schnell (eds.), *Studies in Childhood History: A Canadian Perspective* (Calgary, Alberta: Detselig Enterprises Limited, 1982), p. 89; Patricia T. Rooke and R.L. Schnell, *Discarding the Asylum: From Child Rescue to the Welfare State in English Canada, 1850–1950* (Lanham, MD: University Press of America, 1983), p. 57.

13. Colonial Office Correspondence, MC 416, CO 188/103, Frederick Rogers and Thomas Murdock to Herman Merivale, 8 December 1847, PANB.

14. Colonial Office Correspondence, MC 416, CO 188/101, Benjamin Wolhaupter to John Simcoe Saunders, 2 September 1847, PANB.

15. Colonial Office Correspondence, MC 416, CO 188/102, Report of Moses H. Perley, 31 December1847, PANB.

16. Colonial Office Correspondence, MC 416, CO 188/102, Sir William Colebrooke to Lord Earl Grey, 14 December 1847, PANB.

17. Colonial Office Correspondence, MC 416, CO 188/102, Sir William Colebrooke to Lord Earl Grey, 25 November 1847, PANB.

18. Colonial Office Correspondence, MC 416, CO 188/103, Margin notes on a dispatch from Sir William Colebrooke to Lord Earl Grey, 10 January 1848, PANB.

19. Provincial Secretary Correspondence, RS 13, George Shore (Acting Provincial Secretary) to Commissioners of the Almshouse, 9 October 1847; John S. Saunders to Commissioners of the Almshouse, 22 December 1847. In the latter letter, John S Saunders named the members of the eight man and seven woman committee.

20. I am indebted to Peter Murphy, who transcribed the Saint John Emigrant Orphan Asylum Admittance Ledger. This valuable document is privately held, and Murphy was granted access in the course of completing his Master of Arts Thesis at St. Mary's University. Murphy subsequently published his thesis in manuscript form. The statistics I calculated and tabulated for this study are drawn from his transcription of the Admittance Ledger. See: Peter D. Murphy, 'Poor, "ignorant children": "a great resource, The Saint John Emigrant Orphan Asylum Admittance Ledger in context,' (MA Thesis, St. Mary's University, 1997); Peter D. Murphy, *Poor Ignorant Children: Irish Famine Orphans in Saint John, New Brunswick* (Halifax, St. Mary's University. 1999).

21. Patricia T. Rooke and R.L. Schnell, "Childhood and charity in nineteenth-century British North America," *Histoire Sociale - Social History* 15, 29 (May 1982), pp. 157–179; Charlotte Neff, "The role of Protestant children's homes in nineteenth-century Ontario: child rescue or family support?" *Journal of Family History* 34, 1 (January 2009), pp. 48–88.

22. Very similar admission statistics for half and full orphans were found at Missouri Protestant Orphan homes. Susan Whitelaw Downs and Michael W. Sherraden, "The orphan asylum in the nineteenth century," *Social Service Review* 57, 2 (June 1983), p. 280.

23. *The Morning News*, 6 December 1847.

24. *New Brunswick Courier*, 4 December 1847.

25. *New Brunswick Courier*, 18 December 1847.

26. David J. Rothman, see chapter 9.

27. There was a bell system at the almshouse, which announced times to rise, to eat, and to retire. See: Saint John County Court of General Sessions, RS 156, 12 September 1843, PANB.

28. The length of the school day at the asylum was never identified. The Fredericton Infant School operated from 9am to 3pm. York County Parish School Records, School Inspection Returns, RS 657, Q4d, 1844, PANB. The hours of operation at various Ontario homes ranged from 4.5 to 6 hours. Charlotte Neff, "The education of destitute homeless children in nineteenth-century Ontario," *Journal of Family History* 29, 1 (January 2004), pp. 3–46.

29. New Brunswick Executive Council, RS 7, vol. 32, file 1. Petition of the Saint John Emigrant Orphan School Committee to Sir Edmund Head, 27 May 1848, PANB. Other than the Secretary, Sarah E. Davison, who signed this petition, the members of the School Committee are not known.

30. T.W. Acheson, *Saint John: The Making of a Colonial Urban Community* (Toronto: University of Toronto Press, 1985), p. 164.

31. Caroline Winterer, "Avoiding a 'hothouse system of education": nineteenth-century early childhood education from the infant schools to the kindergarten," *History of Education Quarterly* 32, 3 (Autumn 1992), pp. 289–314.

32. Catherine Fayerweather, like Alice Minette, did not hold a licence to teach school. Infant Schools existed outside the provincial parish school system and were therefore not subject to the same rules or scrutiny.

33. Colonial Office Correspondence, MC 416, CO 188/104, Report of the Benevolent Society of Fredericton, 1848, PANB.

34. Saint John County Parish School Records, RS 657, L11, Free School (Infant School), 1842–1863; York County Parish School Records, School Inspection Returns, RS 657, Q4d, 1844, PANB.

35. Graeme Somerville Collection, MC 2700, Saint John Almshouse, Financial Records, 1843–1853, PANB. The teachers were Eugene Rogan (1846), John McCurt (1847), Eugene O'Regan (1848), Adam Dobbin (1850), Eugene O'Regan (1851–1853).

36. Eugene O'Regan, who taught at the almshouse in 1848, and then again from 1851–1853, could speak the Irish language. It is uncertain whether this capability was an

asset for his teaching duties there. The 1901 Canadian Census contained information related to "Mother Tongue," and this data demonstrates that the Irish language was still spoken in New Brunswick at that time and beyond. See: Bradford Gaunce, 'Challenging the standard interpretation of Irish language survival in the diaspora: The New Brunswick case study' (MA Thesis, University of New Brunswick, 2014).

37. *The Morning News*, 6 December 1847.

38. York County Parish School Records, School Inspection Returns, RS 657.

39. Koral LaVorgna, "Lessons in nineteenth-century New Brunswick teacher careerism," (PhD Dissertation, University of New Brunswick, 2016), p. 166.

40. "The Orphan Asylum," *The Morning News*, 6 December 1847.

41. There was only a single child aged 1 in the asylum at that time, although the reporter indicated that the youngest inmate was 3 months old.

42. Katherine MacNaughton, *The Development of the Theory and Practice of Education in New Brunswick, 1784–1900* (Fredericton: The University of New Brunswick, 1947), p. 119.

43. Provincial Secretary Records, RS 555, Commissioners Smith and Chubb to John S. Saunders, 26 May 1848, PANB.

44. Colonial Office Correspondence, MC 416, CO 188/107, Report of Moses H. Perley, 15 December 1847; CO 188/102, Report of Moses H. Perley, 31 December 1847, PANB.

45. Colonial Office Correspondence, MC 416, CO 188/106, Moses H. Perley to James R. Partelow, 10 October 1848, PANB.

46. Colonial Office Correspondence, MC 416, CO 188/106, Sir Edmund Head to Lord Earl Grey, 25 July 1848, PANB.

47. New Brunswick Executive Council, RS 7, vol. 32, file 1, Petition of the Saint John Emigrant Orphan School Committee to Sir Edmund Head, 27 May 1848, PANB.

48. Saint John County Court of General Sessions, RS 156, 16 December 1848, p. 118, PANB.

49. *The Morning News*, 6 December 1847.

50. Teachers' Petitions, RS 655, Alice Minette, 12 May 1849, PANB.

51. *The Morning News*, 6 June 1849.

52. Saint John County Court of General Sessions, RS 156, 16 June 1849, pp. 225–226, PANB.

53. Whalen, "New Brunswick Poor Law," pp. 16–17; Rooke and Schnell, "Childhood and charity," p. 169.

Representing Trauma

CHAPTER EIGHT

READING THE GREAT HUNGER?

In search of Mary Anne Sadlier's young audience

Stephen Butler

In March 2015, the *Irish Times* published an article by Marguérite Corporaal and Christopher Cusack chronicling the eventful life of an Irish emigrant named Mary Anne Sadlier.[1] Born Mary Anne Madden on 30 December 1820 in Cootehill, County Cavan, she lost her mother early in her childhood and was raised by her prosperous merchant father. She emigrated to Montreal in 1844 after her father's business collapsed and he died. Two years later, she married the prominent Irish-Catholic publisher James Sadlier, with whom she had six children. In 1860, the Sadliers moved from Montreal to New York City, where Mrs. J. Sadlier—this was her pen-name—edited a weekly newspaper, published fiction as well as devotional books, and administered her husband's business after his death. But the intent of Corporaal and Cusack in writing their article was less about sketching Sadlier's remarkable biography than it was about making a case for the significance of her prolific career as a popular novelist. The authors included these words in their final paragraph:

> Writing some of the earliest literary accounts of the Famine, Sadlier played
> a crucial role in disseminating its legacies, to Ireland but especially to the

North-American diaspora. With her works ... she gave voice to the preoc-
cupations of a large section of the Irish-American community, and for this
she deserves to be read.[2]

Calls for a renewed recognition of Sadlier's remarkable life and literary
achievements are not new. As far back as 1944, one finds a letter to the
editor of New York's Irish *Advocate* describing Sadlier as a "forgotten Irish
poetess" and reminding readers that she had "devoted the best years of her
life to the composition of works that shall always contribute to the well-
being of Catholics everywhere."[3] Shortly thereafter, at the 1946 meeting of
the Canadian Catholic Historical Association, Martin P. Reid, a parish priest,
made a case for the heroic virtue of her by-then-forgotten literary labors.[4] In
a note to an article for the 1968 journal of the American Antiquarian Society,
Willard Thorp wrote, "there is no satisfactory account of Mrs. Sadlier's career
(A full-length biography is much needed)."[5] In a 1990 contribution to the
Dictionary of Literary Biography, Michele Lacombe wrote that "there is much
in the documentary mode ... and a rendering of the social climate sufficient
to rescue her novels from the obscurity to which she has been relegated."[6]
And as recently as 2009, in the journal *Legacy*, which focuses on American
women's writing, Sharon M. Harris asked rhetorically: "how is it that this Irish
American immigrant author, who penned sixty books (including 18 novels)
on issues pertinent to numerous avenues of scholarly interest from the Irish
famine to newly arrived immigrants' lives, has remained so understudied?"[7]

Among Irish Studies scholars at least, that obscurity and under-study was
ameliorated in part by Charles Fanning's enlightening discussion of Sadlier in
his influential tome *The Irish Voice in America*. Fanning claimed that Sadlier's
oeuvre, particularly her novels set in mid-19th century America, is "the essential body of fiction for understanding the experience of the Famine immigrants and the conservative Catholic ideology by which many of them lived."[8]
Crucially, Fanning suggested that Sadlier's fiction was not just passively
reflecting the social conditions in which many of these emigrant readers lived,
but actively trying to fashion a pious, patriotic Irish-Catholic identity for

them that could work within North American society. Fanning emphasized that Sadlier was not only a "chronicler" but a "guide" whose fiction provided a "functional ideology" that "worked" for fellow immigrants.[9]

Rather than making another argument for Sadlier's considerable literary, cultural and historical significance in the face of the relative neglect in which her reputation still finds itself among many historians and literary critics, this essay instead tries to begin to explore questions begged by Fanning's insights. Is there any archival evidence that might clarify and/or specify the way in which Sadlier's didactic novels informed the readers' sense of what it meant to be Irish and/or Catholic and/or a Famine emigrant in 19th century America? Does any archival evidence exist that might show or at least suggest how reading Sadlier influenced the creation and/or nourished the maintenance of American Irish-Catholic identity in concrete, individual ways? And more specifically, for the purposes of this collection, are there any historical traces of the young readers who encountered the novels Sadlier wrote about the era of the Great Hunger in Ireland and North America? In attempting to address that last query, this essay focuses its investigation on the reception of four novels written in a roughly 10-year period: *Willy Burke; or, The Irish Orphan in America* (serialized in the *Boston Pilot* and published 1850); *Alice Riordan, the Blind Man's Daughter. A Tale for the Young* (serialized in the *Boston Pilot* in 1850 and then published in 1851); *New Lights; or, Life in Galway* (published in 1853); and *Bessy Conway; or, the Irish Girl in America* (published in 1861).

Before examining these particular novels, let us review what we know about the general audience for Sadlier's writing. Evidence noted in the existing scholarship points to the fact that Sadlier's "works were consumed in huge numbers." In his address to the Canadian Catholic Historical Association (CCHA), Reid reported that "'Sadlier's Library,' a collection of volumes comprising fiction, books of devotion, historical writings and a Catechism... was the stock in trade in every parish library in [Canada]" and that "Her story books were handed out as prizes to two generations, maybe three, of Catholic scholars."[10] Willard Thorpe discovered that "many of her novels were kept in print for 50 years or more" and that "her early novels were evidently read to pieces."[11] Michele Lacombe noted that she "achieved a wide readership in ... North America, as evidenced by the ubiquitous serializations, reprints, and pirated editions of her work."[12] And many scholars also have noted that Sadlier's connections to various periodicals—the *Literary Garland* and the *True Witness* in Montreal, Patrick Donahoe's *Boston Pilot*, Thomas D'Arcy McGee's *American Celt*, and her husband's New York *Tablet*—afforded her unique opportunities for disseminating her fiction, first in the format of weekly serials and then later as bound novels.[13] Clearly then, the handful of scholars who have studied Sadlier's career have amassed considerable circumstantial evidence suggesting that she did indeed achieve a wide readership among Irish-Catholic North Americans. Yet, despite this ample circumstantial evidence, the questions posed earlier about the precise ways in which individual readers within this broad audience were practically influenced by Sadlier's didactic fiction proves more difficult to answer. After all, if her novels were literally "read to pieces"—their brittle pages crumbled and their flimsy spines rent asunder—then the scribbling of readers in margins or the individual commentary they may have appended to the end of a story cannot be recovered as historical evidence. And even more disposable and degradable than Sadlier's books are the actual newspapers in which she initially published many of her stories. Nevertheless, some interesting information about Sadlier's young adult/Famine fiction has been preserved for scholars.

Willy Burke; or, The Irish Orphan in America was published serially in the *Boston Pilot* from 15 June to 17 August 1850.[14] Chapters were placed prominently, typically taking up all the columns of the front page. Upon encountering the story for the first time, readers would have recognized that instead of starting her story in 1850 amid the contemporary context of the Great Hunger, Sadlier began the novel "some twenty years ago" in Tipperary, with a once-strong farmer named Andy Burke deciding to transplant his family to America. His wife resists the move, but Andy argues that between rents and tithes, there is no future for his four children in Ireland. On the ship from Liverpool to New York, Andy contracts a fever and dies. Within a year of arriving, two of the children also die, of cholera. That leaves the mother, Biddy Burke, and her teenage sons, Peter and Willy, as the central characters. Soon enough, Peter is seduced by the commercial Protestant culture of the city, which breaks his poor mother's heart and kills her; Willy, by contrast, stays true to the faith, works hard and is rewarded with an inheritance from his German Protestant boss, who converts to Catholicism on his deathbed. In the end, Willy's good example even leads his prodigal brother, Peter, back to the Church. Sadlier had composed *Willy Burke* in response to a call for a story about an Irish orphan boy made by the Catholic convert and public intellectual Orestes Brownson in his journal, *Quarterly Review*. Patrick Donahoe, the publisher of the *Pilot* turned this suggestion into a competition, with the winning novelist earning $50 and publication in his newspaper. The 22 June 1850 issue of the *Pilot*, in a column titled "The Prize Tale," informed readers that the second and third chapters of the novel were included in the issue and expressed gratitude that the story "has been well received by our patrons." In the Preface to the book-length version of the novel, printed in October 1850 by the publishing firm owned by Donahoe, Sadlier explained her didactic intentions beyond winning the prize and gaining an audience:

> This little work was written for the express purpose of being useful to the young sons of my native land, in their arduous struggle with the tempter, whose nefarious design of bearing them from the faith of their fathers is so artfully concealed under every possible disguise. The most plausible pretence is, that men make their way better in this money-seeking world, by becoming Protestants; and the fallacy of this saying I have endeavored to show, by proving that a man may be a good Catholic, a sincere Christian,— yet obtain both wealth and honor even here below.[15]

In its announcement of the book, the 26 October *Pilot* congratulated Sadlier enthusiastically for succeeding in her goal:

> We commend this little book to all our young friends, and bid them take Willy Burke for their model, and we recommend all Protestants who are

engaged in stealing our children from us in order to train them up as heretics, and to do what they can to check the growth of the Catholic population in this country, to procure it, read it, and to ponder it well.[16]

While the story is obviously contrived propaganda, Sadlier's daughter, Anna, reported that at least one elderly reader took it as documentary truth: "An old Irishman said to Mrs. Sadlier one day: 'I was in Andy Burke's house the night before they left, and I remember the schoolmaster being there.'"[17] According to Anna, *Willy Burke* sold 7,000 copies in the first six weeks after publication.[18] And Fanning claims that three editions had been published by the end of 1851.[19] A copy of that 1850 first edition, published in Boston by Donahoe, can be found in the Library of Congress. It was awarded on July 14, 1853 to Emma Metcalfe of the Academy of the Sisters of Notre Dame, San Jose, California, for Profane History.[20] Another undated edition of *Willy*, published in Dublin by Duffy & Co., can be found in the Thomas Fisher Rare Book Library at the University of Toronto. It was awarded in 1913 to a Hector Andrews of Assumption College, Kilmore, Victoria, Australia, for Geography in 1913.[21] Unfortunately, what Metcalfe or Andrews thought of the book we do not know. But at least we can discover from a letter he sent to the "Uncle Jack's Talks with Boys and Girls" column of the *Sacred Heart Review* that a Henry O'Brien of Clinton, Massachusetts, thought that "Mrs. Sadlier's books are very good. I like 'Willy Burke' the best, it is so much like real life, though I am afraid few boys are as good as 'Willy Burke.'"[22]

In its 7 June 1851 issue, the *Boston Pilot* announced a tale "equal, if not superior, to the story of Willy Burke [sic] by the same authoress." That tale was *Alice Riordan, the Blind Man's Daughter*, which ran from 4 July 1851 to 27 September 1851. Like *Willy*, *Alice* was printed prominently on the front page each week, and also like *Willy*, the novel began, not in the present, but in the recent past, specifically "twelve years ago." The story, set in Montreal rather than New York, opened with a scene of disembarkation. Sadlier described a "crowd of emigrants" with "the rosy hue of health on their weather-bronzed features"—a look, the narrator notes, "far removed from that squalid wretchedness which, of late years, too often marks the appearance of the Irish emigrant." Among these pre-Famine emigrants is Cormac Riordan, the blind man, and his lovely young daughter, Alice, who has been invited to the new world to live with her wealthy uncle and his wife, who are childless. Alice finds that her uncle is a kind and successful businessman who runs a popular tavern, but one who has neglected his religion and wandered off the path to salvation. The novel dramatizes her successful attempts to save his soul by steering him back to the true faith.

Judging by the "Preface" Sadlier composed for the publication of a second edition of the novel, published in 1854 by Thomas B. Noonan and Co., some readers were less interested in the religious moral of the tale than in its seemingly incomplete plot, anxiously asking Sadlier "what became of Alice?"[23] In response, Sadlier added a chapter revealing Alice's "after-life": her wedding to a nice young Catholic man named Tom Richardson and her father's peaceful passing into the next world after dying of consumption. While some read the work as a romantic melodrama, no doubt others regarded it, like Sadlier, as an exemplary moral tale for the young. According to an advertisement for their Catholic Boys and Girls Library series in *The Catholic Quarterly Review*, vol. 8 (1883), Noonan and Co. included *Alice Riordan* and *Willy Burke* in this series, which also included volumes by Cardinal Wiseman, Agnes M. Stewart and Gertrude Parsons. A copy of *Alice Riordan* from Noonan's Catholic Boys and Girls Library can be found in the Thomas Fisher Rare Book Library at the University of Toronto.[24] It was awarded on 24 June 1890 to a 'Miss Mary' of St Mary's Seminary, Bay View, Providence, Rhode Island. But alas, Miss Mary did not leave any evidence as to what she thought of the book. Yet, letters published in the *Sacred Heart Review* from Agnes Knightly of Amherst, Lillian C. McPherson of Charlestown, and Margaret E. Curran of Norwood, all in Massachusetts, all suggest that the book was widely read by Catholic girls.[25]

While Sadlier addressed the Great Hunger only tangentially in *Willy Burke* and *Alice Riordan*, the next of her novels to be printed in book form was the only one of her works to tackle the Famine in Ireland directly.[26] Published in 1853, *New Lights; or, Life in Galway* was set in contemporary Connemara. Sadlier described the village of Killany and environs this way:

> Famine had been busy in the neighborhood, and with it came its handmaid, pestilence, and the misery of the people was great ... Killany was not quite so severely scourged as some other places, but still it had its full measure of sorrow and suffering; and even now, when the famine has exhausted its fury, there is still much destitution existing in that locality.[27]

The novel's central character is Bernard O'Daly, a successful, strong farmer before the Famine, who, in the course of the plot, loses his wife and then is confronted by his anti-Catholic landlord with the choice of eviction or conversion. He chooses to remain steadfast in his faith and loses the farm. O'Daly is saved from utter destitution by the remittances of two sons who have emigrated to Philadelphia.

Fanning claims there were at least eight additions of *New Lights* published by the end of the century, suggesting the book's condemnation of Protestant proselytism and celebration of heroic Catholic suffering earned it an enduring popularity.[28] But the book does not seem to have been marketed toward young readers in the same way as *Willy Burke* and *Alice Riordan*. For instance, *New Lights* was not included in Noonan's Catholic Boys and Girls Library series. Additionally, no copies of the book that had been given out as a school prize could be located, nor was there any reference to this novel among the letters written by children to the *Sacred Heart Review*.

Sadlier was encouraged to re-visit the unequivocally adolescent subject matter of *Willy* and *Alice* by Isaac Hecker, the founder of the Paulists, a man who, like Brownson, had converted to Catholicism and founded a journal, *The Catholic World*. The result of Hecker's request was *Bessy Conway; or, the Irish Girl in America*. In her "Preface" she informed readers that:

> the object of the book is ... simply an attempt to point out to Irish Girls in America—especially that numerous class whose lot it is to hire themselves

out for work, the true and never-failing path to success in this world, and happiness in the next.[29]

This language recalls the "Preface" to *Willy Burke*, as does Sadlier's claim to have written the book:

> from a sincere and heartfelt desire to benefit these young country-women ... by showing them how to win respect and inspire confidence on the part of their employers, and at the same time, to avoid the snares and pitfalls which have been the ruin of so many of their own class.[30]

In concluding the "Preface" Sadlier sought to assure these young girls that "it rests with themselves whether they do well or ill in America, whether they do honor to their country and their faith, or bring shame and reproach to both."[31]

As she did in *New Lights*, Sadlier chose to begin *Bessy Conway* in the immediate post-Famine present, although the scene she paints of "rich and fertile" Tipperary is immediately more promising than famine-ravaged Connemara. Sadlier initially introduces readers to a character named Denis Conway, "a decent man" and strong famer, a characterization that resembles both Bernard O'Daly and Andy Burke. Sadlier explained to readers:

> [Conway] lived through the darkest and most dismal of 'rainy days,' when gaunt famine stared in at the door and pestilence at the window; when a shilling was worth a precious life, and a pound of meal its weight in gold, because of the hunger that was gnawing at the people's hearts, and Denis Conway had seen all that ...
>
> Happily, the dark days of famine and pestilence had passed away without leaving Denis Conway any worse legacy than that of experience. Unlike many of his friends and neighbors he had seen no one belonging to him die the awful death of hunger—reduced to the last necessity as they had been, and for whole days without eating a morsel, still it so happened that relief always came at the right time, justifying the word that was always on the old man's lips: 'God is a good provider.'[32]

In this way, Sadlier used the opening paragraphs to set-up the story of how Conway was saved from eviction, starvation and probable death by Divine Providence acting through his virtuous daughter Bessy. And Bessy Conway's story, like the story of Willy Burke and Alice Riordan, begins "years ago" (i.e., in the pre-Famine 1830s) when she departed Tipperary for America. The American parts of the story duplicate many scenes and themes from the earlier novels, such as the juxtaposition of material abundance and spiritual poverty in the New World, the contrasting behavior of good Irish-Catholics and bad ones, and the attempts by wily Protestants to convert Irish-Catholics. Like Alice and Willy, Bessy makes her way in the New World through hard work, thrift and religious devotion. But unlike Alice and Willy, at the end of her story, Bessy returns home to Ireland, just in time to save her family from the bailiffs. This happy ending is further embellished, like the second edition of *Alice Riordan*, by a marriage. In this case, Bessy weds Henry Herbert, the landlord's son, a kind of tortured Byronic hero who has converted to Catholicism after his own sojourn in America.[33]

According to Fanning, *Bessy Conway* had six American editions in the 19th century, the most of any of her novels set in America.[34] How many of the readers of those six editions were young, working-class, immigrant Irish women, and how many of those women learned from the novel ways of avoiding "the snares and pitfalls which have been the ruin of so many of their own class" is hard to know. No documentation appears to have survived from a single reader of this type, who has left behind a record of her interaction with the novel.

Yet, perhaps answers are hinted at in an 1891 article written about Sadlier for the Catholic magazine *Ave Maria*, then reprinted in 1895 in *The Scholastic*, at that time the University of Notre Dame's weekly student newspaper. Notre Dame awarded Sadlier its Laetare Medal in 1895 so the piece was no doubt intended to help explain to students why Sadlier was being honored with what the university continues to bill as the most prestigious award given to American Catholics. In this essay, the author, William Kelly, attributed to her "an influence which very few Catholic writers of her day wielded" and claimed "it is doubtful if a single [North American Catholic novelist] can be found whose works exerted in their day—and still continue to exert in a certain measure ... a wider, deeper, more beneficial influence."[35] In attempting to illustrate this beneficial influence, Kelly wrote:

> it was demonstrated perhaps by the many letters which came to her from humbler classes of her readers, who wrote to thank her for a moral victory won or a better spirit awakened by the perusal of her books.

The content of this correspondence between Sadlier and her readers is further elucidated in a long passage worth quoting at length:

> Letters came to her from all parts of the world—from every quarter and corner of this country and Canada; from various countries in South America; from all over Ireland, and from all parts of Great Britain, from Continental Europe and far-away Australasia; and in fine, from every locality where the 'sea-divided Gael' had found a habitation ... some glowing with warm praises for her books; others criticizing this or that passage, character or bit of local description in them; these full of the tenderest pathos, and telling of dear but sad recollections awakened by reading her pages; those racy with humorous recital, and thanking the novelist for having so faithfully portrayed some cruel, rackrenting landlord or heartless agent; and each and all bearing indubitable testimony to the incalculable amount of good her gifted pen was accomplishing among the scattered children of her native land, by confirming them and their descendants in the faith and virtuous ways of their father.[36]

At the moment, this potential treasure trove of audience response composed by Ireland's scattered children has been lost, or at least misplaced. While this rich vein of archival material waits to be discovered and mined by scholars, just considering the content of the correspondence described by Kelly suggests, counter-intuitively perhaps, that not all the individual or family stories of eviction and/or emigration that began within the context of the Great Hunger ended in tragedy and despair. And that suggestion alone can enrich our existing understanding of the lives of men and women, and boys and girls who fled Ireland hungry and broken in the decades after 1845.

In the conclusion of his insightful chapter on Sadlier, Fanning writes that the fiercely conservative Catholic ideology housed in her fiction "supports Kerby Miller's evidence that this was a profoundly alienated generation of emigrants."[37] And Miller's primary evidence for that sense of alienation was of course, letters written by Famine-era emigrants. Yet, the letters described above by Kelly suggest emotions besides just angst and alienation; those lost letters suggest deeply human feelings such as pathos, patriotism, faith and even fun. And so, perhaps a simple but useful conclusion for this essay is that the search for Sadlier's readers reminds us that surely there is much, much more for us to discover and learn about the emotional, intellectual and spiritual lives of the generations of Irish people who endured the trauma of the Great Hunger in Ireland and the subsequent shock of journeying across the waves to new worlds around the globe. Importantly also, much remains to be unearthed regarding the experiences of the young readers who encountered Sadlier's novels about the impact of the Great Hunger in Ireland and North America.

NOTES

1. Marguérite Corporaal and Christopher Cusack, "In Praise of Mary Anne Sadlier, a Literary Figurehead of Catholic North America," in *The Irish Times*, 18 March 2015. Web.

2. Ibid.

3. T.D. Curtin, "Old School Days Recalled," in *The Advocate*, 23 September 1944, p. 4.

4. Martin P. Reid, P.P., "Mrs. Jas. Sadlier Canadian Apostle of Catholic Literature" in *Canadian Catholic Historical Association Report*, 14 (1946), pp. 105–113.

5. Willard Thorpe, "Catholic Novelists in Defense of Their Faith, 1829–1865" in *Proceedings of the American Antiquarian Society*, 78 (April 1968), n98.

6. Michele Lacombe, "Mary Anne Sadlier," in *Dictionary of Literary Biography, Volume 99: Canadian Writers Before 1890* (The Gale Group, 1990).

7. Sharon M. Harris, "'Across the Gulf': Working in the Post-Recovery Era" in *Legacy*, vol. 26, no. 2 (2009), p. 290.

8. Charles Fanning, *The Irish Voice in America: 250 Years of Irish-American Fiction*, 2nd Edition (Lexington: The University Press of Kentucky, 2000), p. 114.

9. Ibid., p. 140.

10. Reid, 'Apostle of Catholic Literature', p. 112.

11. Thorpe, 'Catholic Novelists', pp. 98–99.

12. Lacombe, 'Sadlier.'

13. Eileen Sullivan, "Community in Print: Irish-American Publishers and Readers" in *American Journal of Irish Studies*, v. 8 (2011), p. 64.

14. I am indebted to the Boston College Libraries for having created an open-access, browse-able database, containing 485 issues of the *Boston Pilot*. The issues run from 3 January 1846 to 26 December 1857.

15. Mrs. J. Sadlier, *Willy Burke; or The Irish Orphan in America*, (Boston: Thomas B. Noonan & Co., 1850), p. iii

16. 'New Books,' *Boston Pilot*, 26 October 1850.

17. Anna T. Sadlier, "Mrs. Sadlier's Early Life, Her Books and Friends," in *Donahoe's Magazine* (April 1903), p. 334.

18. Ibid., p. 331.

19. Fanning, *The Irish Voice*, p. 120.

20. A scanned image of this copy of the book is available online at the Internet Archive website (https://archive.org/details/willyburkeoosadl), accessed 16 December 2017.

21. Ibid.

22. *The Sacred Heart Review*, vol. 15, no. 3, 18 January 1896, p. 10.

23. Mrs. J. Sadlier, *Alice Riordan, The Blind Man's Daughter. A Tale for the Young* (Boston: Thomas B. Noonan and Co., 1854), pp. 3–4.

24. A scanned image of this copy of the book is available at the Internet Archive website (https://archive.org/details/aliceriordanblinoosadl), accessed 16 December 2017).

25. See the "Uncle Jack's Talks with Boys and Girls" column of the *Sacred Heart Review* vol. 17, no. 4, 3 April 1897 (for Agnes's letter) and vol. 25, no. 16, 20 April 1901 (for Lillian's letter) and vol. 28, no. 5, 2 August 1902 (for Margaret's letter).

26. In the interim Sadlier serialized *The Blakes and Flanagans*—a novel about the public school question—for Thomas Darcy McGee's *The American Celt*. But this work was not published as a book until 1855.

27. Mrs. J. Sadlier, *New Lights; or Life in Galway, A Tale* (New York: D. and J. Sadlier & Co., 1865), p. 6.

28. Fanning, p. 116.

29. Mrs. J. Sadlier, *Bessy Conway; or The Irish Girl in America* (New York: D. and J. Sadlier & Co., 1861), p. iii.

30. Ibid.

31. Sadlier, *Bessy*, p. iv.

32. Sadlier, *Bessy*, pp 5–6.

33. For a rich reading of how Sadlier employs "a different kind of gothic" see Marjorie Howes's "Discipline, Sentiment, and the Irish-American Public: Mary Anne Sadlier's Popular Fiction," in *Eire-Ireland*, vol. 40, nos. 1 & 2 (Spring/Summer 2005), pp 159–166.

34. Fanning, *The Irish Voice*, p. 134

35. William D. Kelly, "A Benefactress of Her Race" in *The Scholastic*, vol. 28, no. 26 (23 March 1895), p. 405.

36. Ibid., p. 408.

37. Fanning, *The Irish Voice*, p. 152.

CHAPTER NINE

"A THIG A THOO GAEILGE?"

Famine immigrants' Irish words remembered by their children[1]

E. Moore Quinn

In the mid 1980s, an elderly Irish-American living in New England reminisced that his father, an immigrant to America from Ireland after the years of *An Gorta Mor*—the Great Hunger [literally, the Great Hurt, or the Great Famine] of 1845–1852—had sung to him when he was a child. He asked, "'*Crúiscín lán.*' What does it mean? My father often sang that to me." I was able to reveal that *crúiscín* is the Irish word for "little jug" and *lán* means "full." In all likelihood, the man's father was singing about the virtues of having a little jug full of whiskey, or perhaps even milk.

Although "it is estimated that between one-quarter and one third of America-bound emigrants (from Ireland) during the famine were Irish speakers,"[2] the Irish language in the United States attenuated as immigrants attempted to acculturate in a new country. Indubitably, workforce demands for monolingual usage in the United States weakened the language.[3] So, too, did the ideology of contempt advanced against it, to be discussed in greater detail below.[4] However, scholars recognize that "Irish speakers have always formed a substantial percentage of Irish immigrants to the United States."[5]

Famine-related emigration "made the language more common in many Irish-American neighbourhoods than it had been earlier in the nineteenth century."[6] Nancy Stenson suggests that " ... Irish speakers must have been a prominent presence among Irish immigrants in the nineteenth century, and one might expect their language skills to have been an important factor in their assimilation to North American life."[7] Likewise, Joseph Callahan reveals that Irish was common in informal use in Irish neighborhoods and "suspended in solution ... [and] present as a possibility" within the communities in which it was uttered.[8] Callahan learned that his parents had "listened in" when Irish was spoken, and could "reel off bits of the language" years later.[9] So, too, could Stenson's interviewees, who acknowledged that they had preserved a passive knowledge of Irish, having acquired it within their domestic domains.[10] One of my interviewees could translate linguistic items bequeathed by her father, such as "going out to pick 'cashlevauns'— (dandelions)."

As shall be noted in the memories that follow, what this person recollected might not have been exactly what her father said. *Caisearbhán*, one translation of dandelion,[11] is similar to *ceannbhán*, something "white-headed" or "whitish."[12] "Cean-a-bhans" are "tiny white flowers dancing over the marshy brown earth" of Irish bogs in May.[13] Although the aforementioned consultant displayed confidence in the accuracy of her pronunciation and translation, others were less self-assured. Like the gentleman who inquired about *crúiscín lán*, many Irish-Americans whose ancestors thronged from Ireland in the mid- to late-19th century could conjure only an Irish word or two.[14] One woman remembered her "Nanna" [grandmother] sending her to purchase "lukeh peena galliah" [*luach pingne gallúnai*], a "penny's worth of soap."

Another revealed:

> She taught me, or I picked up, simple phrases in Gaelic such as 'It's hot/cold,' 'Open/shut the door,' 'How are you?' 'Where are you going?' "Sit down." She and my grandmother (born in Holyoke [Massachusetts] of Irish parents) often spoke Irish together, usually when they didn't want me to know what they were saying. And my father often said to me in Irish, 'You

have no sense and no one will marry you.' I remember the words but have no idea how to spell them.

The last sentence above reflects a truism of Irish-American oral tradition; few individuals, even if they were able to replicate verbally *Tá sé fuar* [It"s cold] or *Dún an doras* [Shut the door], could spell or write the Irish expressions they had heard in their youth. Hardly anyone spoke of having access to Irish language pedagogy, and only rarely did interviewees supply contextual information regarding when and where Irish was spoken. One interviewee said that Irish seemed "like a fairy language or something equally mysterious, and in a way, forbidden." These attributes imbued the language with covert prestige, as if knowing it might be a link to the lost worlds of their adult relatives, and perhaps even to *An Gorta Mór*.

In immigrants' talk, the Great Hunger was referenced indirectly in what I have labeled "coming over narratives" and "sound bite memories."[15] They survive in mere one- or two-line recollections: "1845–1847. Famine. Irish fled to America." "My great grandfather came during famine. Nine children scattered to Australia and [the United States]; one stayed [behind] to care for parents." "[My] maternal grandfather's family came to [the United States] as a result of [my mother's] father's death and [the] Potato Famine."[16]

More obliquely, the legacy of the Famine surfaced in immigrants" attitudes and relationships to food. For instance, the expression "There is eating and drinking in that" was said about anything that deserved praise. A widening girth was interpreted as a sign that life's circumstances were improving. One consultant revealed, "It was a compliment to hear, 'You're getting fat, God bless you,'" adding, "I suppose the saying went away back to the [F]amine days." It was noted that one immigrant thought the epitome of being well-off was to be able to afford roast beef. Whenever he saw a new invention he would say, "I bet the man that got that up et [ate] roast beef!" In this instance, we are apprised of the long-term ideological consequences of *An Gorta Mór*, for during that time, the Irish were accused of consuming "morally inferior" food (i.e., potatoes).[17] The anecdote is indicative of how one man's sense of his own intelligence was affected by such propaganda. Wasting food was considered unethical and morally suspect; in light of that fact, the decision to "let the captive go free," uttered in choosing not to save leftovers, takes on special significance. I was told that, were a visit to be paid to a new home for the first time, a gift of food would be brought "to insure that [the family] would never go hungry."

Many consultants talked about *An Gorta Mór* within larger contexts of their parents' and grandparents' inimical feelings toward the practices and policies of England. One consultant wrote:

> ... a hatred toward the English for the inflictions of their race. Loss of religious practice; suppression of [the] Gaelic language; starvation; killings; loss of homeland; etc.

Others recalled acrimonious sentiments voiced by elders. One woman recalled that a person who was very bitter and fiercely opposed to the English was described as "black as a *carog*'s [beetle's] kitten." Another consultant recalled family members saying, "The only good Englishman is a dead Englishman." By way of explanation, he added, "[The words were] said with much bitterness left over from [the] Famine. Family Split up. Tragedy." Still another recalled his father's grace: "This is the grace my father said after each meal: 'Thanks be to God for the next meal; I'm sure of this one now.'" The consultant added, "Must be a throw-back to the Famine days." Still another indexed how "the decline in Christian charity" played out at this family's dinner table:[18]

> God bless me and my wife,
> My son John and his wife,
> Us four,
> And no more.
> Amen.[19]

Such restrictive sentiments exemplify how post-Famine trauma endured on a day-to-day basis within some Irish-American homes. These brief fragments attest to what was often said in interviews: "They didn't talk much about it." Their silence is not unlike the aforementioned memories of the Irish language, which was spoken in secret, when adults sought to obscure certain topics from children.

Considering that many were reluctant to pass on their mother tongue, it becomes all the more significant to examine the corpus of linguistic materials retained in folk memory by immigrants" descendants. Irish language words, phrases and fragments were collected from approximately 1985 to 2000. During that time, Irish-Americans residing in New England completed questionnaires, posted letters and participated in a variety of face-to-face interviews. The method was to set down approximations of the sounds, "words," and "expressions" which descendants of post-Famine (i.e., 19th century and early 20th century) Irish immigrants recalled hearing when they were young.[20] The data provide opportunities to examine linguistic repertoires, to examine spoken words remembered, and to conjecture as to the meaning of the corpus for language maintenance and survival.

Although the aforementioned "cashlevaun" does not seem to have passed into English usage, many other Irish words did, and without much fanfare.[21] English borrowed a number of Irish words and names that, after frequent use, lost specific associations. These include "galore," from the Irish *go leor*, enough or plenty; "bog," from the Irish *bogach*, "soft ground"; and "gob," the Irish word for mouth.[22] "Slew" and "slue," are variants of *slua*, meaning host, crowd, or throng.[23] "Smithereens" comes from s*midiríní*, Irish for "small fragments."[24] In Irish, "banshee" is *bean sí* or *bean sighe*, a female death messenger, often associated with the fairy world. "Spree" has its Irish equivalent, *spraoi*, meaning fun or sport.[25] Other words like "poteen" [*poitín*, "moonshine," a homemade alcoholic brew],[26] appear in random places, including song lyrics. Generally, however, the aforesaid go unrecognized as Irish words.[27]

So, too, does "hubbub," an English word that may have derived from the Irish *hububú*, "a confused crying or wailing"[28] or from the Irish *ub ub*, "a war cry, noisy confusion."[29] "Ballyhoo" was recalled by one interviewee as meaning "a lively good time"; Espy defines it as "a clamorous advertising; [a] noisy uproar." He adds that the word may have derived from "Ballyhooly," a place in Ireland where one could "probably expect [the] singing and roistering to continue into the dawn."[30] In terms of sense of place, "ballyhoo" may derive from the Irish *báile*, meaning home, place or township, and/or from the name of a clan chief or important figure.[31] In the United States, "ballyhooly" is also defined as "advertising or publicity, especially of a raucous or colourful sort [and] exaggeration, hype."[32]

In spite of many linguistic borrowings, Irish became associated with poverty and backwardness.[33] When a language becomes devalued, eventually its speakers fear being heard, the equivalent of being "found out" or "discovered." As Callahan notes, there was a reason why "Fionn Mac Cumhaill never walked in the St. Patrick's Day Parade."[34] Negative stereotyping gained sway among Famine and post-Famine immigrants such that they became ashamed of their language. Irish words—to say nothing of the poems and stories that had comprised their former soundscape—were discarded. My grandmother told me that her mother never had "the brogue."

The word *bróg* is Irish for shoe. Some have said that it became a reference to Irish talk because speakers sounded as if they had "a shoe on their tongue."[35] On the other hand, Irish lexicographer Patrick Dinneen associates the Anglo-Irish word *brogue* with Irish *barróg*, "a hold ... a tight grip"; he describes it as "a stiff, grippy way of speaking English."[36] Montgomery adds:

> From the mid-18th century on, the Irish of Boston talk not just of the *brogue* but of the *brogue on the tongue*. [It] in fact was originally the difficulty experienced by Irish speakers in getting their tongues round the alien English sounds.[37]

Like so many others, my great-grandmother believed that conquering non-habitual English sounds would accelerate her ability to "pass" into American life. She had learned that "the brogue" marked the Irish language in general and her dialect in particular as different.

Consultants" remembrances of commands of silence, with their concomitant estimations of linguistic unworthiness, help us to understand how Irish immigrants in America socialized their youth—and one another—to life in America. In a variety of contexts and for a number of reasons, not the least of which was the acquisition of upward mobility, they monitored their offspring"s speech habits, encouraging quiescence on many topics. The Irish command *Ná bí ag caint* [the negative imperative singular form of the verb to talk], is an expression that survived in Irish-American vernacular. The sentence means "Don't be talking." One consultant recalled the reprimand, "Don't be talking a tear!" [*Ná bí réabadh cainte faoi*]. To this day, especially in parts of Massachusetts, one can hear *Ná bí caint* [*sic*] uttered in terms of future behavior, as in the sentence, "We"ll be "*ná bí caint*" (i.e., regarding a certain subject) when we get there," or "I"d be "*ná bí caint*" about that if I were you." (The pronunciation of the preposition *ag* disappeared). Collectively unsure of what *Ná bí* [*ag*] *caint* meant in Irish, interviewees had little doubt as to its English translation: "It's a good idea to keep (your) mouth closed." For one particular consultant, *Ná bí caint* carried an extended sense: "[It's] better to keep your mouth closed and be thought a fool than to open it and remove all doubt."

Hearing the expression *Ná bí* [*ag*] *caint* was understood as a warning—or at the very least, an encouragement—to behave in a manner that parents and/or grandparents considered apt. Such silencing strategies and monitoring practices led to questions regarding linguistic identity and self-definition. They go some distance toward providing an explanation as to why immigrants' children and grandchildren retained only fragments of the Irish language. Another correspondent revealed her perception of the levels of literacy that her father and his brother possessed:

> When my father and uncle did not want the children to know what they were saying, they would speak in Gaelic, but their knowledge of the language was very limited because they had very little education.

In all likelihood, my consultant was referring to knowledge of the *written* language. Kenneth Nilsen states that "most Irish speakers who landed on [American] shores were illiterate in their native language ... This is especially true of the thousands of poor Irish speakers who arrived during and after the Famine."[38]

Hiberno-English, sometimes referred to as Anglo-Irish[39] and defined as "the Irish use of English,"[40] is the term applied to the variety of non-standard English terms spoken by the Irish. Although the English were inclined to treat Hiberno-English expressions as amusing, it is worth noting that they reflected an almost verbatim adherence to Irish language grammatical constructions. Interviewees could reproduce syntactical structures that demonstrated how the influence of the Irish language had affected their parents" English, and to some extent, their own. These included the use of the present habitual tense, as in "I do be (or "I bees) going to work every day" and copula constructions like "Twas a rough journey, so it was"; "Tis a fine day, it is"; and "Tis no bargain unless you need it, sure it isn't." Ironically, the use of Hiberno-English may have provided immigrants to America with a linguistic "leg up," in the sense that their expressions lent color and imagination to their speech and aided in their attempts at self-definition. Consultants recalled single words more often than phrases, revealing that, as children, they made little distinction between Irish and English words. One recalled, "My mother spoke of my father"s pipe as his 'dudeen.'" The diminutive −ín forms a suffix for the Irish word *dúid*, a short-stemmed pipe, usually made of clay.[41]

Although words like *dúidín* entered Irish-America relatively intact, the collection is comprised of other words of a more garbled and/or fragmented nature. For example, one interviewee recalled his father's reprimand, "Don't be a 'doegan.'" This may have been a reference to the Irish *dogairne*, "a cross, crude person or thing."[42] However, other possibilities deserve consideration: first, present tense constructions for the Irish *dóigh*, which means "to burn," include *dóghann. Dóigh* can mean "idling" or "wasting time."[43] "Don't be a 'doegan'" may have been advice not to procrastinate. On the other hand, the

Irish prefix *do-* means "impossible, extremely difficult...ill, evil."[44] *Do-* may have been prefixed to *duine*, Irish for person. Thus, "doegan" may have been how a child heard his father"s remonstration not to be a *do-dhuine*, "inhuman, wicked person."[45]

Úcaire, the Irish word for a "fuller,"[46] someone who pounds cloth with a club (or by stamping), may be the origination of the Irish-American nickname "Dooker," described as "[one who was] always fighting."[47] Other variations of this term include bellicose challenges like "Put up your 'dooks'" [hands or fists] and "Let's 'dook' it out." Úcaire also may be the source of the expression, "I"m gonna 'ooker' it out of you" (i.e., force you to tell it).

Another word with many spelling variants that entered the realms of everyday Irish-American speech was "kibosh." Interviewees remembered "He put the kabosh [kiebash] on that" and "Someone put the "cabash" on something." Although some suggest that "kibosh" may have derived from Irish *faigh bás*, meaning, literally, "to get or to find death" (in other words, to die), Padraic Colum"s explanation may be more plausible:

> 'Kibosh,' I believe, means 'the cap of death' and it is always used in that sense— 'He put the kibosh on it.' In Irish, it could be written [as] '*cie báis*'— the last word pronounced 'bosh,' the genitive of '*bas*,' death.[48]

Appearing in an English-Irish Dictionary, "kibosh" is defined as "putting the end on something" [*deireadh a chur le rud*].[49] Bernard Share associates its nominative usage to the 1798 Insurgency in Ireland, when the British used it to mean "cap of death" or "pitch cap."[50] Even now in Ireland, it is common to hear that someone "put the kibosh on" a thing or event, although "it is never [put] on a person."[51]

A last word remembered more than any other, perhaps because it was simple to say in a number of situations, was *Sláinte*, meaning good luck, good fortune and good health. Consultants" spellings (if the word was written) and oral deliveries took a variety of forms, including "Slahnke" and "Slahnteh." The three-word Irish expression, *Sláinte mhaith agat*, "Good health to you," was

delivered as "Slahncheh wallaguh!" and "Slahncheh maw agoot." One correspondent wrote: "Expression when drinking: 'Slainte A Wallacha'"[sic]. *Sláinte
geal go mór* [Fine health [to you], was approximated as: "Slanta geal go mor."
The toast *Sláinte agus saol fada agat* [Health and long life to you], was written as
"Slainte agus saoghal fada agut." One consultant remembered hearing *slán* and
wondered if it were the same as the English "so long."[52] Griffith argues in the
affirmative, suggesting that this is how *slán* entered into English.[53] Another
reason for *sláinte*"s great staying power may have been its representation of
the opposite end of the emotional spectrum, for if "kibosh" reflected the
death of something, *sláinte* indicated the desire for life. In Ireland, the clos-
ings *Slán leat* and *Slán agat* [Good health until we meet again] are spoken
formulaically by those coming and going.

In addition to remembering terms that reflected the antinomies of life and
death, consultants recalled expressions suffused with the concerns of living,
such as "*Sé do bheatha* [Lit. It"s your breath, life], a welcome. Proverbs like
"A pig of his age is no *bonham*" [a young pig] were remembered; so, too, were
prayers and curses. *In anam an mhic* [In the name of the Son] was remembered,
as was the "mild expletive" *M"anam an deel* (or *diabhal*) [My soul to the devil].[54]
One consultant recalled hearing a relative say "I'm feeling very "flahtile""
[*flaithiúlach*, overflowing with abundance], a word that Joyce argues was
connected, especially in the south of Ireland, with "the old Irish chiefs [who]
kept full houses, with full and plenty for all who came."[55] Michael McCarthy
adds that defining a person as *flaithiúlach* "personifies a value we on occasion
nostalgically associate with a real or imagined past world whose language has
given us this word."[56] Irish-Americans defined "screeshting" as "coming in for
a fireside chat," a description imbued with the cultural values of hospitality
and comradery. The Irish *scríste* is a variant of *scíth*, meaning rest.[57] Apparently,
rest and favorable company went "hand in hand" in Irish-America.

Those who provided verbal items for this collection recalled that their
parents and grandparents utilized Irish to comment on distinguishing charac-
teristics and/or personality traits of friends, neighbors and family members.

"Mother," said one, [would say] 'Here comes Hathamor'" [*hata mór*], referring to a woman with a big hat, and "Here comes 'Cota fada' [*cóta fada*]," identifying a man in an overcoat. The proverb "Black cat—black pusheen" [*píscíne*, kitten], was recalled, as was the expression "the good *sagart*," described as an "insult." The latter is the Irish word for priest; its being remembered as a form of disparagement may mean that it referenced a person of the cloth (or otherwise) behaving "holier than thou" or "forgetting where he came from."[58]

If these descriptions were deployed to register satire or derision, others were utilized to evoke sympathy.[59] A "poor anky shor," with its "poor annie sore" variant, is a case in point:

> When my aunt and mother would be talking, they often said someone was a "poor Anky-Shore." The spelling is mine (phonetic). I am sure that is not the correct Irish version.

It is probable that "Anky-Shore" was derived from Irish *aincíseoir* [variant *ainniseoir*]. Although one consultant related that it referred to "a person to be pitied," another suggested that it meant "a peevish person." Still another revealed that an "angoshure" was "a forlorn person or child." The latter is in keeping with the word"s sense of "wretch."[60] Ó Dónaill defines *aincíseoir* as "a miserable, mean person."[61] For Diarmuid Ó Muirithe, however, "angashore" means "a miserable, sickly person; a foolish, wretched person." In Irish-America, "Anky-Shore" and its variants seem to have been applied to cantankerous individuals as well as those experiencing hard circumstances.[62] A "widdastrua" is perhaps Hiberno-English for *A Mhuire, is trua*, "Oh Mary, it"s a pity."[63] For some, the moniker aroused little sympathy, for a widdastrua was described as a woman constantly "connie-shuring," a word that may have derived from the Irish *cáinseoireacht*, "the act of fault-finding, scolding."[64] On the other hand, one consultant translated "connie-shuring" as "gossiping (usually women)."

Piseóg is Irish for charm, spell, or superstitious practice.[65] Patrick Kennedy describes "pishrogues" in the similar sense of "witchcraft or [superstition]."

In Ireland, the word could refer to "wise women" who had charms.[66] Yet in Irish-America, it acquired several other meanings, including fairy tale, hearsay, and "old wives' tale."[67] One consultant recalled "old pishrogues" being told; another revealed that "pishogues" were "made up stories." The words "straile" and "streel" referenced a "sloppy person" or "untidy girl." The source(s) may be one or a combination of Irish words, including *sraoille*, an unkempt woman, *striel* or *straille*.[68] The Irish word *straille* describes a "slattern."[69] The Irish expression "*Bíonn snáth fada ag sraoill*" means "A slattern has a long thread" (i.e., sews untidily). One Irish-American mentioned seeing "stríos" on a person," described as "whining, "[needing to] dry tears," and "being red with crying." This may have been how *strus*, the Irish for stress or strain,[70] was remembered. "Lisheen" was a term used in reference to a section of the cemetery where unbaptized children were buried. To this day, it has the same meaning in Ireland. The Irish *liosín*, the diminutive of *lios*, is an enclosed ground of an ancient dwelling house, also thought to be a fairy mound.[71]

The word "gom," as in "He's a big gom," referred to a fool, "an idiot," "a retarded person," or someone with undesirable traits. In addition, the words "gomeril" and "gomeral" were recalled.[72] All three may derive from *gamal*, the Irish word for lout, simpleton, or fool; in the Irish context, the word references a woman.[73] In Irish-America, however, the admonition, "Don't be playing [or acting] the gom" was said to sons as well as daughters in attempting to restrict behaviors considered to be foolish. I was told that Irish-American mothers referred to their children as "gommels" or "big gommels" when they acted as if they had no sense. In Irish, the word"s adjectival form is *gamalach*, meaning silly or loutish.[74]

Similar to "gom," the word "gidgemeen" carried a pejorative connotation. The word may have derived from Irish *gige*, a variation of *scige*, meaning the act of giggling, tittering, jeering, scoffing, mocking or deriding.[75] On the other hand, the word *gíge*, with its variant spelling *gíog*, means to cheep, chirp or squeak.[76] This word may have reflected the behaviors of children. However, Irish-Americans remembered hearing a rowdy or rambunctious youngster referred to as a "gidgemeen" or "a little gidgemeen." The term, then, may have come from Irish *geidimín*, a variant spelling of *geidín*, meaning "(small) buttocks, tail-end, rump, scut."[77] Ó Muirithe notes that the word means "an unlikable character; generally a social nuisance ... there is no known female specimen."[78] Although consultants mentioned no gendered usage of "gidgemeen," its various meanings may have become conflated in Irish-America, producing a word that could be applied in a number of contexts to a variety of individuals. "Amadahn" [*amadán*], another word for fool and one that specifies males in the Irish context, was applied to both genders in Irish-America. One correspondent wrote, "insult: 'omhadawn.'" Others recalled hearing, "She's an 'amadahn'" and "You [big] 'amadan.'" A woman remembered, "[My] mother called me an 'omodon' at times." Another remembered being called "oonshuk" [*óinseach*], an Irish word that specifically references a female fool.[79]

Irish Americans also recalled "gluggen." Terence Patrick Dolan describes such a person as fearful and timid; Joyce says the term was "applied very often in a secondary sense to a vain empty foolish boaster."[80] In Irish, "gliogar" means "an addled egg" and *ubh ghlugair*, a "bad egg."[81] In New England, I heard "She's a 'bad egg,'" although it is doubtful that the speaker knew of its Irish equivalent. Along with "goms," "amadahns," "oonshuks," gidgemeens" and "gluggers," one person remembered that "arrald" referred to "someone mentally mixed up." Perhaps this was a garbled version of *earráid*, the Irish word for "error, mistake, errancy, aberration." It also means "wrong-headedness" and "eccentricity."[82] One consultant recalled "foor-hay," described as an "eejit," an idiot who had "not the slightest "splinc" of sense." Splinc is said to derive from Irish *splanc*, a gleam or glimmer. *Níl splanc aige* means "He hasn't the slightest intelligence."[83]

The label "foor-hay" requires that one consider Irish *púir*, meaning loss, tragedy, cause of sorrow. The word has a proverbial application in the copula: *Is mór an phúir é*: "What a pity about him!"[84] In Irish, the pronunciation of *phúir* is similar to the English pronunciation of "foor." Therefore, a person identifying the "foor-hay" might have been referring to someone pitiable.

One consultant recalled "foostering about"; another remembered being labeled a "big faustuke." They both might be garbled versions of *fústaire*, still used in Ireland to mean "searching about aimlessly."[85] On the other hand, "faustuke" may have come from *fústrach*, meaning fussy or fidgety. Some sources list the latter as a noun: *fústrach* [variant *fústaire*] with the identical meaning of "a fussy, fidgety person." Joyce defines "footer" as "hurry, flurry, fluster, great fuss; Irish *fústar*, same sound and meaning."[86] *Fostúch* means "a grownup youth, an idle, lazy fellow."[87] Once again, elision may have occurred.

Like some of the aforementioned Irish words, *ciotóg* denotes a sense of awkwardness; it characterized the subject of the following anecdote.[88]

> There was [a] Mrs. Tivnan who used to make her own bread. She had a pail [of] about fourteen quarts with some kind of mixing device attached. She used to 'con' the kids in the neighborhood into turning the crank to mix the dough until one day a left-handed kid had the honor of turning the crank and was doing a fair job of it until Mrs. Tivnan noticed he was turning the wrong way. [She chased the child away with the words] 'Get out of that, you *kithouge* [sic]; you"re taking the twist out of me bread.'[89]

One of the meanings of *ciotóg* is "left handed person."[90] The practice of turning the handle with the dash was known in Ireland as "taking a brash." Anyone entering a dwelling where such work was underway was expected to engage in the work briefly by taking a few turns for good luck.[91] Yet someone moving in the left-handed direction was thought to be on the "wrong" side of the good spirits, that is to say, on the side of the devil. In this anecdote, the Irish word was remembered within the context of a customary Irish practice. Moreover, here one finds the blending of two prepositions, "out," and "of" (i.e., "out of me bread"). Prepositional blending is a common feature of Irish speech in English.

Although many interviewees mentioned the name or label "Bubba," the exact meaning was unknown to them. The Irish expressions *bambairne a dhéanamh de dhuine* and/or *bob a bhualadh ar dhuine* may provide inklings into how "Bubba" survived. The first means to make a fool of someone and the second, to play a trick on (or make a fool of) someone.[92] Also, *bambairne fir* and *bambairne mná* mean "big strong man" (or woman, respectively); Irish *bobaire* means a practical joker, a trickster.[93] Thus, a gullible, bulky, and/or practical joking individual may have been called "Bubba." Over the course of time, although specific meanings disappeared, the usefulness of "Bubba" for naming purposes remained.[94]

Another word that may have lost its particular reference in New England was "spalpeen" [*spailpín*]. In Ireland, it meant a seasonal hired laborer or migratory farm worker. It also indexed a "person of low degree; a rude person; scamp."[95] In Irish-America, "spalpeen" referred to any lad, fellow, chap, or even one or more son(s). Like the Irish word *cailín*, "girl" (or when spelled "Colleen," a girl's name), "spalpeen" retained its application to a specific gender. The Irish word for boy, *gasúr* (also *garsún*) gave rise to the Hiberno-English word "gossoon," used in Irish-America to refer to young male children.[96] *Bodach*, Irish for churl,[97] may have produced the nicknames "Bud" and "Buddy"; both were in common parlance among descendants of Irish immigrants; both indexed a "close friend" and "someone who could be trusted." On the other hand, *boddagh* is another possibility for the origin of Bud; it means "a rich, churlish, clownish fellow."[98]

Nicknames with possible Irish language roots include "Pudvers" and "Pluther." For "Pudvers," the consultant provided an aside: "I suspect pudding is the source." Perhaps "Pudvers" is a very garbled version of *púdarlach*, "a fat, lubberly person."[99] Due to the fact that he was described as being constantly intoxicated, a person named "Pluther" may have called to mind Irish words for mud, including *pluda*, mud or slush, *pludach*, muddy or slushy, and *pludar*, the sound of splashing in mud.[100] "Pluther" was also used in Irish-America as a verb, as in "to be pluthered," i.e., to be intoxicated, "sloshed," or in Ivor Brown"s description, confronted with "the dull swish of a heavy blow."[101] The word "spawgs" was described as "feet, probably large." *Spág* means a "broad, flat foot; (a) big, clumsy foot."[102] "Brogans," as in the sentence, "Father put on the brogans," may have been the conflation of *bróg*, Irish for boot or shoe, and *broganta*, the adjective for sturdy.[103] "Threetheens," another consultant"s word for shoes, is thought to be Hiberno-English for *troithíní*, "unsoled stockings, a term used in the west of the country."[104] K.E. Younge defines the word in the singular as "step or spade"; Joyce suggests *troigh*, meaning foot; its diminutive –*ín*, produces *troighthín*.[105]

One consultant recalled "mulla molla," an expression of his mother, which he defined as meaning "shiftless." This may be how he remembered being scolded with the words *míle mallacht*, "a thousand curses [on you]," as in the expression, *Mo sheacht mile mallacht ort* [My seven thousand curses on you].[106] Alternatively, the Irish expression *mille maide* described "someone who couldn't work a trade well."[107] Those trying to do just that found themselves using Irish in certain public workplaces.[108] The following correspondence was received from a man who grew up in Norwood, Massachusetts:

> [L]et me tell you this little anecdote. The foreman of the PWD [Public Works Department] workers who used to give my brothers dimes in order to talk Gaelic with him was himself Irish-American. Still, whenever he would come to inspect the work, the watchword would be given, "Dig down deep, boys, '*ta sé*.' And anyone resting on his shovel set to work.

The polysemic *tá sé* means "he is" or "it is"; it functions as an entry-level item for language beginners, providing an affirmative answer to the present-tense question of the verb to be. It acquired unique and particular meanings in certain Irish counties; for example, in Cork, it indexed "a "yes man" forever answering yes to everyone, particularly those in authority."[109] *Tá sé* also refers to the expression and performance of labour, for in Ireland, "working like *tá sé* means "to work very quickly."[110] In the aforementioned anecdote, we are afforded a glimpse of the use of Irish in work-related settings. Although it is clear that, in this consultant's memory *tá sé* was a nickname, it also functioned as a warning, a coded linguistic expression that meant, for the working crew, "Do not rest on your shovel now, for the boss is near." In this context, and especially in terms of keeping one's job, talk was anything but cheap. Moreover, the fact that the foreman was willing to offer monetary recompense to his crew for speaking Irish equates to a unique form of language preservation, his own, and perhaps that of his charges as well.

If Irishmen spoke Irish in specific work communities, they did the same at sporting and recreation-oriented events. Consultants provided the variants "Fog la bail" and "Fag an ballagh." One interviewee attended a boxing match in his youth and heard "Fog la bail" uttered repeatedly. The term could be the garbled *Fág le bolg é* or *Fág lena bholg é*, meaning "Leave it (or put it) in (his) belly" ("Hit him in the belly!"). Another revealed that *Fág lena bholg é* was the motto for the Massachusetts 69th Infantry Regiment in the American Civil War. The Royal Irish Fusilliers' war cry, "Fag an Bealach," inspired the group"s nickname, the "Old Fogs" (due to the pronunciation of *fág*). Thus, the expression *Fág an bealach*, "Clear the way," may have entered Irish-America unaltered. In Ireland, the interjectory phrase *Fág an baile* means "Leave the town!" or "Get out." It was "commonly used in faction fighting" and may have become confused with *Fág an bealach*. [III]

Related to fighting was defeat. The word "banjaxed" was defined as being "totally overcome" or "beat." Additional meanings include "being ruined, stymied, or destroyed." A number of sources list the etymology of "banjaxed" as unknown. Dolan suggests that it is a combination of "bang" and "smash." [112] Interestingly, to "get smashed" in some Irish-American usages means to become drunk. [113] Others trace "banjaxed" to Hiberno-English used in the first half of the twentieth century and to being "tired, shattered [or] cream crackered." [114] Thinking along these lines, one might suggest that *bánéadanach*, meaning white-faced or white-fronted, [115] was the source for "banjaxed," used in contexts of being "made pale," whitened, "creamed" or overwhelmed by circumstances.

If the Irish were defeated at times, they also found occasions to triumph. I recall my father's narrative concerning Daniel O'Connell, who was about to be murdered by eating toxic meat (in other versions, The Liberator was on the brink of drinking poison). However, an Irish server intervened, warning him with, in my father's rendering of the Irish, "A thig a thoo Gaeilge?" [*An dtuigeann tú an Ghaeilge? Do you understand Irish?*]. When O'Connell answered in the affirmative, she bade him avoid the contaminated substance. In terms of overcoming a near calamity, my father stressed that it was the ability to "thig a thoo Gaeilge" – comprehend Irish – that saved Daniel O'Connell's life. [116]

Like "A thig a thoo Gaeilge?" Irish terms of endearment seem to have functioned as a lifeline, even as they solidified impressions that the Irish were affected, insincere, and full of "blarney."[117] Particularly in domestic settings, endearing words released tension, comforted and amused. Direct address terms like "machree" [*mo chroí*, my heart], "mo cushla" [*mo chuisle*, my pulse], "mavourneen" [*mo mhúirnín*, my darling], and "a vic og" [*a mhic* óg, young son] were recalled by descendants of Irish immigrants. Although unable to render literal meanings, they approximated and recollected hearing the terms in occasions of fondness, affection, and coaxing. To "butter (someone) up" was, as one consultant explained, to "plau mase" [*plámás*, act of flattering, flattery, soft talk, cajolery].[118] In a discussion of her Irish-born aunt, another revealed, "Whenever she wrote to me, she addressed me as "My dear peteen bawn" [*peatín bán*, fair little pet]." The English word "pet" derives from Old Irish *peta*, a tame or domesticated animal.[119] As mentioned previously, the English suffix –een (Irish –ín) functions as a diminutive. "Bawn" is the Anglicized spelling of *bán*, meaning blonde or light-skinned.

Sometimes the meaning of Irish words failed to transfer from private to public domains, resulting in misunderstanding. One consultant revealed:

> We never referred to "breaking wind" or "farting" in our house. The act was called a "fusin." I thought that that was Standard English and was laughed at in school because of it ... . Perhaps it"s Irish?

The word "fusin" may have been either the Irish word *fúsc* or *fúscadh*; both are variations of úsc, a verb meaning (among other things) "to exude" and as a noun, "exudation."[120] Thus, "fusin," as a diminutive of *fúsc* (i.e., *fúsín*), may have referred to flatulence, or more euphemistically, "a small puff of air." As part of an intimate lexicon, the word would have been uttered at a remove from public realms, where, as this consultant attests, it was interpreted as ludicrous. Another humorous recollection of the Irish language used "behind closed doors" surfaced in the following:

My father called me his little girl. I remember him (now and then) hugging me and saying something that sounded like 'Pugga ma horn.' I was small, maybe four or five, and I'd try to repeat it, and he'd laugh and laugh. Well, it seems as though years later, one of my brothers told me that it was Irish: (*Póg mo thóin* meant 'Kiss my a___').[121] I never really found out if this was true. But if it was, no wonder my father laughed when he heard it coming out of my mouth. It's not very nice, but it's from my memory [*sic*].

This anecdote is remarkable for the lack of understanding of its meaning until years later, and then, for the questioning of its veracity. Although deemed not very nice, it had been remembered since childhood and reproduced as a memory of the Irish language.

Conclusion

As Irish immigrants who escaped from the horrors of *An Gorta Mór* attempted to assimilate into the New World [*an t oileán úr*], they are said to have "abandoned their language with a haste and endeavor that was as spectacular as the rate of emigration."[122] Painful memories of The Great Hunger were barely mentioned, or, if they did emerge, discussed in whispers in the hushed tones of the Irish language. The fact that *any* linguistic item survives testifies to the cultural importance that the mother tongue held for those who settled in New England. By not putting the "kibosh" on sayings like "Slahncheh wallaguh" or queries like "A thig a thoo Gaeilge," immigrants bequeathed to their offspring words for judging character, respecting silence, behaving properly and conveying affection. Although many utterances were rendered and remembered in fragmented or incomplete forms, they provoke speculations as to the probable contexts within which they were uttered and the manner by which they were preserved in the mnemonic soundscapes of their children.

NOTES

1. Acknowledgments are extended to Angela Bourke, John Brougham (RIP), Patricia Curran, Brad Huber, William Mahan, Kenneth E. Nilsen (RIP), Liam Ó Cuinneagáin, Marius Ó hEarcáin, and Séamus Pender, the consultants who made this research possible. *Go raibh mile maith agaibh go léir.*

2. Quoted in Brian Ó Conchubhair, 'The Global Diaspora and the "New" Irish (Language),' in Caoilfhionn Nic Pháidín & Seán Ó Cearnaigh (eds.) *A New View of the Irish Language* (Dublin, 2008), p. 239.

3. Nancy Stenson, *'Beagáinín:'* The Use of Irish among Immigrants to the United States" in *New Hibernia Review/Iris Éireannach Nua*, ii, no. 2 (1998), pp. 116–131.

4. Ralph D. Grillo, *Dominant Languages: Language and Hierarchy in Britain and France* (Cambridge, 1989), p. 173.

5. Kenneth E. Nilsen, 'Thinking on Monday: The Irish Speakers of Portland, Maine,' in *Éire-Ireland, A Journal of Irish Studies*, xxv, no. 1 (1990), p. 7.

6. Kevin Kenny, *The American Irish: A History* (Harlow, 2000), p. 138.

7. Nancy Stenson, 'Speaking Irish in America: Language and Identity' in P. Sture Ureland (ed.), *Global Eurolinguistics: European Languages in North America, Migration, Maintenance, and Death* (Tübingen, 2001), p. 436.

8. Joseph Callahan, 'The Irish Language in Pennsylvania,' in Thomas Ihde (ed.) *The Irish Language in the United States: A Historical, Sociolinguistic and Applied Linguistic Survey* (Westport, 1994), pp. 18–26.

9. Ibid., p. 23.

10. Stenson, "Speaking Irish in America," p. 439.

11. Tomás De Bhaldraithe, *English-Irish Dictionary*, p. 168.

12. Niall Ó Dónaill, *Foclóir Gaeilge-Béarla*, p. 207.

13. Delaney, *Of Irish Ways*, p. 127. 'Cannavaun' is 'bog cotton, common cotton grass.' See Diarmuid Ó Muirithe, *A Dictionary of Anglo-Irish* (Dublin, 1966), p. 56. *Ceannabhán mona*, bog cotton, was used for stuffing pillows if feathers were hard to come by in Ireland. See Kevin Danaher, *Irish Customs and Beliefs* (Dublin, 2004), p. 77.

14. Kenneth E. Nilsen, 'Irish in Nineteenth Century New York,' in Ofelia Garcia & Joshua A. Fishman (eds), *The Multilingual Apple: Languages in New York City* (Berlin, 1979), pp. 59–60, and Brian Ó Conchubhair, "The Global Diaspora," p. 224.

15. E. Moore Quinn, '"She Must Have Come Steerage": The Great Famine in New England Folk Memory,' in David A. Valone (ed.), *Ireland's Great Hunger: Relief, Representation and Remembrance* (vol. 2; Lanham, 2010), pp. 161–180.

16. Ibid., p. 165.

17. Mary E. Daly, 'The Operations of Famine Relief, 1845–1857,' in Cathal Póirtéir (ed.) *The Great Irish Famine* (Cork, 1995), pp. 123–134.

18. Roger J. McHugh, 'The Famine in Irish Oral Tradition,' in R. Dudley Edwards and T. Desmond Williams (eds.) *The Great Famine: Studies in Irish History 1845–1852* (Dublin, 1994), p. 435.

19. Quinn, 'She Must Have Come,' p. 166.

20. For a discussion of deeply entrenched and enduring post-Famine poverty and emigration, see F. S. L. Lyons, *Ireland Since the Famine* (London, 1985), pp. 68–69.

21. David Rattray, ed. *Success With Words: A Guide to the American Language* (New York, 1983), p. 360; p. 62; p. 682.

22. Ó Muirithe, *A Dictionary*, p. 113. The word gob refers to the mouth and the lips. See Patrick Weston Joyce, *English as It is Spoken in Ireland* (Dublin, 1991), p. 263. Deriving from the Celtic word *gobbo-*, it 'has been in use since the mid-fifteenth century.' See Linda Flavell & Roger Flavell, *Idioms and Their Origins* (London, 1996), p. 197.

23. Ó Donaill, *Foclóir Gaeilge-Béarla*, p. 1115.

24. Terence Patrick Dolan, *A Dictionary of Hiberno-English* (Dublin, 1999), p. 248.

25. De Bhaldraithe, *English-Irish Dictionary*, p. 694.

26. One definition of *poitín* is 'illicit whiskey,' as compared to 'parliament whiskey,' upon which a duty was exacted. See Ó Muirithe, *A Dictionary*, p. 152, and Dolan, *A Dictionary*, p. 202.

27. Immigrants borrowed words like 'moonshine;' one return emigrant confessed that he had succeeded in America by making it. 'Moonshine is poteen,' he said, and 'not everyone knew what a good drop [of it] should taste like.' See Paddy Linehan, *Yesterday's Ireland* (Devon, 2003), p. 183.

28. Ó Muirithe, *A Dictionary*, p. 119.

29. Dolan, *A Dictionary*, p. 141.

30. Willard R. Espy, *Thou Improper*, p. 194.

31. Ó Dónaill, *Foclóir Gaeilge-Béarla*, p. 76.

32. Bernard Share, *A Dictionary*, p. 11.

33. Maureen Wall, 'The Decline of the Irish Language.' In Brian Ó Cuiv (ed.), *A View of the Irish Language* (Dublin, 1969), pp 81–90.

34. Callahan, 'The Irish Language,' p. 22.

35. Dolan, *A Dictionary*, p. 42.

36. Patrick S. Dinneen, *Foclóir Gaedhilge agus Béarla* Irish English Dictionary (Dublin, 1904), p. 58. celt.ucc.ie//Dinneen1.pdf, accessed 29 January 2018.

37. Michael Montgomery, *From Ulster to America: The Scotch-Irish Heritage of American English* (Belfast, 2006), pp 30–31.

38. Kenneth E. Nilsen, 'Irish Language in the U.S.,' in Michael Glazier (ed.), *The Encyclopedia of the Irish in America* (Notre Dame, 1999), p. 472.

39. Patrick John Dowling, *A History of Irish Education* (Cork, 1971), p. 73.

40. Dolan, *A Dictionary*, p. 121.

41. Ó Muirithe, *A Dictionary*, p. 88. Ó Muirithe notes that the Irish spelling of this word is *dúidín*.

42. Ó Dónaill, *Foclóir Gaeilge-Béarla*, p. 427.

43. Ibid., p. 429.

44. Ibid., p. 423.

45. Ibid., p. 427.

46. Ibid., p. 1294.

47. The etymology of 'dooks' and its counterpart 'dukes' remain unconfirmed, although the terms appeared in slang dictionaries as early as the mid-19th century.

48. Quoted in Charles Earle Funk, *A Hog on Ice and Other Curious Expressions* (New York, 1985), p. 22. See Dolan, *A Dictionary*, p. 153.

49. De Bhaldraithe, *English-Irish Dictionary* (Dublin, 1987), p. 388.

50. Share, *Slanguage* (Dublin, 1997), p. 157.

51. Patricia Curran, personal communication. Some scholars argue for a Jewish origin, a claim that indexes the international nature of folk materials. 'Kibosh' is still deployed whenever something must be brought to a final conclusion or whenever someone must have "the last silencing word." See worldwidewords.org/articles/kibosh.htm.

52. See Dolan, *A Dictionary*, p. xxi.

53. Francis Griffith, 'Irish Usage in American English' in *Irish-America* (1986), pp 34–35.

54. Ó Muirithe, *A Dictionary*, p. 82.

55. Joyce, *English as it is Spoken*, p. 257.

56. Michael McCarthy, "What Hiberno-English May Be Telling Us about Ourselves" in *Skibbereen and District Historical Society Journal* xii (2016), p. 65.

57. Ó Dónaill, *Foclóir Gaeilge-Béarla,* p. 1055.

58. A similar example is found in James Joyce: '*Sagart* can self laud *nilobstant* ...' See Ó Muirithe, *A Dictionary*, p. 163.

59. Gabriel Rosenstock, *Irish Proverbs in Irish and English* (Cork, 1999), p. 20.

60. Ó Muirithe, *A Dictionary*, p. 25; Share, *A Dictionary*, p. 5; Joyce, *English as It is Spoken*, p. 211.

61. Ó Dónaill, *Foclóir Gaeilge-Béarla* (Dublin, 1977), p. 24.

62. Dolan, *A Dictionary*, p. 10.

63. Willard R. Espy, *Thou Improper, Thou Uncommon Noun* (New York, 1978), p. 3; Ó Muirithe, *A Dictionary*, p. 140; Dolan, *A Dictionary*, p. 288; and Joyce, *English as it is Spoken*, p. 351.

64. Ó Dónaill, *Foclóir Gaeilge-Béarla*, p. 174. *A Mhuire is trua* was "a connection of the Blessed Virgin with the sorrow." See Joyce, *English as it is Spoken*, p. 351.

65. Ó Dónaill, *Foclóir Gaeilge-Béarla*, p. 953; De Baldraithe, *English-Irish Dictionary*, p. 726.

66. Patrick Kennedy, *Legends of Witches and Fairies* (Dublin, 1976), p. 90; Arthur Henry Singleton, 'Dairy Folklore and Other Notes from Meath and Tipperary' in *Folklore: a Quarterly Review of Myth, Tradition, Institution, and Custom*, xv (1904), p. 159.

67. These interpretations also surface in Ireland.

68. De Bhaldraithe, *English-Irish Dictionary*, p. 807.

69. Rosenstock, *Irish Proverbs*, p. 20; Dolan, *A Dictionary*, p. 255.

70. Ó Dónaill, *Foclóir Gaeilge-Béarla*, p. 954.

71. Ibid., p. 791. Alternative spellings include *lisín*, lisseen, and lisheen. See Ó Muirithe, *A Dictionary*, p. 127.

72. Ó Muirithe, *A Dictionary*, p. 105.

73. De Bhaldraithe, *English-Irish Dictionary*, p. 269; Ó Dónaill, *Foclóir Gaeilge-Béarla*, p. 609, for other gender distinctions.

74. Ó Dónaill, *Foclóir Gaeilge-Béarla*, p. 609. *Gamal* is 'also Irish for a camel and used all over Ireland.' Joyce, *English as it is Spoken*, p. 205.

75. Ó Dónaill, *Foclóir Gaeilge-Béarla*, p. 105.

76. Ibid., p. 633.

77. Ibid., p. 626.

78. Ó Muirithe, *A Dictionary*, p. 108.

79. De Bhaldraithe, *English-Irish Dictionary*, p. 269.

80. Dolan, *A Dictionary*, p. 127; Joyce, *English as It is Spoken*, p. 263.

81. De Bhaldraithe, *English-Irish Dictionary*, p. 216.

82. Ó Dónaill, *Foclóir Gaeilge-Béarla*, p. 480.

83. De Bhaldraithe, *English-Irish Dictionary*, p. 300; Dolan, *A Dictionary*, p. 255.

84. Ó Dónaill, *Foclóir Gaeilge-Béarla,* p. 975.

85. Marius Ó hEarcáin (personal communication) suggested that "faustuke" might be a garbled version of *fústaire*.

86. Joyce, *English as It is Spoken*, p. 258.

87. Dolan, *A Dictionary*, p. 96.

88. Seán Gaffney and Séamus Cashman (eds), *Proverbs and Sayings of Ireland* (Dublin 1979), p. 113.

89. Joyce, *English as it is Spoken*, p. 44.

90. Ó Dónaill, *Foclóir Gaeilge-Béarla*, p. 233.

91. Séamus Ó Catháin, *Irish Life and Lore* (Dublin, 1982), p. 25.

92. Ó Dónaill, *Foclóir Gaeilge-Béarla* p. 83; p. 117.

93. Ibid., p. 83; p. 117.

94. I have collected this moniker in parts of the American South and heard people refer to themselves as "Bubbas," meaning "'good ol'' country boys (or men).'

95. Ó Dónaill, *Foclóir Gaeilge-Béarla*, p. 1138.

96. The Irish word was derived from *garçon*, a French word with the same meaning (Angela Bourke, personal communication).

97. Ó Muirithe, *A Dictionary*, p. 40; Frederic Gomes Cassidy and Joan Houston Hall, *Dictionary of American Regional Speech* (Cambridge, MA, 2007).

98. Joyce, *English as it is Spoken,* p. 218.

99. Ó Dónaill, *Foclóir Gaeilge-Béarla*, p. 974.

100. Joyce, *English as It is Spoken*, p. 303; Ó Dónaill, *Foclóir Gaeilge-Béarla*, p. 959.

101. Ivor Brown, *No Idle Words and Having the Last Word* (New York, 1951), p. 129.

102. Ó Dónaill, *Foclóir Gaeilge-Béarla*, p. 1137.

103. Ibid., pp. 143–144.

104. Dolan, *A Dictionary*, p. 243.

105. K. E. Younge, 'Irish Idioms in English Speech' in *An tEaglaiseach Gaedhealach* iv, no. 5 (1922), p. 46; Joyce, *English as It is Spoken*, p. 343.

106. Ó Muirithe, *A Dictionary*, p.133.

107. Seán Ó Súilleabháin, *A Handbook of Irish Folklore* (Dublin, 1942), p. 63.

108. Stenson, 'Speaking Irish,' p. 438.

109. McCarthy, 'What Hiberno English May Be,' p. 66.

110. Ó Muirithe, *A Dictionary*, p. 195.

111. Ó Muirithe, *A Dictionary*, p. 92; Margaret E. Maloney, *Fág an Bealach: Clear Out of the Way: the Irish Contribution to America and Especially to Western Pennsylvania* (2nd edition, Pittsburgh, 1977).

112. Dolan, *A Dictionary*, p. 15.

113. Harold Wentworth and Stuart Flexner, *The Dictionary of American Slang* (New York: 1975), p. 492.

114. 'Banjaxed.' allwords.com, accessed 10 February 2018.

115. Ó Dónaill, *Foclóir Gaeilge-Béarla*, p. 84.

116. "*A Dhónaill Uí Chonaill, an dtuigeann tú Gaeilge?*"
   [Daniel O"Connell, do you understand Irish?].
   '*Tuigim go maith í, a chailín ó* Éirinn' [I do, and well, Irish girl].
   '*Tá nimh i do chupán a mharódh na céadta!*' [There is poison in your cup that would kill hundreds].
   '*Maith tú, a chailín, is tabharfaidh mé spré duit*' [Well done, girl; I will reward you [lit. give you a dowry].
   '*I hóg sé a chupán féin agus chuir sé anonn é go tiubh agus thóg sé cupán eile. Maraíodh fear eile ansin ina ionad féin.*' [He took his own cup and put it aside from him on the sly and took another one. Another man died then, in Daniel's place].
   Translated by this author. See The Daltaí Discussion Forums, 6–7 January 2009.

117. George Potter, *To the Golden Door*, p. 101. In 1602, with 'sweet talk' and 'a harp in his throat,' Lord Blarney, a MacCarthy from Cork, was said to have stalled Queen Elizabeth's siege on his territories by using flattering words. Allegedly, Elizabeth declared that he was 'Blarney, Blarney, nothing but Blarney.' His name became associated with chattering nonsense; the word is still used in this sense both in Ireland and Irish-America.

118. Ó Dónaill, *Foclóir Gaeilge-Béarla*, p. 954.

119. Ó Muirithe, *A Dictionary*, p. 148.

120. Ó Donnaill, *Foclóir Gaeilge-Béarla*, p. 1307.

121. The Irish word for bottom or backside is *tóin*. '[It is] used through a sense of delicacy instead of the more vulgar English equivalent.' See Ó Muirithe, *A Dictionary*, p. 108.

122. Quoted in Ó Conchubhair, 'The Global Diaspora,' p. 224.

CHAPTER TEN

CHILDREN AND LOCAL MEMORIES OF THE GREAT HUNGER 90 YEARS ON

Stories from the Irish Folklore Commission's "Schools' Collection" (1937–1938)

Salvador Ryan

In 1937–38, an ambitious and far-sighted project entitled "The Schools' Scheme" was initiated in Ireland by the newly founded Irish Folklore Commission under the direction of Séamus Ó Duilearga and Seán Ó Súilleabháin, honorary director and registrar of the commission respectively, in conjunction with the Department of Education. The scheme, which made use of the extensive network of National Schools and their teachers, envisaged enlisting the assistance of children, aged 11 to 14 years, in collecting local folklore from their parents, grandparents, relatives and neighbors and recording it in their copybooks after which a selection of the material (to avoid repetition) would be transcribed into official copybooks which would be returned to the Folklore Commission for deposition in its archive. To this end, in 1937 the commission prepared an information booklet, *Irish Folklore and Tradition*, for teachers, which provided hundreds of sample questions that the pupils might use, and these questions ranged over 55 topic headings. The foreword to the booklet of instructions deemed the project no less than a "work of national importance" and remarked that it was:

> ... fitting that in our Primary Schools the senior pupils should be invited to participate in the task of rescuing from oblivion the traditions which, in spite of the vicissitudes of the historic Irish nation, have, century in, century out, been preserved with loving care by their ancestors.[1]

In the period from September 1937 to June 1938, school time usually devoted to English composition (in English-speaking areas) and Irish composition (in Irish-speaking areas) would now be reassigned to the business of recording in their copybooks the material that the children had collected. Thereafter, a small number of children (those who were known for their competence in writing and spelling) were given the task of transferring a selection of this material into the official notebooks provided by the Department of Education.[2] By late January 1939, over 20 tons' worth of copybooks had been returned to the commission.[3] By the close of the project, more than 50,000 children from 5,000 schools in the Irish Free State had contributed to the scheme which would result in 1,128 numbered and bound volumes, not counting some 40,000 of the original copybooks of the children.[4] In recent years, the collection has been digitized and is searchable.[5]

Children Recording Memories of the Famine

One of the general headings that the commission suggested schoolchildren address when speaking to their informants was "Famine Times" and it provided a host of sample questions that might be asked. The information booklet issued at the outset of the project concluded that "great importance is attached to the writing down by children of events which occurred locally during the famine years as in these short and apparently trivial stories the background of this National Disaster is clearly pictured."[6] Few scholars today would make so bold a claim in the wake of the subsequent explosion of interest in memory studies. Indeed, Niall Ó Ciosáin points to the work of scholars such as Cormac Ó Gráda, Carmel Quinlan and Patricia Lysaght who focus, instead, on "the inaccuracies of oral testimony, on evasions, elisions and distortions."[7] He argues that folk material represents a composite of three types of memory: local memory, popular memory and abstract or global memory—the latter influenced by written accounts of the Famine. In this kind of material, the chronology also can be somewhat loose, incorporating memories of food shortages that occurred outside of the period of the Great Famine.[8] In one instance from Cappagh, County Galway, the informant confuses the Famine period with that of the Penal Laws by remarking: "Around that time the priests were not allowed to say Mass."[9] In a 1996 article, Cathal Póirtéir admitted that there are advantages and disadvantages pertaining to the use of folklore as an historical source, noting that, while it is neither analytical nor objective, it is "nevertheless rooted in the mentality of the people in a way that no other account is."[10] More recently, he has argued that the folklore of the Famine has a value in allowing us "to hear local voices, recall local events" and offers "glimpses of how the cataclysm made a lasting impact on a community's past and its understanding of it." Beyond the descriptions it provides, it affords us "access to the feelings and interpretations which accompanied the events and their aftermath;" it also "humanises statistics with vivid, heart-felt descriptions."[11]

The present chapter, written by a non-specialist in studies of the Great Hunger, takes its inspiration from Póirtéir's words. It is not so much concerned with whether the events related in these accounts actually happened in precisely the way the accounts describe, if at all; rather, it is interested in the *mentalités* uncovered in what Guy Beiner terms "alternative vernacular histories."[12] Given the volume of material, the stories included here represent a mere sample from across a number of counties.[13] Furthermore, for the most part, general descriptions of Famine conditions have been overlooked here in favor of stories concerning particular individuals and events, which cast light on a local area and its inhabitants and thus allow us to access perceptions of more general conditions through that local lens. These vignettes are gathered under a number of thematic headings, although there is often a degree of overlap, which renders such categorizations as anything but neat. It is also noteworthy that these are tales that were told to children between 11 and 14 years of age and, by virtue of their inclusion in the official copybooks, which were returned to the Folklore Commission, it is to be presumed that this material was deemed suitable by their teachers (for, as noted above, a selection process was employed in the transmission of the raw material to the official copybooks). Yet this, too, is instructive for, in some cases at least, efforts to sanitize the subject matter seem to have been minimal.

Describing Hunger

On 23 July 1997, on the occasion of the dedication of the first American Famine Memorial in Cambridge, Massachusetts, John Flaherty, president of the Cambridge Celtic Arts Society, drew upon familiar imagery associated with the Irish Famine when he spoke of the necessity of rightly remembering our painful history: "We *remember*, we *remember* the children who died with their mouths stained green from eating the grass ...."[14] The image of the starving Irish resorting to eating grass, nettles and shoots is a common one and is found widely in the accounts recorded in the Schools' Collection.[15] An account from Ballinderry, County Galway, notes that "the people began to eat grass like wild animals they were so hungery."[16] One report from Newtown in County Tipperary paints a more gruesome picture still: "people were so hungry that they ate grass by the roadside, and were often seen lying dead in the ditches with the green juice of the grass coming out of their mouths."[17] Mary O'Connor from Lagganstown, County Tipperary, relates how her grandmother was traveling to Golden during the Famine times and passed a woman dying by a fence on the roadside. On her way back, the coroner was already there and "near her they found a glass of water and protruding from her mouth was a fist of half masticated grass."[18] A variation on this image comes from Clooncah, County Roscommon in which 87-year-old Mrs. L. English told her collector that "one time a man was ploughing and these two boys had a fight about the thraneen that grows on the scrape of the plough. If you scrape the root of the thraneen and wash it and roast it is very nice and sweet to eat. But these two boys didn't roast the thraneen they ate it raw."[19] Twelve-year-old Annie Egan, at school in Ballinlass, County Galway, put it more simply still: "People dived on the water cress. In fact it got very scarce around that time."[20] A 72-year-old informant from Woodford in County Galway informed his collector that a certain "Catherine Conroy of Tipperforgu, whose death occurred only about ten years ago at the age of 96 years" recalled similar examples from around the district at that time: "She often saw the poor people coming into her own yard to pick up the skins of turnips and mangolds in order to eat them."[21] There is also the lovely vignette from Killomoran, County Galway, which recalls how, in 1848, "they also gave Indian meal and when little boys saw it they cut the buttons out of their little pants to buy a little of the yellow meal as they called it."[22]

Many of the stories go to great lengths in describing the depths of deprivation endured by the Irish, often employing a good deal of exaggeration in the telling and, indeed, it could be said, occasionally some black humor. For instance, it is difficult to take seriously the tale collected from the Mercy School in Tulla, County Clare, which relates how a man was found dead on the road to Ennis and, the people having performed an impromptu post-mortem on him, "all the food they discovered in his stomach was one grain of wheat."[23] A variation on this story from Drumgarly, County Monaghan, speaks of a man found dead by a hedge who, when opened by a doctor, was found to have "nothing in his stomach but a half pint of water."[24] Other tales stretch credulity both in the way they are set up and their denouement, prompting one to wonder about the role of humour in remembering the Great Hunger. In the following tale from Lowertown, County Cork, a certain Mr. Cotter "had nothing to eat and was dying of starvation." The story continues:

> He crawled on his face and hands to Schull to get something to eat. When he arrived in Schull all he could get was a hard crust of bread. He then started for home but when he was about a mile from the town he died. It was the hard crust of bread that choked him.[25]

Proselytism and "Soupers"

John Flaherty's 1997 Famine Memorial address went on to state that "We *remember* the soup being extended but only if you would give up your land or religion." This image of the dispensing of food (and clothes) in return for embracing another religious faith is very vivid in Irish folk memory and is widely found across the stories collected in the Schools' Scheme. It is perhaps described most simply by Patrick Lyons, a child at school in Ballydehob, County Cork, who explains it as follows: "Catholics used to change into Protestants for soup, and they were called soupers."[26] Ó Ciosáin has observed that many instances (especially those that mention specific names of converts) represent local memory in those regions in which proselytism was a phenomenon. However, he points out that more generalized accounts of proselytism are also found in regions where there is no evidence of such activity having taken place, and that this more likely reflects a "Catholic meta-narrative," whether accessed directly in written or printed form, or indirectly through sermons or speeches.[27]

Many of these stories focus specifically on the act(s) of renunciation of one's own faith that was involved in accepting the soup, whether temporary or otherwise. Perhaps the most well-known of these is that found across many counties and, in this version, from Newmarket in County Cork, which recalls how:

> A poor man when very hungry before going to the Protestant church for soup, paid a visit to the Catholic church and standing at the door and looking very mournfully at the Altar was heard to say 'Goodbye Almighty God until the praties will grow again.'[28]

These tales often present the protagonist as a relatively reluctant convert, even a latter-day "church papist," as in the case of the following account collected in Kilcomane, County Cork, which relates how the local Protestant clergyman, Mr. Fisher, used to distribute clothes to Catholics who would turn Protestant, which prompted the bishop to send a very strict priest to the parish, a Father Holland, who preached a stern sermon to the people and threatened to curse those who turned Protestant, after which Fisher found a heap of returned clothes outside his door. One man defied the priest's ban on accepting clothes and stated that he would go to whatever churches he wished to, regardless of the wishes of the bishop. The tale recounts how "the man died before the end of the day and his son was killed by his own horse within a week." The account continues with the following case:

> There was one man in Toormore that went to the Protestant Church but he also went to Mass before going there. Mr. Fisher found this out. He met him one day and asked him why he was going to Mass and also going to Church. He said he was going to Mass to save his soul and that he was going to Church to save his body.[29]

Some stories, such as this cautionary tale from Kilcoosy, County Leitrim, include reference to a quite specific act of renunciation of one's Catholic faith and the portent of otherworldly displeasure that a person could elicit should they choose to comply:

> Once upon a time there lived an old man in Cloonquin and his name was William McMorrow. During the famine an old lady went into the house

with a can of soup and told the man that if he would turn Prodstant [sic] she would bring him soup every day. The man agreed and she gave him the can of soup. Then she gave him a book to read certain prayers from the book. Three times a day he was to say 'I disone the blessed Virgin and all belonging to her'. One day he knelt on a flag to read the prayers and one day while he was reading the prayers from the book the flag on which he was kneeling split in two pieces.[30]

An account from Cloonkeen Kerrill, County Galway, states more explicitly still that:

there was a woman living in Monivea, Athenry, County Galway named Lady Hall. She was a protestant and she distributed clothes, money, and food to all those who spat on the statue of the Blessed virgin that she kept for the purpose.[31]

Perhaps most disturbing of all is the following tale from Jamestown in County Leitrim, which details the lengths to which some of the faithful were prepared to go in resisting the urge to convert. The informant, a Mrs. Hunt, speaks of "a woman named Nellie Kelly who lived in Corrigeenroe near where I was born, (during the Famine). I knew her myself later on." It continues:

This poor woman had a big family, and they fell sick, in ones and twos from starvation. The neighbours ... advised her to go to Kilmactranny to the Parson's for the Indian meal. She knew well, she'd have to 'turn' [Protestant] or at any rate, pretend she was going to turn, before she'd get it. So sooner than do that, she let them all (her children) die. She lived herself on water-grass [cress]. When I was a child, I saw her going round begging—the poor thing lost her land with everything else. No one would refuse her and everyone respected her, even though she was only a beggar. I often heard her telling about her children. She never regretted letting them die. 'Better to die than be damned', she'd say. She knew they were in Heaven. 'Casfaidh siad orm sna bhflaithis,'[32] she'd say.[33]

That was more than could (presumably) be said for the old woman who became a Protestant in an account from Whitegate in County Cork, which relates how "when she died a black moth flew into the room and quenched the six candles that were lighting at the foot of the bed."[34]

Theft

Many of the accounts of the "Famine Times" in the Schools' Collection deal with the phenomenon of theft and its punishment; however, these tales vary a good deal in how they present both those who stole or were tempted to steal and those who came upon them in the act of stealing. An account from Mullagh in County Clare speaks of the poor visiting gardens at night time and "darting" for potatoes and turnip roots. It recalls how "a poor man named Martin Killeen was caught 'darting' for turnip roots in a garden belonging to a farmer name O'Dwyer. He was tied to a horse and cart and drawn through the street and publicly whipped."[35] A report from Ganty in County Galway by Mr. Patsy Dempsey, aged 85, recounted how "any girl that was found stealing [turnips] there was tar put on her head."[36] Meanwhile, a fanciful story told to Bridie Dillon in Aill in County Galway by Tom Flaherty, aged 73, presented Michael Hynes, a Robin-Hood-type figure from Athenry who "used to steal sheep from the rich people and share them with the poor" and was finally captured near Loughrea. To gain his acquittal, he was given the option of outrunning the hounds of the local gentlemen while allowing smoked fish to be tied to his feet, a challenge he accepted and won.[37] Another sheep-stealing tale—from Dunmore in County Kilkenny—is introduced as a "funny but true story of the Famine":

> A certain man starving with the hunger came out to Dunmore to steal a sheep. He borrowed an ass and car, also his mother's cap and cloak. He cut

a sheep's throat put the cap and cloak on her and put her in the car. He met one of Lord Ormonds men on the way home. The Lords man said what have you in the car. He said my mother she is sick I am bringing her to hospital. The Lords man was letting him pass when the sheep who was not half dead gave a little bawl. The Lords man heard her. The thief started to run the guard after him the ass bolted the guard ran back to ketch the ass in the end all got away.[38]

In Ballynacarriga, County Cork, the story was told of a man who was shot at a grinding mill while trying to procure some flour for his family. His body was left lying on the wall of the bridge near the castle as a warning to other would-be thieves, and was afterwards dragged by horse into Dunmanway where it was set up in the market square.[39] One gruesome tale told by 95-year-old Mr. William Tierney to a collector from Ballingeary East, County Tipperary, relates how, at that time, robberies were so common that one member of a family would always remain at home when others were at Mass. The story details how one man protected himself and his goods from robbery one Sunday morning by keeping a bill-hook in his hand inside the door. When a knock came to the door the man pretended to be a little child and, in a child's voice, said "put in your little fingie through the keyhole, and push back the bolt." As the robber, delighted at his good fortune did as he was told he had his finger swept clean off by the bill-hook. The man then continued "put in your other little fingie now."[40]

Some accounts, however, offer a glimpse of humanity, even from land-owners, with respect to the theft of their goods. A story collected from William Carrigan, aged 70, by a pupil of Grange school, Clonmel, told of how Carrigan's grandfather, who was working for a local landowner, had to make a quick decision when he spied a woman gathering "kippens" (firewood) with her two- or three-year-old son, who stole a small turnip. At that moment, he decided to turn a blind eye, but word of this got back to Mr. Adams, the steward. Carrigan relates that "the excuse my grandfather had was that the woman appeared to be very near her confinement and that he was afraid to frighten her by saying anything to her. Right enough she had a baby the day after." Presumably his excuse was accepted for the informant relates that "that's what saved my grandfather from getting the sack."[41] Others were said to have even gone beyond the realm of clemency in dealing with those who were engaged in theft. One informant, Diarmuid Ó Duibhir, records how his grandmother often told him a story about the "famine of '48" and a theft of turnips at her family home in Drombane, County Tipperary. She spoke of how her brother Johnny was keeping an eye on the turnips one night when

> a half-starved fellow came into the garden and filled a bag with turnips. He tried to lift them on his back but fell on his knees. He tried again but failed. Johnny was so moved with pity for the poor fellow that the shouted out 'hold on poor fellow, I'll carry 'em home for you'. He then took the turnips home for the starving man and his starving children.[42]

Although theft features regularly in these accounts, there are also entries such as this one recorded by Annie Egan from Ballinlass, County Galway, which noted that, "Some of the people died by the ditches because of the hunger. They were very proud and they would die by the ditch rather than steal anything from their neighbours."[43]

Miracles as a reward for generosity

Folk memories of the Famine often include stories of divine intervention, usually in the form of a miracle, which accompanies the generosity of an individual who chooses to share or give away what little food he or she has. Many of these tales have biblical parallels. One example concerns a certain Mrs. Nyhan from Enniskeane in County Cork and relates how:

> she had a tin of oatmeal and the starving people came to her for food. They came so plentifully that by night-time the bin was empty. She was in a

terrible state that night for she had no food for her husband's breakfast next morning but she prayed hard and next morning their bin was full of meal. This was a miracle.[44]

A similar story is told of the nuns at the Sacred Heart Convent in Roscrea, County Tipperary, where, during the Famine, a barrel of food miraculously kept replenishing itself as they handed provisions out to the poor.[45] In Dunmanway, County Cork, the following tale was recounted by 73-year-old Mrs. Landon:

> Mr McGivern had a very good crop of potatoes which he generously gave to all who came for them. An old man reproved Mr McGivern for his generosity telling him that he would let his own family starve. Mr McGivern replied that as long as the potatoes lasted, he would not allow anybody to starve. Mr McGivern gave and gave from his supply which, like 'the widow's cruise' was never exhausted.[46]

The "widow's cruise" here refers to the story of the widow of Zarephath as recounted in 1 Kings 17:16 in which her jar of flour was not used up nor did her jug of oil run dry. An Irish-language tale from Ballyferriter, County Kerry, draws its inspiration from the same source. It relates how a local woman was very generous and used to give all the milk she had to her neighbors. The more she gave, the more people came to her looking for milk. One evening her husband tells her that they have an early start in the morning as a group of men were due to come by to cut turf. "And I don't have a drop of milk!" she exclaimed. When her husband finds out why, he remonstrated with her for her actions: "Yeah, give something to the neighbours and remain yourself a stupid woman," he chides. But the woman maintains that "God's help is nearer than the door," and when the morning broke, the keelers (vessels for holding milk) were full to the brim.[47] Other tales were quick to point out when a person did not adequately trust in God's providence—and these too drew loosely on biblical injunctions such as that found in Matthew 6:34. A story from Bodyke in County Clare recounts how:

There was an old woman living in one village who would be 100 now if she lived. Who told me her mother told her of the hardships of the people in the time of the famine. She had rationed out the food for herself (some potatoes) and she came to the last meal. She said to some one I'll leave these till tomorrow but when tomorrow came 'she was dead'. My friend said, she had a right to eat the meal for the day before and leave the [future?] to God to provide.[48]

Concern with the spread of disease

Before beginning our discussion of the next two sections, it is perhaps worth remembering that at the outset of the project, Seamus Ó Duilearga seems to have been concerned that children might be preserved from contact with material of an inappropriate nature; indeed, at a conference in Tipperary in 1938, he noted that "the children in Tipperary could gather material about the Famine without going into any gruesome details."[49] However, the evidence from the following two sections suggests that this did not always work out as planned. The following stories often contain quite vivid descriptions of the very real concern that people had surrounding the spread of disease and, consequently, the fear of coming in contact with those—alive or dead—who might be contagious. Francis Saunders from Mullagh National School, County Clare, records how:

> Bad as was the hunger the cholera swept the majority of the people. It must have raged terribly in the district because one of the worst curses people use in Irish at Quilty is 'Cholera Ort'.[50] There were cases where people were buried alive who had the cholera. It used come 'like a shower of fog' and strike the people. The people so stricken would be 'as black as the hob' in a very short time.[51]

A report from Knockvicar, County Roscommon, states that "if a person was dying in the house, all the rest of the household went out working because they were afraid of the fever."[52]

A report from Newtown in County Tipperary notes that it was the sickness that came with the Famine that caused the most deaths: "it was so dreaded that even brothers and sisters would not go near a dead father or mother to bury them. When a member of a family got this disease the other members of the family fed him or her at the end of a long pole."[53] This claim is also found in an account from Dunmanway in County Cork, which relates how

> one old woman was found by the roadside infested with vermin and disease. So awful was her plight nobody dared do anything to alleviate her suffering. At length somebody thought of building a house all round the suffering woman. This was done, a thatched roof was put on, and a small window was made. A long-handled vessel was then procured and by this means, food was put in to the poor woman who eventually recovered.[54]

Another story recalls how an old woman died in a cabin near Sillahertane School, County Cork, and was dead for several days before anyone found her. When her remains were discovered "the corpse was in such an awful state of decay that they could not remove it, they simply knocked in the little cabin on it."[55] One response to the fear of being press-ganged into contact with the dead is cited in an account from Gortnadeeve West, County Galway, as the origin of a funeral custom that still survives in some areas:

> The people used not to have any help to bring a corpse to the grave yard. When they would get tired they would go into a house to see if there was anyone that could help them. When the people of the houses would see a funeral coming they would close the doors and put the blinds on the windows so that the people who would be carrying the corpse would not go in for anyone to help them. Even to this day the doors are shut and the blinds put on the windows while a funeral is passing.[56]

The terror that disease struck in people also provided the opportunity for tales of heroism. The story is told of cholera raging in Tulla in County Clare and people being terrified to go anywhere near the dead bodies. The local priest, Rev. Daniel Corbett, often coffined the bodies and took them to the graveyard. Upon asking for assistance, only one man by the name of Whelan was prepared to come forward and was rewarded afterwards for his efforts:

> He told him that there was no fear that he'd 'take' the cholera. Whelan day and night carried the bodies to the graveyard and though constantly in contact with the cholera he never fell a victim to it. He lived to a great age, and it is remarkable that while others who refused to assist died at an early age and scarcely left any descendants to perpetuate their names, the name of Whelan is very common in Tulla and the surrounding districts all having large families.[57]

This seemingly divine preservation from disease accorded to those who were willing to bury the dead is also reported during an outbreak of cholera in Castledermot, County Kildare, and, once again, a local priest plays a central role in the story: "it is told that Archdeacon Dunne told the people to go into the affected houses & carry out the dead & bury them & they would be none the worse for it. Those who obeyed his order were never stricken with the dread disease."[58]

Not all stories show human nature at its most heroic, however. The following tale comes from Abbeytown Convent, Boyle, County Roscommon, and was recorded by a pupil whose teacher was a Sister M. Columbanus:

> There was a lady living in Boyle who kept a governess for her children. The girl became very ill of the fever. She was unconscious for days. The lady, fearing that her children might take the fever, got her servants to make a wooden box in which they put the girl alive and intended to bury her. While they were putting the clay over the coffin, she screamed, and in order to stop her terrific screams they opened the box. When they opened, the girl was almost dead from the nails that went through her, and she was covered over with blood. After a few hours she died and they buried her.[59]

One wonders about the effectiveness of the vetting process for stories recorded in this school given the graphic description above. This is somewhat confirmed in the line (also found in this section) that "the children who were sent out to play while their parents were dying inside took a great delight in poking rods in the eyes of dead people." Most alarming of all, perhaps, is the inclusion of material relating to incidences of infanticide and cannibalism in an Irish language account from Grianán, County Mayo.[60]

Burial Alive

One of the very common features of folk tales of the Famine is the "memory" of people being buried alive. In Caherlustraun, County Galway, Michael Curry recorded how his father, Pat Curry, aged 63, told him "of a man named Ned Conolly who died on the streets with his head resting on a stone and froth from his mouth ... and of others, certified by doctors to be dead and ordered to be buried immediately, who were not dead at all."[61] An account from Killaghtan, County Galway, collected by Mary Kearns, also refers to the idea that during Famine times, people were being buried alive:

> Some people weren't let go cold until they were (but stirring) in the Coffin going to the graveyard. One evening they were carrying a person to Killaghton grave-yard and they felt him stirring (in the) in the coffin. When they came to the gate they looked in and he was turned mouth under.[62]

A story from Ballyroddy in County Roscommon, the informant being Nora Connor aged 86, runs, with no little black humour:

> On one occasion the doctor pronounced sentence of death on so many of the patients the man for burying them was hustling all the corpses into a mat, when this man spoke in a weak voice and said 'I'm not dead yet. 'It's no matter', says the man in charge 'the doctor says you are', and he bundled all away and buried them.[63]

One of the more well-known tales concerning the burial of someone who was still alive concerned a certain Tom Gearn, who was reportedly buried alive near Skibbereen.[64] Mary O'Sullivan from Dunbeacon school in County Cork relates how:

> It is said that a man by the name of Tom Gearn was buried alive in Skibbereen. He was taken to the graveyard with many others who died of hunger and fever. He broke his two legs trying to come out and from that time he had to walk with crutches.[65]

John Murphy from Bantry relates a slightly different version of the tale:

> During the time of the Famine there lived in Bantry a boy named Tom Gearns. One night he fainted with hunger in a street, and next morning the car, which was collecting the dead bodies was going around, and he was thrown into the car, and he was thrown into the Famine Pit. His legs were broken by the fall but after a while he regained consciousness, and he got out of the pit and crawled home, and during his life-time afterwards his legs were crooked.[66]

In other accounts, the name of the main protagonist is not recalled. John McFarlane, who attended Lowertown school, County Cork, related the story as follows:

> This is another story about a man who was dying on the roadside. There was a man going around with a horse and car taking up the dead bodies. The man came to the dying man and thought he was dead and he threw him into the car. When he was burying the bodies he put the dying body in also. He hit the bodies with a shovel to pack them and when he struck the dying man he groaned. The man then took him out of the grave and took him to the Workhouse and he recovered in a few months but was lame in one leg. The man hit him on the leg with a shovel and broke it. This man is only about twenty years dead. He was an inhabitant of Long Island but I do not know his name.[67]

In these three accounts alone, there are three versions of how the individual came to have a leg injury afterwards: 1) injured while trying to come out of the grave; 2) injured while being thrown into the grave; 3) injured by being hit on the leg with a shovel as the bodies were being packed in. Such discrepancies are useful reminders of the fluid nature of much of this material.

Pathos in the Schools' Collection

The accounts discussed above fulfilled a number of functions: some were constructed to provide a sense of general conditions during the Famine; others were salutary tales regarding those who had forfeited their faith for food; still more held up heroic figures to be remembered; and there were also stories whose sole purpose, despite the grim subject matter, was to entertain. But the Schools' Collection also contains a large number of Famine stories that can only be described as heart-wrenching. These often concern the deaths of loved ones, and especially children. It is here, perhaps most of all, that the collection "humanises statistics," in Cathal Póirtéir's words cited above, offering a poignancy and inviting an emotional response that cannot be accessed while poring over demographics.

A story from Bantry, County Cork, relates in a matter-of-fact manner how:

> there was a man living in the Quay during the time of the Famine and he had a large family. One night, two of his children died, and the mother and the father carried them in a sack to the Famine pit in the Abbey and threw them into the pit. When they returned home, they found that three more of the children had died.[68]

A tale from the same region collected by Mary O'Donovan is just as stark:

> There is a very interesting story told about a poor family that lived in this district. They had nothing to eat and the two eldest daughters died, so the

father went to work in a mine near Cork and he sent five shillings every week to support the wife and son that remained at home. One week the money did not come so the woman waited for a few weeks and in the end the hunger pressed heavily upon both again so that they set out for Cork. On the way the son died of hunger and weariness and to the poor woman's great distress when she arrived at the husband's working place she was told that he had died two weeks previously. She got such a fright that she died in a few hours and was buried in the pit where the husband was.[69]

Ó Gráda states that accounts such as these "are at the heart of the Famine story. They make it "a palpable thing,' adding context to the matchstick scavengers portrayed in the *Illustrated London News* in 1847 and 1848, and widely reproduced since."[70]

Some tales, for instance, offer tantalizing glimpses of male emotional responses to the ravages of hunger in a young family, such as the account from Scoil na mBráthar, Thurles, County Tipperary, which relates how:

There was such a famine that the little children used to be crying with the hunger and their fathers used to go away out around the field and not come back until night when it was time to go to bed because they could not bear to be listening to the children crying.[71]

This is not an isolated reference and can be found in reports from other parts of the country.[72] The same source adds another commonly recalled image, that of "the mothers of the children [who] used to fill a pot of stones and water and let on to the children that they were potatoes."[73] Stories such as these are given added poignancy when the names of the individuals are included, as in the case of the following tale from Kilbegnet, County Roscommon, collected by Una Ní Chuinn:

There is another graphic story told about one widow named Peggy Griffin that was dying without fire, food or clothes and seven young children dying around her. While she was dying a neighbouring man named Mr O'Kelly called to comfort her in her last hours. And the man said 'O Peggy, isn't it hard', and she said 'welcome be the will of God. Soon I will be happy myself and my little ones'.[74]

Other accounts of people preparing for death communicate the sense of isolation that accompanied the person who was left alone to face the end, such as the following report from Clonmel, County Tipperary, where, "there were 7 or 8 people found dead from Kilsheelan. When they were all dead except for one man he had to go into a house and lock the door so that pigs or dogs would not eat him."[75]

Side by side with the pathos evoked in sometimes quite intimate accounts, however, there was also to be found in many quarters a certain distancing of one's own native place from the horrific events that were described. Carmel Quinlan speaks of a "detached attitude to those who died or were dispossessed ... there is frequently a perceptible 'othering' of the victims by depicting them as 'strangers' or people who died in 'other places.'"[76] Quinlan also draws attention to the number of references to people coming across strangers dead in their locality.[77] One good example of this from the Schools' Collection is from Curreeny school, County Tipperary:

> There is no account of any people dying around here except one poor scholar whose name is unknown was found dead near Kilcommon. It is believed he died after eating some porridge because his bowels were not able to stand the strain of the strong porridge. He came from the Doon side & was nearly dead from hunger when he arrived here.[78]

Máire MacNeill, writing about the folk memory of the Famine, captures this ambivalence when she claims that, "the horror went deep but there was also a wish to forget it ... perhaps the seeming detachment came originally from the wish of the survivors to suppress its memories."[79]

Conclusion

The Schools' Collection of 1937–38 constitutes a remarkable repository of folk memory concerning the period of the Great Hunger some 90 years before. The foresight of Ó Duilearga and Ó Súilleabháin in entrusting such a data-gathering exercise, in the first instance, to schoolchildren (even given the precise instructions laid out) was remarkable for its time. The vignettes presented above represent a small sample of the richness of this, to date, underutilized source. It is to be hoped that this will be rectified in the future, especially since the collection has now been digitized and is very easily navigable. These stories provide a unique window into perceptions of the past, which were very long-lived, indeed, surviving in many instances to the present day. Cathal Póirtéir captures this very well when he concludes that:

> It is within the folklore material that we discover that stories of individual cruelty and kindness outlasted the Famine itself by generations and that it was the actions or inactions of people at a local level which were vividly recalled rather than government policy or its national administrators who were far removed from their communities.[80]

NOTES

1. Mícheál Briody, *The Irish Folklore Commission, 1935–1970: History, Ideology, Methodology* (Helsinki: Finnish Literature Society, 2007), p. 261. The language used here evoked what were understood to be earlier historic efforts at the preservation of an endangered culture; both Ó Duilearga and Ó Súilleabháin drew comparisons with the Annals of the Four Masters compiled in the 17th century. See Mary E. Daly, '"The State Papers of a Forgotten and Neglected People": the National Folklore Collection and the Writing of Irish History,' *Béaloideas* 78 (2010), 61–79; at 62, n. 4.

2. Briody, pp. 264–5.

3. Briody, p. 267.

4. duchas.ie/en/info/cbe, accessed 22 March 2018.

5. It can be accessed at duchas.ie/en.

6. Stuart McLean, *The Event and its Terrors: Ireland, Famine, Modernity* (Stanford: Stanford University Press, 2004), p. 23.

7. Niall Ó Ciosáin, 'Approaching a Folklore Archive: The Irish Folklore Commission and the Memory of the Great Famine,' *Folklore* 115 (2004), 222–232; at p. 224.

8. Niall Ó Ciosáin, 'Famine memory and the popular representation of scarcity', in Ian McBride (ed.), *History and Memory in Modern Ireland* (Cambridge: Cambridge University Press, 2001), pp. 116–17.

9. An Cheapach. The Schools' Collection [henceforth SC], vol. 0046, p. 0144.

10. 'Ach ta sé préamhaithe i meon an phobail ar bhealach nach bhfuil aon tuairisc eile', Cathal Póirtéir, 'Pictiúr Briste: Seanchas faoin Drochshaol,' *Comhar* 55:2 (Feb. 1996), 9–12.

11. Cathal Póirtéir, 'The folklore of the Famine: Seanchas an Drochshaoil,' *Atlas of the Great Irish Famine* (Cork: Cork University Press, 2012), pp. 604–5.

12. See Guy Beiner, *Remembering the year of the French. Irish Folk History and Social Memory* (Madison: University of Wisconsin Press, 2007), cited in Daly, p. 77.

13. When one types the word 'Famine' into the search engine of the digitised Schools' Collection, some 2,368 stories are returned. This does not include 245 returns for the word 'Drochshaol', and 87 for 'Gorta', its Irish language equivalents. This study, with a couple of exceptions, has purposely limited itself to English language returns.

14. E. Moore Quinn, '"She must have come steerage": the Great Famine in New England Folk Memory,' in David A. Valone (ed.), *Ireland's Great Hunger: Relief, Representation and Remembrance* (Lanham, Maryland: University Press of America, 2009), p. 12x (ebook). He also went on to say 'We *remember* the soup being extended but only if you would give up your land or religion.'

15. For the influence of this image of eating grass in children's literature see Karen Hill McNamara, 'The potato eaters: food collection in Irish famine literature for children,' in Kara K. Keeling and Scott T. Pollard (eds), *Critical Approaches to Food in Children's Literature* (New York: Routledge, 2009), pp. 152–3.

16. Baile an Doire, County Galway. SC, vol. 0021, p. 0260.

17. Baile Nua, Gabhal tSulchóide. SC, vol. 0578, pp. 083–084.

18. Lagganstown, New Inn. SC, vol. 0576, pp. 206–208.

19. Radharc na Sionainne, Clooncah, County Roscommon. SC, vol. 0260, p. 104. 'Thraneen,' from *tráithnín*: a blade of grass, a straw, a rush, a sop of hay.

20. Baile an Leasa, County Galway. SC, vol. 0037, pp. 0216–0217.

21. An Clochar, Gráig na Muilte Iarainn. SC, vol. 0050, pp. 0433–0435.

22. Killomoran. SC, vol. 0047, pp. 0268–0270.

23. Clochar na Trócaire, An Tulach. SC, vol. 0589, p. 207.

24. Druim Garlaigh. SC, vol. 0950, p. 037.

25. Lubhghortán (Lowertown), Scoil Mhuire. SC, vol. 0289, pp. 366–377.

26. Béal an Dá Chab. SC, vol. 0290, p. 231.

27. Ó Ciosáin, 'Approaching a Folklore Archive,' p. 228.

28. Áth Treasna (C.), vol. 0353, p. 056. (By contrast, the same informant relates how 'I heard a story about a woman. All the hunger never weakened her faith she never missed Sunday mass. In the finish she was not able to walk there and she crawled on her face and hands and she died in front of the altar'). A similar version from Carrigtohill, County Cork, recalls how a 'man, driven during the Famine period by hunger to accept the hospitality of the "Soupers" had to pass the Catholic Church on his way there. He turned back, took off his "caubeen" and said "Goodbye Almighty God, till the praties grow"'. An Charraig, Contae Thír Thuathail, SC, vol. 0385, p. 113.

29. Cill Thiomáin, Durrus, Bantry. SC, vol. 0288, p. 020. Regarding this sort of tale, Niall Ó Ciosáin refers to 'types of "trickster" stories, whereby people get the benefit of the food on offer without abandoning their previous religion, outwitting the proselytisers through continuing to go to mass in the Catholic church even while attending a Protestant service, through having a rosary in their pockets during those services, blessing themselves before eating'. Ó Ciosáin, 'Approaching a Folklore Archive,' p. 228.

30. Cill Chuisigh. SC, vol. 0200, p. 159.

31. Cloonkeen Kerrill. SC, vol. 0078, p. 312.

32. 'They'll meet me in Heaven.'

33. Cill Srianáin (Jamestown). SC, vol. 0210, pp. 412–413.

34. An Geata Bán, Whitegate, vol. 0393, pp. 025–026.

35. Mullach, Sráid na Cathrach. SC, vol. 0624, pp. 107–108.

36. Ganntaigh. SC, vol. 0034, pp. 0193–0195.

37. An Aill (Aille). SC, vol. 0059, pp. 0469–0471.

38. Dunmore, Kilkenny. SC. vol. 0863, pp. 233–234.

39. Béal na Carraige, Béal Átha Fhinghín. SC, vol. 0310, p. 041.

40. Baile an Ghaorthaidh, Cluain Meala. SC, vol. 0569, p. 033.

41. An Ghráinseach, Cluain Meala. SC, vol. 0571, p. 067.

42. Ros Mor, County Tipperary. SC, vol. 0584, p. 094.

43. Baile an Leasa. SC, vol. 0037, pp. 0216–0217.

44. Mawbeg East, Bandon. SC, vol. 0315, pp. 047–048.

45. Corbally, Roscrea. Corville. SC, vol. 0548, pp. 137–139. The account is then brought up to date with the lines: 'The Sacred Heart nuns are still in Roscrea. They have a beautiful convent. The old custom is still to be seen. Any poor person that goes to the convent seeking alms, they get it, although it is not out of the wonderful barrel.'

46. Naomh Éamoinn, Dúnmaonmhuighe. SC, vol. 0304, p. 377.

47. Baile an Fheirtéaraigh, County Chiarraí. SC, vol. 0419, pp. 470–71.

48. Lúbán Díge (Bodyke). SC, vol. 0591, p. 376.

49. Caoimhe Ní Lochlainn, '"A work of National Importance": Child–Adult Dynamics in Bailiúchán Na Scol/The Schools' Collection, 1937–1939,' *The Journal of the History of Childhood and Youth*, 9:2 (Spring 2016), 203–211; at p. 204.

50. 'May you have cholera!'

51. Mullach, Sráid na Cathrach. SC, vol. 0624, pp. 107–108.

52. Naomh Pádraig, Knockvicar. SC, vol. 0233, pp. 502ff.

53. Baile Nua, Gabhal tSulchóide. SC, vol. 0578, pp. 083–084.

54. Naomh Éamoinn, Dúnmaonmhuighe. SC, vol. 0304, p. 377.

55. Sailcheartáin (Sillahertane), Dúnmaonmhuighe. SC, vol. 0304, p. 123. A similar story is told of a family of 'Hannas' in Kilmichael parish in which the house was tumbled in and the bodies mingled with earth and debris before they were eventually buried. Seana-chaiseal, Maghcromtha. SC, vol. 0340, p. 126.

56. Gort na Díogha. SC, vol. 0016, pp. 109–110.

57. Clooney, Cuinche. SC, vol. 0593, pp. 447–48.

58. Castledermot (C.). SC, vol. 0782, p. 093.

59. Abbeytown Convent, Boyle, County Roscommon. SC, vol. 0235, pp. 206–7.

60. Grianán, County Mayo. SC, vol. 0094, p.208. See also Cormac Ó Gráda, *Eating People is Wrong and Other Essays on Famine, Its Past and Its Future* (Princeton: Princeton University Press, 2015).

61. Cathair Loisgreáin, vol. 0022, p. 0253. Pat Curry related that he heard this story from his own father.

62. Cill a' Lachtáin, vol. 0028, p. 0246.

63. Ballyroddy, County Roscommon. SC, vol. 0250, p. 177. A close variation of this tale is found in Ballinderry, County Galway. Baile an Doire. SC, vol. 0021, p. 0260. The informant, a Mrs Cullinan, explains: 'the people were dying by thousands. There was

no time to make coffins they were dying so fast. They were even burying them before they died at all, so that they would be out of their way.'

64. This story is also recounted by Susan Campbell Bartoletti in her *Black Potatoes: the story of the Great Irish Famine* (New York: Houghton Mifflin, 2001), p. 103: 'grim stories circulated about people buried alive. "Tom Gearins was a young lad at the time of the Famine," said Margaret Donovan from County Cork. "With many others he was taken and thrown into the Famine hole in Skibbereen Alley. He was not dead and somehow he was able to raise his hand." Tom was rescued but both his legs had been broken in the fall. After that it was said that Tom "arose from the dead."'

65. Dún Bhéacháin (Dunbeacon), vol. 0290, pp. 172–173.

66. Beanntraighe (B.), vol. 0281, p. 140.

67. Lubhghortán (Lowertown), Scoil Mhuire, vol. 0289, pp. 366–377.

68. Beanntraighe (B.). SC, vol. 0281, p. 140.

69. Ceann Caorach, Cill Crócháin. SC, vol. 0286, pp. 032–033.

70. Cormac Ó Gráda, *The Great Irish Famine* (Cambridge: Cambridge University Press, 1995), p. 32.

71. Scoil na mBráthar, Dúrlas Éile. SC, vol. 0552, pp. 131–132.

72. See Ballyroddy, County Roscommon. SC, vol. 0250, pp. 176–177; also Ballinameen, County Roscommon. SC, vol. 0238, pp. 412–13.

73. Scoil na mBráthar, Dúrlas Éile. SC, vol. 0552, pp. 131–132.

74. Kilbegnet, County Roscommon. SC, vol. 0262, pp. 010–012.

75. Newtownanner Demesne, Clonmel. SC, vol. 0568, p. 125.

76. Carmel Quinlan, '"A Punishment from God": The Famine in the Centenary Folklore Questionnaire', *The Irish Review* 19 (spring-summer 1996), 68–86; at p. 68.

77. Quinlan, '"A Punishment from God", p. 81.

78. Curreeny, Dolla, Nenagh. SC, vol. 0537, p. 30.

79. Máire MacNeill, 'Irish Folklore as a Source for Research,' *Journal of the Folklore Institute of Indiana*, 2 (1965), p. 347.

80. Cathal Póirtéir, 'The folklore of the Famine,' p. 604.

CHAPTER ELEVEN

CREATING THE GREAT IRISH FAMINE CURRICULUM IN NEW YORK

Maureen Murphy

The Great Irish Famine Curriculum was launched from both sides of Washington Avenue, the narrow street in Albany, New York, that separates the center of New York State government from the headquarters of the New York State Education Department. In 1996, the State Education Department began to distribute copies of its new performance-based New York State Learning Standards, created to improve the quality of education in the State's public schools. The new set of assessments was designed to ensure that all pupils in grades four, eight and eleven could demonstrate appropriate standards of competence in each of the middle and secondary school subjects. Because the assessments would be performance-based, no curricula were provided for the new standards. (Learning Standards had been replaced during President Obama's administration with the "Common Core", which emphasized basic literacy and numeracy.)

The following year, the 150th anniversary of the worst year of the Great Irish Famine, Ann Garvey, president of the American Irish Teachers Association, approached Joe Crowley, then an assemblyman in the New York

State Legislature, to urge him to advocate that a study of the Great Irish Famine be added to the required strands in the State Education Department's Human Rights Curriculum. At that time, the required strands were the Atlantic Slave Trade and the European Holocaust. Crowley introduced the motion and steered it through the legislative process where it had enthusiastic bi-partisan support. The Legislature and the Office of the Governor provided funding to develop the curriculum.[1] Hofstra University was selected, by way of a competitive bidding process, to develop the curriculum.

Our primary goal in developing the Great Irish Famine Curriculum was to write Ireland into the teaching of global history, a required course in the secondary schools in New York state. We designed our history and social studies lessons and our lessons in the other disciplines by framing students' learning with the newly minted New York State Learning Standards in each subject. The finished curriculum offered teachers 150 interdisciplinary, project-based lessons, which engage students with material from civics, economics, geography, history, language, arts, math, science, technology, performing arts, fine arts and family and consumer science. The Great Irish Famine Curriculum, as one of the strands of the State Human Rights Curriculum, was designed to ask students to look at common themes: human suffering and the development of policies and strategies to remedy or ameliorate conditions responsible for slavery, famine and genocide. Because the 150 lessons were self-contained units, with readings, handouts and references to additional resources, there was no racing around by teachers to find additional sources. Furthermore, permission for copyrighted materials to be reproduced for classroom use had been obtained.

The Great Irish Famine Curriculum asked students to consider a number of major questions: What forces shaped Ireland and the world before the Great Irish Famine? (Answers include the Columbian exchange, the Reformation in Europe, the European colonization of Africa, South America and Asia, and the Industrial Revolution.) These themes invited students and teachers to read, think, speak and write about some of the big questions in world history.

How can an event or an object transform history? What role does religion play in human history? How does technology change the way people live and work? Are famines caused by acts of nature or are they the result of decisions made by people and governments? What are the consequences of prejudices? What is a government's responsibility during a time of disaster? What is the responsibility of the media when it reports the news? What are the responsibilities of individuals when they are faced with injustice or calamity? What are the origins and consequences of imperialism? What constitutes human rights and how are they protected? What is genocide? Can individuals and groups shape the future?

The question of whether the Great Irish Famine is an example of genocide was the most sensitive question in the curriculum. It was raised when the curriculum was first mooted, and John Kerr, the then British ambassador to the United States, objected to New York Governor George Pataki's statement, made on 9 October 1996, claiming that the Famine resulted from "...a deliberate campaign by the British to deny the Irish people to food they needed to survive."[2] The context of this public dispute was significant, as the Peace Process was in its early stages and it had been put in serious jeopardy when the Irish Republic Army's 17-month ceasefire had come to a violent end in February 1996, with a bomb in London.[3] Consequently, relationships between the Irish and British governments were fragile. The debate over the Famine Curriculum was viewed by some as reviving traditional resentments. The influential London *Times*, for example, claimed that Pataki was motivated by a desire to win the Irish American vote, and that his knowledge of Irish history was derived from, "the Fenian propaganda version which ambitious American politicians tend to prefer."[4] Again, however, external political events, most notably the resumption of the Peace Process, was changing the context in which the curriculum was operating. The official British party line was altered in Tony Blair's 31 May 1997 message to the people of Cork, which included the assertion:

> The Famine was a defining event in the history of Ireland and Britain. It has left deep scars. That one million people should have died in what was then part of the richest and most powerful nation in the world is something that still causes pain as we reflect on it today. Those who governed in London at the time failed their people.[5]

It was the first public admission by the British government of culpability. A further symbolic gesture of the softening of relations between Ireland and Britain occurred on 19 May 2011, with a speech made by Queen Elizabeth II at Dublin Castle, which began, *A hUachtarain agus a chairde*.[6] She then spoke of the complexity of the shared history of the Republic of Ireland and the United Kingdom and the "troubled past," which prompted her reflection about "things she wished had been done differently or not at all."[7] Regardless of these sensitivities, and shifting political positions, the question of genocide became the document-based question, a key component of the state's Social Studies Regents Exam of the time, which asked students to examine a variety of primary source documents and write an essay taking a position based on their analysis of the evidence. We did not require them to take "our" position.

The curriculum included several lessons that asked students to examine questions about a government's response to the crisis. Was the Great Irish Famine an example of genocide? Did the government's policy of letting food leave the country constitute an act of genocide? What about the ejectment notices served to some 974,930 people between 1849 and 1854, the implementation of a harrowing policy that produced mass homelessness, which did not stop in 1854.[8] The document-based question considered the matter of definition of the term "genocide." Students discovered that genocide is a recent term, one coined by Raphael Lemkin in his book *Axis Rule in Occupied Europe* (1944). We framed the lesson with the United Nation's Convention on Prevention and Punishment of the Crime of Genocide, 1951, which stipulated that genocide consisted of:

Any of the following acts committed with intent to destroy in whole or in part a national, ethnic, racial or religious group, such as

a) killing members of the group;

b) causing serious bodily or mental harm to members of the group;

c) deliberately inflicting on the group conditions of life calculated to bring about its physical destruction in whole or in part;

d) imposing measures intended to prevent births within the group;

e) forcibly transferring children of the group to another group.[9]

Using the United Nations definition of genocide and other primary source documents, students were asked to compare British policy during the Great Irish Famine with a choice of two other 20th-century events that resulted in high mortality to particular people: in Armenia, in Europe during the Holocaust, in Bosnia, in Rwanda and in East Timor. Students examined print and non-print primary source documents including graphs, charts, maps, photographs, illustrations and political cartoons to determine which events met the criteria of the United Nations definition of genocide. Students were required to provide supporting evidence for their choices. The culmination of the genocide lesson was an activity developed by Alan Singer and Michael Pezzone called a "democratic dialogue," a formal discussion of a complex issue that follows a protocol that requires students to support their opinions with evidence from primary source documents. There is no declared winner of the dialogue; instead, the emphasis was on clarifying and understanding complex issues, which help empower students to become active and engaged citizens.

Experience with the Famine dialogues demonstrated that students found the question of genocide and the Great Irish Famine was complicated because the United Nations requires that the charge of genocide, as defined by them, is based on intentionality, on deliberate action taken by members of a group against members of another group. The UN does not mention groups or governments that fail to act during famine conditions. Students did not find evidence of British intentionality, but they were highly critical of the British policy that failed to provide timely and appropriate relief to the Irish. It was an important insight for students. They concluded that we are responsible not only for what we do, but we also are responsible for what we fail to do. As a result, after the democratic dialogue, students spent time discussing how to frame language to bring charges against people who fail to act or to act appropriately. Students' conclusions about the question of British Famine policy generally agree with the prevailing expert opinion. While genocide continued to inform some versions of the nationalist narrative, it is not the interpretation that is accepted by most historians today.

The curriculum did not, on the other hand, excuse British culpability. Students deconstructed Blair's message to the Irish people in 1997. Many students concluded that while Blair's message was not an apology, it constituted an implicit apology since Blair expressed regret and took responsibility on behalf of the British government. Blair's message was revisited later in the curriculum when it talked about reconciliation and forgiveness as the last step in any permanent peace process.

Having identified government leaders who failed to take appropriate action, we were equally concerned with providing students with models of compassionate and responsible behavior. Students re-created the relief organizations that New Yorkers found to aid the Irish and discussed how best to organize such relief campaigns. They read simulated grant applications and debated how to allocate their funds to realize "the greatest possible good."

The lessons in the final section of the curriculum consider the legacy of the Great Irish Famine: folk legends of hospitality rewarded, proverbs like *A scáth a cheile, a mhaireann na daoine* that remind students of our obligations to each other.[10] Lessons about art, music and literature provided further opportunities to reflect on the losses of the Famine decade that continue to survive in the Irish landscape and in its oral and written tradition. The monuments, both local and national, created to mark the 150th anniversary of the Great Irish Famine, offered students opportunities to study and to evaluate the way that such commemorations help mourners live with loss. Students also had opportunities to think about cultures of commemoration and to design their own Famine or diaspora memorials.

The closing lessons of the Great Irish Famine Curriculum draw students' attention to examples of hunger in other parts of the world. While it may appear that lessons asking students to look at the Great Irish Famine comparatively with famines in places like India and sub-Sahara Africa is a departure from our original brief to create a curriculum that teaches students about the Great Irish Famine, the model of Margaret Kelleher's pioneering study *The Feminization of Famine. Expression of the Inexpressible?* (1997) demonstrated that studying the Great Irish Famine comparatively is an effective way to situate the Irish Famine in a study of hunger and homelessness. This approach anticipated Cormac Ó Gráda's integrative methodology in *Famine. A History* (2009), his analytical history of world famines.

Our three lessons about famine in the world today, used with the permission of the Irish relief organization *Trócaire*, focus on hunger in sub-Sahara Africa. In addition to these lessons, additional ones were designed to raise awareness of hunger in our own communities, some of which are among the most affluent communities in the country.[11] Students were asked to identify the hungry in their own communities and the causes of local hunger, and to create a plan of action to recruit volunteers for local hunger related service projects. They were encouraged to take advantage of school, church or scouting organizations that required or enabled service learning and to consider responding to this most basic need.

The Great Irish Famine Curriculum ends with a meditation about hunger in memory and how people experience, remember and reconcile the traumatic events in their past. This lesson provides a way to examine the trauma of the Great Irish Famine with other narratives of loss and suffering. Students examine the different narratives of national trauma using new methodologies and models that integrate a variety of primary source documents.[12] Students were left with the words of Hannah Arendt who spoke about being liberated from the past by forgiving and, at the same time, being bound to the future by promising.[13] In the spirit of Arendt, the curriculum concludes with a lesson about planning an annual student hunger Remembrance Day with a

Proclamation and a promise to work with others to do something to eliminate the poverty that causes hunger and homelessness.[14]

As the lesson drafts were completed, they were field-tested in diverse settlings: in inner city schools, in rural areas of New York state and in various suburban settings. Since Hofstra University was involved with placing and supervising students in student teaching sites, there was an opportunity to work with students who brought a variety of backgrounds, experiences, interests and abilities to the classroom. We learned to make our Famine curriculum and materials accessible to those students. In some cases, two or three versions of texts were created to provide content rich texts for students of different reading levels. These texts allowed students to participate fully in class discussions and to be active participants in learning activities.

The degree to which all students were engaged never failed to impress those who came to observe the curriculum in the classroom. One of the test sites was a Queens middle school with a high failure rate on the 8th grade social studies exam. One of the teachers used the Famine lessons with his students. His finding? That attendance improved among the disadvantaged high-risk students. Under the new Common Core Curriculum, any modified text is not allowed; instead, lessons focus on making the primary text accessible to every student.

Since the students are taught to differentiate between fact and opinion, we asked those interested in evaluating the efficacy of the curriculum to examine the accounts of observers like Harry Browne of *The Irish Times* who watched students working with the curriculum ("U.S. using the Irish Past to Shape its Future") in The Education and Living Supplement, *The Irish Times*, 24 April 2001. The national Ancient Order of Hibernians historian Mike McCormick monitored the curriculum closely and visited school sites when we field-tested the lessons. He concluded that while our curriculum differed from the one he and others had envisaged, and while he would have preferred coverage of topics like the Penal Laws, having seen the curriculum in the classroom, he endorsed it. He was present in Phoenix when the curriculum was awarded the National Council of the Social Studies Project Excellence Award in 2002.

The curriculum, however, was not without its detractors. It was criticized in the pages of *The Irish People* for being too easy on the British government. It is a criticism that failed to appreciate the difference between a curriculum that involves a narrative to be mastered and a curriculum that asks students to think critically like historians. Both curricula use primary sources; however, while the curriculum envisaged by critics would instruct students how to interpret the sources, the Great Irish Famine Curriculum invited students to examine the sources and to draw their own conclusions. As educators, we trusted the integrity of the sources and the ability of our students to read with understanding, to draw conclusions based on primary source evidence, and to speak and write with clarity. Faced with a variety of historical evidence and given a variety of ways to approach the material and to make meaning of it, students exposed to the curriculum learned what the lessons of the Great Irish Famine have to teach us today about hunger and homelessness. In addition, the Curriculum sought to enhance students' understanding and engagement in their roles as members of a democratic society and to develop their awareness and appreciation of the experiences and identities of diverse peoples.

The curriculum had an influence beyond the classroom. In 1999, when Governor Pataki charged the Battery Park City Authority with creating a memorial to the Great Irish Famine on a half-acre site within the shadow of the World Trade Center, the Great Irish Famine Curriculum helped to influence the decision not only to commemorate the Famine and the diaspora, but also to raise awareness about world hunger. The dual purpose of the memorial is reflected in its name: The Irish Hunger Memorial. The texts and audio loops with passages in Amharic, English, German, Irish, Russian and Spanish speak to the Great Irish Famine and to other historical examples of famine in other parts of the world.

Below are a number of examples of lessons from the Great Irish Famine Curriculum. They address the questions: "What forces shaped Ireland and the world before the Great Irish Famine?"; "Was the Great Irish Famine an act of nature or an act of man?" and "How did the Great Irish Famine affect Ireland and the world?." Throughout the lessons, an overarching question is, "What can we learn about the challenges of hunger and homelessness from the Great Irish Famine?"

1. PRE-FAMINE HOUSING CONDITIONS IN IRELAND

The important 1841 census gives us a snapshot of Ireland on the edge of the Famine. It included a survey of housing with the number of houses of each type:

Class 1: better housing than a class 2 house (40,080)
Class 2: a good farm house or a house in town with five to nine rooms
   and windows (264,184)
Class 3: better built mud cabin with two to four rooms and windows
   (533,297)
Class 4: mud cabin with one room (491,278)
Would your house be a class 1, 2, 3, or 4 type of house?

Create a chart or graph of the house types. Consider two data points: the total number of houses surveyed was 1,328,839 which means 50 percent would be 664,419. Class 3 and 4 accounts for more than 1,000,000 houses).

2. ARABLE LAND AND POPULATION DENSITY

If you were part of a team asked to predict the areas of Ireland most likely to suffer during the Great Irish Famine, what information would the survey of house types provide?

3. FOOD EXPORTS DURING THE GREAT IRISH FAMINE:

The matter of the export of food during the Great Irish Famine has been of great interest to famine historians. Christine Kinealy has written in *This Great*

Calamity about the effectiveness had an embargo been placed on food leaving Ireland. She concluded, "There was no shortage of resources to avoid the tragedy of a famine. Within Ireland itself, there were substantial resources of food, which, had the political will existed, could have been diverted, even as a short-term measure, to supply the starving people."[15] Kinealy's conclusion echoes the theory of the Nobel Laureate in Economics Amartya Sen that famines are caused not by food shortage but by access to food.

The economic historian, Cormac Ó Gráda, identified the critical moment in regard to food supply as being late 1846 when there was still a significant export of oats and before the American corn arrived. "A temporary embargo on grain exports coupled with restrictions and prohibitions on brewing and distilling" would have helped to alleviate suffering in the worst months of the famine."[16]

Part of the *laissez faire* policy was NOT to restrict legal distilling. According to Elizabeth Malcolm's *Ireland Sober. Ireland Free. Drink and temperance in nine teenth-century Ireland*, in 1847, with the price of grain sky high, the production of legal spirits fell 25 percent from eight million to six million gallons.[17] How much grain does it take to produce one gallon of 80 proof spirits? How much grain does it take to produce 6,000,000 gallons of spirits? How many servings of grain-based cereal could have been produced if the grain had been diverted from the production of spirits? One source says 100 kilograms (222 pounds of grain will produce 21 to 23 gallons of 80 proof alcohol).

4. "AN OLD WOMAN OF THE ROADS": EVICTION AND HOMELESSNESS IN IRELAND

The New York Learning Standards as well as the Common Core ask students to compare an information article with a literary piece. Students read and compare Asenath Nicholson's description of an eviction in Newport, County Mayo, with Padraic Colum's poem "An Old Woman of the Roads" and, working in pairs or groups, write a response to the two texts that reflects on the long-range consequences of eviction and homelessness.

5. THE GREATEST POSSIBLE GOOD: FAMINE GRANTS

Students simulate the kinds of grants the Central Committee of the Society of Friends solicited and received during the Great Irish Famine. All applications are worthy. Students must establish the criteria for awards, evaluate applications and decide which grants to award and whether applicants should get all the money requested or just a percentage of the amount. Students will work in groups, report their awards and the basis for their choices.

6. WHAT DO WE KNOW ABOUT HUNGER?

Students will conduct research on current hunger crises and discuss the similarities between the Great Irish Famine and current famine conditions in Sub-Sahara Africa and the Middle East. Students might work with an article such as, "Cholera, Famine and Girls Sold into Marriage: Yemen's Dire Picture" from the *New York Times*, 30 May 2017.

7. PREPARING FOR EMIGRATION

Students will read Liam O'Flaherty's short story "Going into Exile," and analyze the relationship between characters and identify the difference between the public and private behavior expressed in the verbal and non-verbal behavior of Mr. and Mrs. Feeney, Michael and Mary. Why is dance such an important feature of the American wake?

8. THE EMIGRANT'S TRUNK

Students read from Máirtín Ó Cadháin short story "The Year 1912."

What things does Mary put in her trunk for America? What is the significance of each? What would you take?

The Blasket Island storyteller Peig Sayers said, "Going to America was the nearest thing to death." Do you agree? What are the positive aspects of emigration?

Students interview their immigrant families and ask what family members chose to take with them when they emigrated to the United States.

9. PLACE IN POETRY

Eavan Boland's poem "That the Science of Cartography is Limited," suggests that conventional mapmaking cannot always adequately represent the historical reality. In her poem, Boland talks of the starving people who worked building "famine roads" until they died and the road just stopped. What kind of maps can students design to represent the kind of human reality to which Boland's poem refers?

10. HOW HISTORY BECOMES POETRY: MAKING POEMS FROM PROSE

Students will read the passage from Cecil Woodham-Smith's *The Great Hunger* that describes the Whitehall reprimand given to Sir. James Dombrain, Inspector General of the Coast Guards, for disregarding orders to transport grain to Westport depot and instead giving the meal free to the hungry people of Westport. Students were asked to distinguish between the moral and civil law in that instance and to identify and discuss other examples of civil disobedience (*Antigone*, "Civil Disobedience," Rosa Parks).

The teacher reads the Woodham-Smith passage a second time asking students to list in a column words that strike them as especially vivid. Students use their lists, and perhaps a few additional readings to compose a pyramid poem:

Example:
Skeletons
Emaciated, half-dead
Staring, imploring, starving

Students are asked to read Seamus Heaney's poem "For the Commander of the *Eliza*," a poem that alludes to that episode in The *Great Hunger*. How has Heaney used Woodham-Smith's text to create his poem? Notice that he turns Woodham-Smith's text into a narrative, the eyewitness account of the unnamed commander of the *Eliza* who is presented with a dilemma: does he follow orders to ignore the suffering around him or does he disregard orders and give food to the hungry? The poem suggests a third choice: the commander reports the conditions around the Killeries to his superior, Sir James Dombrain. (Students, who often feel powerless, can talk to a responsible adult.)

NOTES

1. Thomas J. Archdeacon's essay, "The Irish Famine in American School Curricula," examines closely the politics of the New York State adoption of the Famine Curriculum legislation including the exchanges between Governor George Pataki and Ambassador for the United Kingdom John Kerr. *Éire-Ireland*, XXXVII, 1 & 2 (Spring/Summer 2002), pp. 130–152. Archdeacon's essay also considered the claims of James Mullen's New Jersey Irish Famine Curriculum and Mullen's criticism of the New York Great Irish Famine Curriculum.

2. Archdeacon, 'Irish Famine,' p. 140.

3. 'IRA smash ceasefire', *Guardian*, 10 February 1996.

4. The *Times,* 13 October 1996.

5. 'Blair issues apology for Irish Potato Famine', the *Independent*, 1 June 1997.

6. Irish language phrase meaning 'President and friends'.

7. 'The Queen in Ireland: Dublin Castle speech in full,' the *Telegraph*, 28 November 2017.

8. Tim O'Neill, "Famine Evictions," *Famine, Land and Culture in Ireland.* Carla King (ed.), (Dublin: University College, Dublin Press, 2000), p. 40.

9. Article 2 of the *United Nation Convention of Prevention and Punishment of the Crime of Genocide.*

10. The Irish proverb translates as *'People live in each other's shadows.'*

11. In developing a course for undergraduates on the Great Irish Famine, I developed a survey of local hunger and a requirement to visit one of the local food aid

organizations and do 20 hours of service. Later, I added an optional extra credit "week on food stamps" experience.

12. Since the curriculum was created, a new development in understanding the trans-generational impact of famine and trauma has been developed, in the Irish context by Oonagh Walsh. See her chapter on 'Epigenetics' in Kinealy, King, Reilly (eds) *Women and the Great Hunger* (Quinnipiac UP and Cork UP, 2016).

13. Paul Rincoeur, "Memory and Forgetting," in Richard Kearney and Mark Dooley, eds. *Questioning Ethics: Contemporary Debates in Philosophy.* New York: Routledge, 1998. p. 10. The Arendt reference is to *The Human Condition* (1992).

14. Since 2008, the National Famine Commemoration Day (*Lá Cuimhneacháin Náisiúnta an Ghorta Mhóir*) has been organized annually by the government of the Irish Republic.

15. Christine Kinealy, *This Great Calamity. The Great Famine in Ireland* (Dublin: Gill and Macmillan, 2006), p. 359.

16. Cormac Ó Gráda, *Black '47 and Beyond: the great famine in history, economy and memory* (Princeton, NJ: Princeton University Press, 1999), p. 174.

17. Elizabeth Malcolm, *Ireland Sober. Ireland Free. Drink and Temperance in Nineteenth Century Ireland* (Dublin: Gill and Macmillan, 1986).

CHAPTER TWELVE

SHAMROCKS, HAWTHORN TREES, AND BLACK POTATOES

Writing for children and young adults about Ireland's Great Hunger

Robert A. Young .Jr.

In an essay published in 2015, the Irish historian Ciarán Reilly made the following observation about the impact that the 150th anniversary of Ireland's Great Hunger had in relation to academic scholarship and the public memorializing of what is now considered the greatest humanitarian crisis of 19th-century Europe:

> The mid-1990s witnessed an explosion of interest in the Great Irish Famine, from the local to the international, evidenced not only in the scholarly publications which emerged, but also in the memorials and sites of commemoration developed across the world. This "re-awakening" of scholarship was broadly welcomed, as the "great silence" which had pervaded for decades was also reflected in the dearth of publication on the subject. The period since the sesquicentenary commemoration in 1995 has continued to be a fruitful one for Famine scholars, and, indeed, within the last five years a number of important publications have emerged.[1]

In addition to the scholarly studies that Reilly references, the 1990s and the early years of the 21st century increasingly saw the publication of other types of literature about the Great Hunger, including fiction and popular nonfiction books that were written not only for adults, but specifically for children and adolescents. It is the books written for young people, those between the ages of approximately 5 to 18, that this chapter will examine. In particular, it will focus on the sub-collection of Great Hunger books written for the young that are part of the larger Lender Family Special Collection, which is housed at Quinnipiac University's Arnold Bernhard Library. The Lender Family Special Collection, also known as the An Gorta Mór collection, is a repository of primary and secondary resources, and consists of over 750 books, 4,000 British Parliamentary Papers, and 250 handwritten letters.[2]

While most of the materials in the Lender collection have been acquired through a partnership that Quinnipiac established with Kenny's Bookshop and Art Galleries in Galway, the acquisition of juvenile literature was initiated by the library's collection management librarian, June DeGennaro. In addition to fulfilling the goal of establishing and maintaining the largest collection of Great Hunger publications in the United States, the addition of books written for young people also enhanced the collection of materials that had been acquired to support the university's School of Education curriculum. When possible, the library always purchases two copies of a juvenile title, one copy is added to the An Gorta Mór collection and the other to the curriculum collection.

As I began to review the library's juvenile collection, from the perspective of a librarian, the following questions arose:

1. Does an up-to-date published bibliography exist for the fiction/ nonfiction titles written for young people about the Great Hunger? (The books in the Lender Family Special Collection were listed in the library catalog as part of the whole collection but were not grouped separately.)
2. Are there additional titles that the library still needs to acquire?

3. Has there been any academic or general studies written about this type of literature, and do those studies include some of the factors that prompted authors to write books about the Great Hunger for the young? For example, had reading scholarly works influenced writers?

4. Do the books written for children, especially the fiction, share certain commonalities in plot, characterization, etc.?

5. What are the various formats and genres of the books?

6. Are there fiction and nonfiction titles that have received critical acclaim or present the Great Hunger story in unique and compelling ways?

When I searched for published bibliographies and studies about Great Hunger literature written for the young, I found one listing of fiction books and two critiques reviewing fictional works. I could find no bibliographies or studies of nonfiction publications. The fiction bibliography, which was annotated, had appeared in a 2003 issue of the Irish studies journal *Foilsiú*.[3] The author, Karen Hill McNamara, was at the time a student in the doctors of letters program (D.Litt.) at Drew University. The bibliography listed 38 titles, and checking the list against what was held at Quinnipiac, I discovered that 24 of the titles were not in the Lender Collection. (Those titles have since been ordered.) McNamara's bibliography served as an inspiration and basis for creating an updated annotated bibliography of fiction and nonfiction, which will be included as a reference resource on the Lender Family Special Collection library webpage. While not yet annotated, the bibliography is found at the end of the chapter. Its creation provided some statistical information and interesting insights into Great Hunger books written for young people:

Number of Books Published, 1940s–2010s: 80 titles
Fiction Titles: 60 titles
Nonfiction: 20 titles

Breakdown by Decade:

1940s – 1 fiction title

1950s – 1 fiction title

1960s – 1 nonfiction title

1970s – 8 fiction titles

1980s – 7 fiction titles

1990s – 23 fiction titles, 4 nonfiction titles

2000s – 17 fiction titles, 12 nonfiction titles

2010s – 3 fiction titles, 3 nonfiction titles

At the same time that the annotated fiction bibliography was published, Karen Hill McNamara also wrote her doctoral dissertation, "Telling Bridget's Tale of Hunger: Children's Literature of the Great Irish Famine." McNamara credits the impact that scholarly studies on the Great Hunger have had, in particular mentioning that a number of the authors she interviewed said that a "dominant text" had been Cecil Woodham-Smith's pioneering 1962 book *The Great Hunger: Ireland 1845–1849.*[4]

Authors that McNamara interviewed also were influenced by other factors, most notably:

1. Family heritage: ancestors had experienced the Great Hunger.[5]
2. Exposure to primary materials that document the Great Hunger.[6]
3. Visiting sites related to the Great Hunger: gravesites and workhouses.[7]
4. Noticing that there was a paucity of literature for the young about the Great Hunger.[8]
5. Becoming aware of the Great Hunger during the 150th anniversary.[9]

Additional influences that McNamara cites as having a possible impact in the increase of children's literature included: the rise of multicultural curriculums in elementary and upper level school systems (including the recent creation of curriculum modules specifically about the Great Hunger)[10] and the rise of feminism (the protagonists of many Great Hunger books are frequently young girls or women).[11] In regard to the gender of the authors, women are better represented, with the bibliography below showing 56 of the books were penned by women, compared with 32 by men.

The commonality of a central female character is something that I also had noted, and the following assessment by McNamara describes many of the fictional works that have been written:

> Before reading a Great Famine story for children I can now usually predict a few things about the protagonist. The narrative will most likely center on a young spunky, Irish Catholic peasant girl who is missing at least one parent. She will eventually survive the Famine by emigrating from Ireland, and become a maid in America. The protagonists are consistently youthful, spirited, resourceful, courageous, and independent. Determined to create new and better worlds for themselves, these heroes learn to endure and to seize every chance for survival. Even the fictitious names are repetitive with the reader encountering numerous Kates, Marys, Noras, and Bridgets.[12]

Besides feminism being a factor, McNamara looked at a number of other possible reasons that females were often the central character, including: the gender of the author— as 71 percent of the authors studied were women, it could be surmised that women might self-identify and have more of a connection to a lead female character.[13] Publishing trends were noted as girls' interest in reading historical fiction had recently increased. The historical record that authors referred to frequently pointed out that many Irish young women did emigrate out of Ireland during the Great Hunger and afterward.[14] In fact, recent scholarship demonstrates that, uniquely, a higher number of females than males left Ireland in the post-Famine decades. As Maureen Murphy, curator of the 'Mission Girl' exhibition, has highlighted, between 1883 and 1908, 307,823 single Irish girls arrived at the port of New York alone. These intrepid women, she argues, became the backbone of Irish America.[15]

McNamara's dissertation also examined some of the basic plot patterns and settings found in juvenile fiction, revealing that frequently key historical details are woven into the narratives.[16] Works often begin with the early stages of the potato blight's appearance in 1845, followed by the starvation and hardships that ensue over the course of the next several years as the crop failure continues to be a regular occurrence. The setting is often the western areas of Ireland, which was the part of the country most severely impacted by the catastrophe. Although, it should be noted, that scholarly work by Christine Kinealy and Gerard MacAtasney has shown that no part of the country, including the predominantly Protestant northeast region, escaped the catastrophe.[17] The cruelty of landlords and the British army are frequently highlighted, two factors that point out the prejudice that was directed at the Catholic poor, as well as the inadequacies and often inhumane conditions that were encountered by those who turned to the workhouses for assistance. Many of the young characters experience the death of siblings, one or both parents, or witness scenes of death in the Irish countryside. One common plotline depicts characters who are forced by their situations to leave home, often traveling by foot to coastal ports where they ultimately obtain passage on a "coffin ship" to America. In a number of cases, authors expand upon an original work, writing a sequel or trilogy. The continuation of a narrative often finds the main characters adjusting to life in a new country, with an emphasis on navigating an unfamiliar urban environment such as New York City.

An example of the multivolume format is the acclaimed trilogy of linked novels written by award-winning Irish author, Marita Conlon-McKenna. Beginning with *Under the Hawthorn Tree* (1990), which depicts the journey of orphaned siblings, two sisters and their brother, who make their way across Ireland to find their aunts, it was followed by *Wildflower Girl* (1991), and *Fields of Home* (1997). The later novels are about the post-Famine lives of the three children in both America and Ireland. The popularity of the first volume led to a television film adaptation, and the publication of a grade school study-guide for both the book and film.[18] Moreover, its success proved to be international, it being translated into over a dozen other languages, including Arabic, Bahasa, French, Dutch, German, Swedish, Italian, Japanese and Irish.[19]

In addition to what might be described as a "typical" or "standard" Great Hunger story, there are a number of books that focus on other historical events of note. For example, one of the earliest works is the American novel, *The Shamrock Cargo: A Story of the Irish Potato Famine* by Anne Colver (1952), which is about three fictional teenage characters living in Boston, who play a part in the American Famine relief that was provided by Captain Robert B. Forbes and the U.S.S. *Jamestown* in 1847.[20] There are also two books that relate the story of how the American Choctaw Indians sent monetary aid to Ireland during the Great Hunger, the Irish novel, *Trail of Tears* by Colin Vard (1997),[21] and the American picture book, *The Long March. The Choctaws Gift to Irish Famine Relief* by Marie-Louise Fitzpatrick (1998).[22] Two pop-up books have been written that also examine specific topics, the American pop-up, *Life on a Famine Ship: A Journal of the Irish Famine, 1845–1850* by Duncan Crosbie (2006),[23] and the Irish pop-up, *Irish Famine Workhouse: A Young Boy's Workhouse Diary* by Pat Hegarty (2011).[24]

A second study that reviews works of fiction was an essay written in 2002 by the Irish writer Siobhán Parkinson. Titled "Children of the Quest: The Irish Famine Myth in Children's Fiction," it was published in the children's literature trade publication, *The Horn Book Magazine*. Parkinson is a well-known author of children's fiction, and she served as Ireland's first Laureate na nÓg from 2010 to 2012, a position established by the Arts Council of Ireland to promote children's literature. While her article about Great Hunger juvenile fiction does not address the reasons that more books began to be written during the 1990s and afterward, it does make some intriguing points and observations. For example, Parkinson makes the case that the nationality of an author, whether it be American, British or Irish, can have a significant impact on a fictional work's perceived verisimilitude and authenticity. She also points out that the fiction written for young people often draws upon what she refers to as the "the Irish Famine myth," and by "myth," she means that authors frequently highlight and draw upon those historical details that have resonated the most powerfully with them. Parkinson contends: "To call it a myth is not to disrespect the suffering of those who lived through and died in the Famine but is simply to recognize that historical events acquire their own psychic momentum and influence the thinking, sense of identity, and stories of people generations removed from those events."[25]

Surprisingly, there have been no studies written about nonfiction juvenile books about the Great Hunger. Titles that fall into this category are fewer in number than their fiction counterparts. Currently only 20 nonfiction titles have been published, versus 60 fiction titles. And, except for one book that was published in the late 1960s, all works of nonfiction have been written since the 1990s. An examination of nonfiction juvenile titles in the Lender Collection reveals that many of them cited scholarly works as sources. Moreover, primary sources were at times not only referenced but incorporated as visual elements into the books. In a few cases, authors used primary sources from repositories that had not been available before the 1990s, such as the National Famine Museum at Strokestown Park in County Roscommon. An example of a book that effectively and engagingly presents primary materials to readers is *Journey of Hope: The Story of Irish Immigration to America, an Interactive History* by Kerby A. Miller and Patricia Mulholland Miller (2001). It includes a number of facsimile documents that detach from the volume and can be read and examined separately. Some of the materials reproduced include tenant eviction notices, passenger ship tickets, and personal letters written by immigrants.[26] This "three dimensional" approach, which is firmly rooted in historical sources, is perhaps not surprising given that Miller is one of the leading authorities on Famine emigration.[27] Another book that referenced primary sources effectively is Susan Bartoletti's award winning 2001 volume *Black Potatoes: The Story of the Great Irish Famine, 1845–1850*. Throughout the volume, Bartoletti includes many of the well-known documentary illustrations that were published in the *Illustrated London News* during the 1840s.[28] A number of nonfiction books include photographs as well, and while photography was in its infancy during the years of the Great Hunger, and no actual images documenting the tragedy exist, photographs of Irish peasant life from later in the 19th century are often used, as are modern views of abandoned cottages and workhouses.

Specialized subject series have included books about the Great Hunger. For example, Power Kids Press (NY) has a series called Spotlight on Immigration and Migration, which includes a volume about the Great Hunger, as does Benchmark Books (Utah) with its Great Journeys immigration series. Books about the Great Hunger also have been included in series focusing on disasters, such as Cause & Effect Disasters published by Lerner's (MN), and Great Disasters: Reforms & Ramifications by Chelsea House Publishing (NY). Many of the nonfiction works provide a general historical overview of the catastrophe, covering the same key details that have been incorporated into the plots of works of fiction. A number of works include listings of "additional readings," that cite scholarly works and, in some cases, other juvenile nonfiction titles.

Both works of fiction and nonfiction that have been written for young people about the Great Hunger appear in a variety of different formats and genres.

Formats:
1. Picture Books
2. Easy Readers
3. Chapter Books
4. Graphic Novels
5. Pop-Up-Books

Genres:
1. Historical Fiction
2. Historical Nonfiction
3. Fantasy Fiction (Fairies included in plot)
4. Supernatural Fiction
5. Time Travel

Reviewing the bibliography below it is clear that the dominant format is Chapter Books, and the dominant genre is Historical Fiction. Books that fall into the Chapter Books/Historical Fiction category frequently present the story of the Great Hunger following the common plot patterns already reviewed. Outside of what one most often encounters in Great Hunger fiction for the young are works that have been written in other genres popular in children's literature, but which might at first seem surprising. As listed above, those genres are fantasy fiction, supernatural fiction, and time travel.

Of the atypical genres, the most popular are stories about time travel. Four books have been written in which the main characters are physically transported back to the years of the Famine: *The Mine of Lost Days* by Mark Brandel (1974),[29] *Trail of Tears* by Colin Vard (1997),[30] *The Quest of the Ruby Ring* by Yvonne McGrory (1999),[31] and *The Grave* by James Heneghan (2000).[32] The supernatural tale *Black Harvest*, which is about English siblings who are haunted by ghosts from the time of the Great Hunger while on vacation in Ireland, was published as both a novel by Ann Pilling (1983),[33] and as a play (adapted from the book) by Nigel Gray (1986).[34] Fairies make an appearance, and provide assistance to those suffering during the Famine, in the novel *Knockabeg: A Famine Tale* by Mary E. Lyons (2001),[35] and the picture book *The Wee Christmas Cabin of Carn-na-ween* by Ruth Sawyer, with illustrations by Max Grafe (2005).[36]

The inclusion of visual elements in nonfiction juvenile works is commonplace, but they are also used throughout works of fiction. One of the most beautifully illustrated books is *Across the Sea from Galway* (1975) by the award winning American author/illustrator Leonard Everett Fisher. The book tells the story in stark black and white drawings, reminiscent of woodcuts, of emigrants who sailed from Ireland in 1849 on the ill-fated ship, *St. John*, which was wrecked off the coast of Cape Cod on a stormy night, with the survival of only 27 of the 143 onboard.[37] The picture book, *Katie's Wish,* by Barbara Shook Hazen (2003), is illustrated with the beautiful water-color drawings of artist Emily Arnold McCully, and is told from the viewpoint of a young girl and her family's struggles that end with emigration to America.[38] One of the most original, and recent, visual publications is the first graphic novel about the Great Hunger, *The Bad Times: An Drochshaol* by renowned Famine scholar Christine Kinealy and graphic artist John Walsh. Kinealy's inspiration for the novel was the 1847 oil painting "Irish Peasant Children" by Irish artist Daniel MacDonald. The children's characters in the graphic novel, Brigit, Daniel and Liam, are based on the three unidentified children in MacDonald's painting.[39] The book also has been published in Irish as *An Drochshaol.*[40]

As mentioned at the beginning of this chapter, it is part of a larger project to create an annotated bibliography of juvenile titles that will be accessible through the Lender Family Special Collection website, and which will serve as an informational resource for educators, students, academics and general readers interested in books written for young people about the Great Hunger. In addition to providing an alphabetical listing, separate listings of the books by date, age level, subject, genre and format will be created. As new titles are written they will be added to the list.

In conclusion, while books that could be categorized as children's literature about Ireland's Great Hunger first began to be published during the mid–20th century, it was not until the 1990s that there was a surge of interest by authors and publishers to produce fiction and nonfiction works for young people about this tragic and pivotal moment in Irish history. A number of factors played a part in why it was not until this time that the Great Hunger titles began to appear in increasing numbers, mirroring fresh scholarly interest. While fiction titles predominated, the appearance of a variety of nonfiction titles, that often cited and made use of scholarly works and primary documents, was a welcome and important development.

In my role as the librarian who provides access to materials in the Lender Family Special Collection, I plan in the future to more actively promote and direct scholars and researchers to juvenile works about the Great Hunger when appropriate. The creation of a continuously updated annotated bibliography of Great Hunger juvenile book titles will provide an introductory resource that will always be available at the Lender Family Special Collection website, and which will allow those interested to see a descriptive listing covering this particular type of literature. These works provide a valuable, yet often over-looked, introduction to the Irish Famine to a new generation of readers.

A Bibliography of Literature for Children & Young Adults

FICTION
1940s

Judson, Clara Ingram. *Michael's Victory: They Came from Ireland*. New York: Follett, 1946.

FICTION
1950s

Colver, Anne, and John Gretzer (illustrator). *The Shamrock Cargo: A Story of the Irish Potato Famine*. Philadelphia: Winston, 1952.

NONFICTION
1960s

Holland, Ruth, and Charles H. Waterhouse (illustrator). *From Famine to Fame: The Irish in America*. New York Grossett & Dunlap, 1967.

FICTION
1970s

Bolton, Carole. *The Search of Mary Katherine Mullo*. Nashville: T. Nelson, 1974.

Brandel, Mark, and John Verling (illustrator). *The Mine of Lost Days*. Philadelphia: Lippincott Williams & Wilkins, 1974.

Branson, Karen, and Jane Sterrett (illustrator). *The Potato Eaters*. Kirkwood, New York: Putnam Publishing Group, 1979.

Bunting, Eve. *The Haunting of Kildoran Abbey*. London: Frederick Warne, 1978.

Cummings, Betty Sue. *Now Ameriky*. New York: Atheneum, 1979.

Fisher, Leonard Everett. *Across The Sea From Galway*. New York: Four Winds Press, 1975.

Hall, Aylmer. *Beware the Moonlight*. New York: Avon, 1970.

Perez, Norah A. *The Passage*. New York: Lippincott, 1975.

FICTION
1980s

Branson, Karen. *Streets of Gold*. Kirkwood, New York: Putnam Publishing Group, 1981.

Gray, Nigel. *Black Harvest: A Play*. London: Collins Educational, 1986.

Langford, Sondra Gordon. *Red Bird of Ireland*. New York: Atheneum, 1983.

Morpurgo, Michael. *Twist of Gold*. Kingswood: Kaye & Ward, 1983.

Pilling, Ann. *Black Harvest*. New York: Harper Collins Children's Books, 1983.

Ranson, Candice F. *Kathleen*. New York: Scholastic, 1985

Reiff, Tana. *Hungry No More*. Belmont, CA: David S. Lake Publishers, 1989

FICTION
1990s

Avi. *Beyond The Western Sea (Book I)*. New York: Avon, 1996.

Avi. *Beyond The Western Sea (Book II)*. New York: Avon, 1996.

Brocker, Susan. *Journey to The New World*. Auckland, NZ: Shortland Publications, 1999.

Charbonneau, Eileen. *Rachel Lemoyne*. New York: Forge Books, 1998.

Conlon-McKenna, Marita, and Donald Teskey (illustrator). *Under The Hawthorn Tree*. Dublin: O'Brien Press, 1990.

Conlon-McKenna, Marita, and Donald Teskey (illustrator). *Wildflower Girl*. Dublin: O'Brien Press, 1991.

Conlon-McKenna, Marita, and Donald Teskey (illustrator). *Fields of Home,* Dublin: O'Brien Press, 1997.

Dennenberg, Barr. *So Far from Home: The Diary of Mary Driscoll, an Irish Mill Girl*. New York: Scholastic, 1997.

Doyle, Malachy, and Greg Gormley (illustrator). *The Great Hunger: A Tale of Famine in Ireland*. London: Watts, 1999.

Fitzpatrick, Marie-Louise, and Gary White Deer (ed.). *The Long March: The Choctaw's Gift to Irish Famine Relief.* Hillsboro, OR: Beyond Words Pub, 1998.

Harrison, Cora. *The Famine Secret.* Niwot, Colo: Wolfhound Press: Irish American Book Co, 1998.

Hodges, Margaret, and Paul Brett Johnson (illustrator). *Saint Patrick and the Peddler*. New York: Orchard Books, 1993.

Holland, Isabelle. *Behind the Lines*. New York: Scholastic, 1997.

Kositsky, Lynne. *Rebecca's Flame*. Montreal: Roussan Publishers, 1999.

Kroll, Steven. *Mary McLean and the St. Patrick's Day Parade*. New York: Scholastic, 1991.

Lally, Soinbhe. *The Hungry Wind*. Dublin: Poolbeg, 1997.

Lutzeier, Elizabeth. *The Coldest Winter.* New York: Holiday House, 1991.

McCormack, Colette. *After the Famine*. Dublin: Attic Press, 1996.

McCormack, Colette. *Mary-Anne's Famine*. Dublin: Attic Press, 1998.

McGrory, Yvonne, and Terry Myler (illustrator). *The Quest of the Ruby Ring*. Dublin: Children's Press, 1999.

Smith, Michael, *Boston! Boston!* Dublin, Poolbeg, 1997.

Vard, Colin. *Trail of Tears (Key to the Past)*. Dublin: Mentor Press, 1997.

NONFICTION

1990s

Barber, Irene. *Under the Hawthorn Tree: The Great Irish Famine; A Study Guide to the Film and Novel*, Dublin, O'Brien Press, 1998.

Cush, Cathie. *Disasters That Shook The World,* Austin, TX: Raintree Steck − Vaughn, 1994.

Gallagher Carmel, Trevor Parkhill, and Christine Kinealy (eds). *Evidence in Ireland for the Young Historian: Making Sense of History.* Belfast, Northern Ireland: Ulster Historical Foundation, 1990.

Nardo, Don, and Brian McGovern. *The Irish Potato Famine.* San Diego, CA: Lucent Books, 1990.

FICTION

2000S

Arrigan, Mary. *Esty's Gold.* London: Frances Lincoln Children's Books, 2009.

Crosbie, Duncan, and Brian Lee (illustrator). *Life on a Famine Ship: A Journal of The Irish Famine, 1845–1850.* Hauppauge, NY: Barron's Educational Series, Inc., 2006.

Drinkwater, Carol. *The Hunger: The Diary of Phyllis McCormack: Ireland 1845–1847.* London: Scholastic, 2001.

Hazen, Barbara Shook, and Emily Arnold McCully (illustrator). *Katie's Wish.* New York: Dial Books for Young Readers, 2003.

Heneghan, James. *The Grave.* New York: Farrar, Straus and Giroux, 2000.

Lutzeier, Elizabeth. *Bound for America*, Oxford: Oxford University Press, 2002.

Lyons, Mary E. *Knockabeg: A Famine Tale,* Boston, MA: Houghton Mifflin, 2001.

Neal, Cynthia G. *The Irish Dresser: A Story of Hope During the Great Hunger* (An Gorta Mor, 1845–1850). Shippensburg, PA: White Mane Kids, 2004.

Neale, Cynthia G. *Hope in New York City: The Continuing Story of the Irish Dresser.* Shippensburg, PA: White Man Kids, 2007.

Nolan, Janet, and Ben F. Stahl (illustrator). *The St. Patrick's Day Shillelagh.* Morton Grove, Ill: A. Whitman, 2002.

Pastore, Clare. *Fiona McGilray's Story: A Voyage From Ireland in 1849.* New York, NY: Berkley Jam, 2001.

Reilly, Patricia. *Maggie's Door.* New York: Wendy Lamb Book, 2003.

Reilly Giff, Patricia. *Nory Ryan's Song.* New York: Delacorte Press, 2000.

Ross, David. *Children of the Great Hunger.* New Lanark, Scotland: Waverly Books, 2002.

Sawyer, Ruth, and Max Grafe (illustrator). *The Wee Christmas Cabin of Carn-na-ween*. Cambridge, MA: Candlewick Press, 2005.

Schneider, Mical. *Annie Quinn in America*. Minneapolis: Carolrhoda Books, 2001.

Stengel, Joyce A. *Katie O*. Dublin: Poolbeg Press, 2000.

Wilson, Mary. *How I Survived The Irish Famine: The Journey of Mary O'Flynn*. New York: Harper Collins Publishers, 2001.

NONFICTION

2000S

Allan, Tony. *The Irish Famine: The Birth of Irish America*. Chicago: Heinemann Library, 2001.

Allan, Tony. *The Irish Famine: The Birth of Irish America* (revised edition). Chicago: Heinemann Library, 2006.

Bartoletti, Susan C. *Black Potatoes: The Story of the Great Irish Famine, 1845–1850*. Boston: Houghton Mifflin, 2001.

Brougham, Feargal, and Caroline Farrell. *The Great Famine*. London: Evans Brothers, 2007.

Dolan, Edward F. *The Irish Potato Famine: The Story of Irish-American Immigration*. New York: Benchmark Books, 2003.

Gallagher, Carole, and Jill McCaffrey. *The Irish Potato Famine*. Philadelphia, PA: Chelsea House Publishers, 2001.

Lyons, Mary E. (ed.). *Feed The Children First: Irish Memories of The Great Hunger*. New York: Athenaeum Books for Young Readers, 2002.

Miller, Kerby A., and Patricia Mulholland Miller. *Journey of Hope: The Story of Irish Immigration to America: an Interactive History*. San Francisco: Chronicle Books, 2001.

O'Neill, Joseph R. *The Irish Potato Famine*. Edina, Minn: ABDO pub. Co., 2009.

Pipe, Jim, and David Antram (illustrator). *You Wouldn't Want to Sail on an Irish Famine Ship! A Trip Across The Atlantic That You'd Rather Not Make*. New York: Watts, 2008.

Seekamp, Gail, and Pierce Feiritear. *The Irish Famine*. Phibsboro, Dublin: Pixie Books, 2008.

Thornton, Jeremy. *The Irish Potato Famine: Irish Immigrants Come to America (1845–1850)*. New York: The Rosen Publishing Group, 2004.

FICTION

2010S

Curtis, Christopher Paul. *The Madman of Piney Woods*. New York: Scholastic Press, 2014.

Hegarty, Pat, and Kay Dixey (illustrator). *The Irish Famine Workhouse: A Young Boy's Workhouse Diary*. Dublin: Gill & Macmillan, 2011.

Kinealy, Christine, and John Walsh. *The Bad Times: An Drochshaol*. Hamden, CT: Quinnipiac University Press 2015.

———. *An Drochshaol. Baile Átha Cliath:* Coiscéim, 2016.

NONFICTION

2010S

Fradin, Dennis Brindell. *The Irish Potato Famine*. Tarrytown, NY: Marshall Cavendish Benchmark, 2012.

O'Donoghue, Sean. *The Disaster of The Irish Potato Famine: Irish Immigrants Arrive in America (1845–1850)*. New York: PowerKids Press, 2016.

Sherman, Jill. *The Irish Potato Famine: A Cause-And-Effect Investigation*. Minneapolis, Lerner Publications, 2017.

See also: libraryguides.quinnipiac.edu/specialcollections

NOTES

1. Ciarán Reilly, "Nearly starved to death": The female petition during the Great Hunger" in Christine Kinealy, Jason King, and Ciarán Reilly (eds), *Women and the Great Hunger* (Quinnipiac University Press, 2016), p. 47.

2. I am the librarian who currently manages this collection and provides assistance to researchers and scholars who wish to access materials in it. My contact information is:

   Robert A. Young, Public Services Librarian
   Arnold Bernhard Library, Quinnipiac University
   275 Mount Carmel Ave.
   Hamden, CT 06518–1908
   Phone: 203–582–3469
   robert.young@qu.edu

3. Karen Hill McNamara, "Children's Literature of the Great Irish Famine: An Annotated Bibliography." *Foilsiú*, 2003, vol. 3, no. 1, pp. 21–31.

4. Karen Hill McNamara, "Telling Bridget's Tale of Hunger: Children's Literature of the Great Irish Famine" (D.Litt dissertation, Drew University, Madison, NJ, 2003), p. 144.

5. Ibid., pp. 136–144.

6. Ibid., pp. 155–162.

7. Ibid.

8. Ibid., pp. 164–166.

9. Ibid., pp. 166–169.

10. Ibid., pp. 15–18.

11. Ibid., pp. 57–60.

12. Ibid., pp. 51–52.

13. Ibid., p. 133.

14. Hasia R. Diner, *Erin's Daughters in America: Irish Immigrant Women in the Nineteenth Century* (Baltimore: John Hopkins University Press, 1983).

15. Maureen Murphy, 'The Mission Girls' Maureen Murphy, Curator, December/January 2010, at: irishamerica.com/2010/01/the-mission-girls/, accessed 10 February 2018.

16. Karen Hill McNamara, "Telling Bridget's Tale of Hunger," pp. 99–102.

17. Christine Kinealy and Gerard MacAtasney, *The Hidden Famine: Hunger Poverty and Sectarianism in Belfast 1840–50* (London: Pluto Press, 2000).

18. Marita Conlon-McKenna and Donald Teskey (illustrator), *Under The Hawthorn Tree* (Dublin: O'Brien Press, 1990). Marita Conlon-McKenna and Donald Teskey (illustrator), *Wildflower Girl* (Dublin: O'Brien Press, 1992). Marita Conlon-McKenna and Donald Teskey (illustrator), *Fields of Home* (Dublin: O'Brien Press, 1997). Irene Barber, *Under the Hawthorn Tree: The Great Irish Famine; a Study Guide to the Film and Novel* (Dublin: O'Brien Press, 1998).

19. 'Marita Conlon-McKenna. About the Author,' *Amazon* at amazon.co.uk/Under-Hawthorn-Tree-Children-Famine-ebook/dp/B00DTWHW2U, accessed 13 January 2018.

20. Anne Colver, *The Shamrock Cargo: A Story of the Irish Potato Famine* (Philadelphia: Winston, 1952).

21. Colin Vard, *Trail of Tears (Key to the Past)* (Dublin: Mentor Press, 1997).

22. Marie Louise Fitzpatrick, *The Long March: The Choctaw's Gift to Irish Famine Relief* (Hillsboro, OR, Beyond Words Pub, 1998).

23. Duncan Crosbie and Brian Lee (illustrator), *Life on a Famine Ship: A Journal of the Irish Famine, 1845–1850* (Hauppauge, NY: Barron's Educational Series, 2006).

24. Pat Hegarty and Kay Dixey (illustrator), *Irish Famine Workhouse: A Young Boy's Workhouse Diary* (Dublin: Gill & Macmillan, 2011).

25. Siobhán Parkinson, "Children of the Quest: The Irish Famine Myth in Children' Fiction," The Horn Book Magazine, Nov.–Dec. 2002, pp. 679–688. Biography at siobhanparkinson.com/bio/, accessed 13 January 2018.

26. Kerby A. Miller and Patricia Mulholland Miller, *Journey of Hope: The Story of Irish Immigration to America: An Interactive History* (San Francisco: Chronicle Books, 2001).

27. Kerby A. Miller, *Emigrants and Exiles: Ireland and Irish Exodus to North America* (New York: Oxford University Press, 1985).

28. Susan C. Bartoletti, *Black Potatoes: The Story of the Great Irish Famine, 1845–1850* (Boston: Houghton Mifflin, 2001).

29. Mark Brandel, *The Mine of Lost Days* (Philadelphia: Lippincott Williams & Wilkins, 1975).

30. Vard, *Trail of Tears.*

31. Yvonne McGrory and Terry Myler (illustrator), *The Quest of the Ruby Ring* (Dublin: Children's Press, 1999).

32. James Heneghan, *The Grave* (New York: Farrar, Straus and Giroux, 2000).

33. Ann Pilling, *Black Harvest* (New York: Harper Collins Children's Books, 1983).

34. Nigel Gray, *Black Harvest: A Play* (London: Collins Educational, 1986).

35. Mary E. Lyons, *Knockabeg: A Famine Tale* (Boston, MA: Houghton Mifflin, 2001).

36. Ruth Sawyer and Max Grafe (illustrator), *The Wee Christmas Cabin of Carn-na-ween* (Cambridge, MA: Candlewick Press, 2005).

37. Leonard Everett Fisher, *Across the Sea from Galway* (New York: Four Winds Press, 1975).

38. Barbara Shook Hazen and Emily Arnold McCully (illustrator), *Katie's Wish* (New York: Dial Books for Young Readers, 2003).

39. Christine Kinealy and John Walsh, *The Bad Times: An Drochshaol* (Hamden, CT: Quinnipiac University Press, 2015).

40. Christine Kinealy and John Walsh, *An Drochshaol* (Baile Átha Cliath: Coiscéim, 2016).

CHAPTER THIRTEEN

WHAT A WRITER SEEKS IN HISTORY

In search of a voice

Michael Collins

Perhaps it is an emigrant lament, but since I left Ireland in 1981, I have felt a growing obligation to better understand what it is to be Irish, given that we are remembered in the historical record as victims—as a people of terrible genocide or Famine. In the summer of 2016, belatedly coming to the tumultuous history of our collective past, I began a month long marathon-a-day run retracing the land passage of some 100,000 immigrants arriving in Canada during the 1847 sailing season as they traveled some 900 kilometers from Grosse Île toward Toronto along the Saint Lawrence.

I did not do so only out of obligation to my heritage. As an emigrant Irish writer, I have been obliged to address the fated historical reality that a disproportionate number of Irish writers have written in self-exile. I might describe myself as such, and although I left for reasons more economic than philosophical, the leave-taking and act of dislocation instigated an intellectual reawakening.

My first collection of stories, *The Meat Eaters,* conceived without a political agenda, sought simply to recapture Irish life through a pastiche of auto-biographical stories. Yet, the dislocation of immigrant life configured a relational distancing between past and present, between here and there. What emerged was a sociological evisceration of a de Valera theocracy, a gestapo Catholicism that had perverted much of Irish life post World War II. It would be years before I understood that what I wrote early on had been informed by a heightened hysteria, a reactionary prose savaging what was then faltering, the controlling influence of the church. I don't discount what I wrote as untrue—*it was true*—but it didn't express the entirety of the cultural influence of the church on our lives. It is difficult to maintain equanimity, especially in the crumbling days of a power structure, when any measure of nostalgia might be taken as an apologist's defense of the indefensible.

There is, in retrospect, the disquieting awareness that my self-ascribed intellectual acuity was a juiced-up, indicting revisionist prose that had cast a myopic eye on all that was good, sanctifying, and life-sustaining—or what had been for a generation of pragmatic-minded Catholics, those who had let the sanctions of moral policing happen outside the domain of open discourse for the avowed belief that to give voice to perceived reprobate behaviors was to corrupt the general morality of all the people.

It was, of course, undemocratic: clandestine politics arguably embodying a willful resistance to an emergent continental modernism best typified by England, that Sodom in Ireland's backyard where the flotsam of Irish teddy boys and loose girls were frog marched to trains bound for Dublin and then taken by boat passage to Liverpool and London. For better or worse, England— then exemplified by the *Star* "Page Three" Girl—while the protectorate of Catholic influence, sanctifying an Irish way of life, kept in abeyance the realities of modern life.

History is a complex intertwining of psychological forces, where the unmasking of apparent incongruities and outright criminal acts must be contextualized. Most always the laws and mores of a society work for the greater majority of its citizens, up until a tipping point when suddenly they don't. It is then easy to unmask what no longer holds true, to tease apart apparent contradictions within a system, to differentiate compassion from brutality, to alight on the innumerable religious scandals that have plagued Ireland, from sex abuse cases to the incarceration of unwed mothers, to the pits of dead babies that might best be described as *The Silence of the Prams*!

It is what makes the study of Irish history such a confounding proposition, be it the Famine, usurping power of the church, or our more immediate incarnation as Europeans. We are not now what we once were, and change within us is most always exemplified in a radical transformation that often outstrips our ability to fully capture the psychological effects of what was so recently assumed gospel. Perhaps a writer of another nation might make the same claim, but oft times we Irish seem the receivers of others' truths, others' agendas, and are not steered by our own ideas. Indeed, in the historical record, a lot is said *about* us, but not much is said *by* us.

Particularly, I am referring to my so far confounding engagement with Irish Famine history. It has been a tough slog this past year and a half. This is my second attempt at understanding and finding a Famine voice that might speak to the horrors of the age. I still have the compiled notes from a welter of a year's research I conducted in my early writing life that eventuated in an incongruous state of intellectual perplexity, where I knew more about our history and at the same time knew less.

In the retreat from the first attempt, I wrote another people's story. Amidst 18-hour days as a programmer at Microsoft, in the dislocation from my early years on athletic scholarship at Notre Dame in Indiana, I published *The Keepers of Truth*. Shortlisted for the Booker Prize and the IMPAC prize, the novel explored the disintegration of the Rust Belt through a noir murder peopled with characters who prefigure a disaffected subculture of what would become Donald Trump supporters, a disenfranchised population left abandoned in the wake of big industry's demise. Five more novels set in the Midwest followed.

And yet, in the hunt for my own sense of self, I was dissatisfied. I returned again and again to the Famine material I had amassed. It was this early failure that had made me loathe to re-engage with our collective history, and although

I embarked on my marathon-a-day run, this time the locus of my attention mediated between a study of the Famine and a history closer to my own life. I thought the intersecting influence of Catholicism on Irish identity might be the conduit to understanding, as this was the fault line that partially ruptured in the years preceding my departure and continued headlong into the innumerable scandals that eventually decoupled Catholicism from the nation's sense of identity.

This might be an emigrant preoccupation and what makes us emigrants such an oddment in the arrested way we latch onto a point of last departure. Yet, somehow, I see the loss of our religion, our Catholicism, as a central impairment in understanding both the psyche of the Famine Irish and our history post-independence under de Valera. I settled on religion as the central issue of differentiation. What possessed our ancestors to resist proselytization for so long against innumerable famines and insurrections that kept them so marginalized? Perhaps all novels have a central theme, and that indomitable fidelity to Catholicism figured in the way a singular questioning will direct a work.

The Voice of the Other—Protestant self-determination and the rise of capitalism

By late 2015, after having spent three months researching the story of the Famine Irish of 1847, I had begun to conceive of the run as an act of pilgrimage, less conjoined with scholarly research and more an homage to those long-suffering victims of our past. I wanted to be on the road with their collective ghosts, to inhabit an exhaustive state and find perhaps some co-union with them. Against the loss of life on that interminable sea passage and amidst calamitous death in the quarantine of Grosse Île and beyond, I asked how they had endured, what had they said and thought. I settled on human questions of the heart as a writer will, because human *wants* and *voice* are the essence of the craft.

Again, in that quest, I intuited that within that older story of endurance and faith was a religious undertow that allowed so many to persist and survive. And yet what was lacking in all I read was the clear voice of those who had endured so much.

Against that curious muting of the actual victims, for the sake of scholarship and finding a point of historical reference in advance of the run, I dutifully returned to the historical records. Most notable were the governmental accounts and rationales of how and why the Famine was managed as it was. I alighted on an insouciant defense of *laissez-faire* capitalism as argued by Charles Trevelyan, who, as government overseer of Famine relief, echoed a dark 19th-century Malthusian politics in addressing the Irish case, declaring:

> I think I see a bright light shining in the distance to the dark cloud which at present hangs over Ireland. A remedy has been already applied... and I hope I am not guilty of irreverence in thinking that this being altogether beyond the power of man, the cure has been applied by the direct stroke of an all-wise Providence... God grant that we may rightly perform our part and not turn into a curse what was intended as a blessing.[1]

It is a damning hymnal to genocide, but in it I heard a voice. No doubt a voice of bureaucracy, but voice is important to a writer. It allows a writer access to the psyche, that clairvoyant intersect with a character where, to paraphrase Atticus Finch in *To Kill a Mocking Bird*, you begin to move around in another's skin. In researching the historical record, in reading the chilling words of Trevelyan, a worldview was communicated that was honest, if calculating, and cruelly so. I despised Trevelyan, but in accessing his own words I knew him better.

Indeed, in trying to understand the greater context of political economic policy toward Ireland, I delved into the historical record to better understand Trevelyan's mindset. In so doing, in the search for the Famine voice of the ordinary people, I was now one step removed, and immersed instead in the voice of British empire. It was frustrating, and yet I rationalized that it was best I understood the explicit doctrine of the age, or came to a general understanding of what I thought people believed during the 19th century.

In seeking to understand Trevelyan, I settled on the specter of population growth, since that had been his great preoccupation, a historical fear that had gripped Europe during the 17th and 18th centuries. It had equally engaged politicians, philosophers, economists and, pointedly, clergy. Indeed, the Anglo-Irish satirist and cleric Jonathan Swift had been so preoccupied with the sprawling overpopulation of Irish destitute that, more than a century before the catastrophic Irish Famine, he had begun his 1729 "A Modest Proposal":

> I am assured... that a young healthy child, well nursed, is, at a year old, a most delicious, nourishing, and wholesome food; whether stewed, roasted, baked or boiled.[2]

Thomas Malthus, another speculative, moralist Protestant cleric, in *An Essay on the Principle of Population*, predicted the inevitable culling of millions through vectors of disease and starvation if population growth remained unchecked. To offset such natural disasters, Malthus argued for moral restraint. Yet, despairing that the poor could ever be so swayed, he sardonically advocated against assisting them in no less unnerving terms than Swift, arguing instead that in:

> our towns we should make the streets narrower, crowd more people into the houses, and court the return of the plague. In the country, we should build our villages near stagnant pools, and particularly encourage settlements in all marshy and unwholesome situations. But above all, we should reprobate specific remedies for ravaging diseases.[3]

Malthus' bombastic hyperbolae owes much to a Protestant-inspired sermonizing rhetoric. Yet the underlying appeal for moral restraint ties to tenets of the Protestant Reformation, namely the direct mediation of the self with God, an idea that would eventually dovetail with the secularist Enlightenment ideas of self-determination, individual rights and self-interested *laissez-faire* capitalism. The Reformation occasioned a socio-political paradigm shift from aristocratic, autocratic rule to enlightened democracy, with emphasis moving from *status* to jurisprudence *contract*.

Resocialization, both moral and economic, lay at the heart of this new enlightenment, as evidenced by another evangelist, Dublin Archbishop Richard Whatley. In his *Introductory Lectures on Political Economy*, Whatley extended sectarian sermonizing beyond veiled notions of salvation toward an argument for economic reform, commenting on the Irish situation that:

> It would be a mistake to suppose that religion or morals alone would be sufficient to save a people. No, they would not be sufficient, if a proper idea of Political Economy was not *cultivated* by that people. A man, even of the purest mind and most exalted feelings, without a knowledge of Political Economy, could not be secured from being made instrumental in forwarding most destructive and disastrous revolutions.[4]

This hybridization of spiritual determinism with secularized Enlightenment and political economy would further influence economic theory. Adam Smith, in his *Wealth of Nations*, penned a proto-Protestant manifesto that argued for unregulated free markets and *laissez-faire* capitalism based on rational self-interest and competition. Without invoking the metaphysical, Smith's theory aligned with Martin Luther's assertion that all Christians served God in their occupations. To quote Luther: "God is milking the cows through the vocation of the milkmaid." In so ordaining work in the temporal world as essentially vocational, Luther ended Catholicism's disjunctive split between the clergy and the laity, where vocation was tied exclusively to acts beyond common human living and marked by chastity. Deconstructing the monastic life, Luther pointedly warned:

> If you find yourself in a work by which you accomplish something good for God, or the holy, or yourself, but not for your neighbor alone, then you should know that that work is not a good work.[5]

Essentially, the rise of the Industrial Age, and with it, a new economy of self-interest inspired capitalism, was facilitated by a radical conceptual shift in the understanding of vocation under the Protestant Reformation. If God commanded the mysteries of the universe, so be it, but there were concerns within the domain of man, namely how he survived and prospered in the temporal world. Smith put it thus in *The Theory of Moral Sentiments*:

> The administration of the great system of the universe … the care of the universal happiness of all rational and sensible beings, is the business of God and not of man. To man is allotted a much humbler department, but one much more suitable to the weakness of his powers, and to the narrowness of his comprehension: the care of his own happiness, of that of his family, his friends, his country.[6]

In anticipating a shift from Catholic emphasis on the transcendent and acts directed to God alone toward Protestant self-actualization in the temporal world, Smith extended Luther's argument for vocations so that the agency of exchange between men could align with principles of self-interest while simultaneously serving a moral function in promoting compassion and advancing happiness. A true Christian could not speak only of faith while overlooking his relationship with his neighbor.

Indeed, Jean-Jacques Rousseau, in *A Discourse,* prefigures the rise of capitalism with the acquisition of property, and argues that the attendant inequality furthered by a commodification of property and wealth was tied to desires, and that such desires or wants were:

> essentially good in that only through them could any improvement in the human condition have come about. While these desires may originally have been narrowly material—more comfortable living conditions, better health, etc., they led dialectically, via the spawning of social interdependence—in fact, via the creation of 'man' as a social being—to the notions of law, justice, civil liberties and popular sovereignty.[7]

Implicit to this inter-relational dependence between the body politic and commerce was the idea of *selfhood* or *self-interest*, all concepts anathema to Catholicism. In his work, *Plutology*, W.E. Hearn extended Rousseau's argument, conceiving self-interest and individualized *wants* as central to driving economics:

> Those nations, and those classes of a nation who stand highest in the scale of civilization, are those whose wants, as experience shows us, are the most numerous; and whose efforts to satisfy those wants are the most unceasing.[8]

As with other political theorists, Hearn's explicit advocacy for economic self-interest served as a Trojan horse, enmeshing capitalism with tenets of Protestantism self-determinism. Hearn would later declare "that research into social science must necessarily lead to the most powerful confirmation of religious truth."[9]

What emerged from this new socio-economic interdependence, this capitalism born of commodity markets and the rise of industrial cities, was a complex amalgam of economic theory, divine providence and enlightenment rationalism that regulated the "rationally self interested individual whose choices and desires invisibly regulate both production and consumption."[10]

Tragically, Ireland was worlds away from this emergent neo-Protestant capitalism of *wants* then spreading across Europe. While the creep of Enclosure Acts elsewhere ended a serfdom medievalism of tenant farming, reorganizing commerce around industrial cities, Ireland was going in the opposite direction.

Specifically, the Irish peasantry's sole reliance on the potato was inextricably linked to arresting economic and moral advancement, condemning denizens of the hinterland to a subsistence life. There was an essential truth and lie within the statement. Firstly, economic advancement was denied the Irish through a conspiracy of Penal Laws that had disenfranchised the Catholic Irish and robbed them of their lands dating to the time of the Protestant Plantation. Driven to rural Ireland in the wake of the brutal conquest of

Cromwell, their numbers conceivably should have fallen in this hinterland of scarcity, and yet it was the potato that saved the Irish. Its confounding alimentary qualities were such that one could survive solely on the potato, with a supplement of buttermilk. The average Irish male in the 19th century ate an astounding 12 to 14 pounds of potatoes daily, and despite overall economic distress, on this singular diet the Irishman was reportedly "half an inch taller than the Englishman and on a Victorian contraption called a dynamometer, his physical strength was measured at 432 pounds compared to 403 pounds for an Englishman."[11]

Indeed, English observers in visiting Ireland were struck simultaneously by the squalor of living conditions, with pigs sleeping alongside families in mud homes, and yet oft noted the beauty of the people, especially women of the lowest class, this despite that fact that even in years of plenty, the potato crop did not last throughout the year. By July the crop was unfit to eat, and most peasants suffered privation before the September harvest.

Charles Trevelyan, in assessing the tragic state of Ireland and her reliance on the potato, put it thus:

> If an enlightened man had been asked what he thought the most discouraging circumstance in the state of Ireland, we do not imagine that he would not have pitched upon Absenteeism, or Protestant bigotry, or Roman Catholic bigotry... or even the system of threatening notices and midday assassinations. These things, he would have said, are evil; but some of them are curable; and others are merely symptomatic. They do not make the case desperate. But what hope is there for a nation which lives on potatoes?[12]

With an eerie premonition of what would eventually unfold, Trevelyan in his work, *The Irish Crisis*, further quotes from a paper by *thinking persons*, published pre-Famine in "Transactions of the Horticultural Society" (1822), that pointedly addressed the effect of sole reliance on the potato:

> The effect of the unlimited extent to which its cultivation may be carried, on the human race, must be a subject of deep interest to the political

economist. The extension of the population will be as unbounded as the production of food, which is capable of being produced in very small space, and with great facility; and the increased number of inhabitants of the earth will necessarily induce change, not only in political systems, but in all the artificial relations of civilized life. How far such changes may conduce to or increase the happiness of mankind, is very problematical, more especially when it is considered, that since the potato, when in cultivation, is very liable to injury from casualties of season, and that it is not at present known how to keep it in store for use beyond a few months, a general failure of the year's crop, whenever it shall have become the chief or sole support of a country, must inevitably lead to all the misery of Famine, more dreadful in proportion to the numbers exposed to its ravages.[13]

Of course, Protestant landlord absenteeism greatly contributed to thwarting the economic advancement of the Irish peasantry and enforced their reliance on the potato. Foodstuff of commercial grade was grown by peasants, but shipped to England as rent payment. Religious and economic theorists were apt to ignore this fact. Rather, the potato was serially demonized as having had an amoral impact on the Irish character, given that the tubers, once sewn, required no maintenance, and thus allegedly contributed to an indolence that abetted an imprudent rise in the Irish birthrate. Prior to the introduction of the potato in the 16th century, the Irish population had stood at 1 million. By the early 18th century, it broached four million. In 1845, on the eve of the Famine, it reached a staggering 8.1 million.

To the outside observer, Ireland was the antithesis of moral restraint, or it was more politically expedient to conflate unremitting birth with Catholicism and Irish ignorance than to seek a deeper understanding of the Irish situation. For the English, the Irish dilemma became less about underlying economics and more representative of a sectarian, attitudinal divide as Protestant self-determinism met the miasma of a wretched Catholic helplessness.

The Fetishizing of Political Economic Theory

Throughout the tumult of the Famine, politicians, philosophers and clerics alike, in a fetishizing of political economic theory, continually identified self-interest as both an economic principle and a spiritual act, further differentiating the religious divide between the Irish and English. Again, Archbishop Whatley drew on Luther's notion of vocation, extending the alliance of individual pursuits so:

> that by the wise and benevolent arrangement of Providence, even those who are thinking only of their own credit and advantage, are, in the pursuit of these selfish objects, led, unconsciously, to benefit others. The husbandman and the weaver exert their utmost industry and ingenuity, to increase the produce of the earth and of the loom; each, that he may be enabled to command for himself a better share of other productions; but in so doing, they cause the community to be better fed, and better clothed. And the effort of each man, with a view to his own credit, to rise, or at least not to sink, in society, causes, when it becomes general, the whole Society to rise in wealth.[14]

Whatley would further his argument, dovetailing self-interest with overall societal advancement, declaring that "in some instances even the most sordid selfishness, are made, in an advanced stage of society, to conduce to public prosperity." In a slow creeping defense of property, capital acquisition and inequity of wealth, Whatley, again in his *Introductory Lectures on Political Economy* cautioned against calls for a redistribution of capital, lecturing the common worker that:

> at first glance, they are apt to imagine, when they see a rich man whose income is a hundred times as much as suffices to maintain a poor man's family, that if he were stripped of all, and his wealth divided, a hundred poor families additional might thus obtain subsistence; which, it is plain, would not be the case, even when the income was spent in such ostentatious and selfish vanity.... [for] in fact, a very large portion of the wealth that exists in a country, is employed in procuring a further increase of wealth; in other words, is employed as Capital.[15]

Another venerable Dublin notable of the time, E. Neilson Hancock, professor of political economy at Trinity College, Dublin and disciple of Adam Smith, indicated a preordained harmony between the laws of political economy and those of God, suggesting that the call for government interference in the price of provisions "arises from the common prejudice, which attributes the rise in price to the conduct of the dealer in provisions, instead of the wisdom of the Almighty."[16]

Hancock continues to invoke the "invisible hand" of God in the miraculous mechanism of economic exchange, pointedly aligning how:

> In the pursuit of this object, without any comprehensive wisdom, or any need of it, [people] cooperate unknowingly in conducting a system, which we can safely say, no human wisdom directed to that end, could have conducted so well – the system by which this enormous population is fed from day to day.[17]

This conflation of political economy and providence would allow those in power to ascribe a *felix culpa* (happy fall) to the Famine, where through the agency of suffering came moral rectitude and civic redemption. Again, it would be Trevelyan, as the high-priest of political economy, and director of Famine relief in Ireland, who would have the temerity to absolve himself and government of responsibility, declaring:

> Unless we are much deceived, posterity will trace up to the Famine the commencement of a salutary revolution in the habits of a nation long singularly unfortunate, and will acknowledge that on this, as on my other occasions, Supreme Wisdom has educed permanent good out of transient evil.[18]

In effect, by the 19th century, one could argue that Hobbes's conceit of life as "short, nasty and brutish" had been reconfigured and sanctified under the unification of a trifecta of emergent ideologies: neo-protestant self-determinism, Darwin's survival of the fittest, and a political economic theory of competition based on self-interest (capitalism).

Sidelining a Claim of Genocide

If there is a charge to be leveled against the British Parliament and with Trevelyan, it must begin with their inaccurate assessment of the Irish society and its underlying economy. And yet, to be fair, the zealous application of a quasi-Protestant economic theory to social and political ills was not peculiar to Ireland. Throughout the 18th and 19th centuries, *laissez-faire* capitalism had sought to make each accountable for their own actions, eschewing government involvement and firmly placing almsgiving among religiously-minded citizens as a stopgap measure against destitution and starvation.

Charles Dickens's "A Christmas Carol," published in 1843, is the classic prototype of this individualized moral transformation of businessmen of means, who achieve salvation, not through parliamentary acts demanding taxes, but through their personal mediation with God. The story begins with Scrooge defiantly protesting almsgiving. He shifts responsibility to the state, demanding, "Are there no prisons... and the Union workhouses... are they still in operation? and ends on a defiantly Malthusian note with Scrooge declaring:

> I don't make merry myself at Christmas and I can't afford to make idle people merry. I help to support the establishments I have mentioned – they cost enough; and those who are badly off must go there... If they would rather die... they had better do it, and decrease the surplus population.[19]

Scrooge, in this opening scene, evokes the sentiment of many British parliamentarians, who, as late as 1832, in a Royal Commission into the Operation of the Poor Laws damningly concluded that existing Poor Laws within England perpetuated a class of subsistence laborers who disrupted the natural laws of supply and demand as employers leveraged this subsistence class to force down wages. In response, efforts were redoubled to ensure that those who entered the workhouse would find conditions worse than the poorest free laborer found elsewhere.

Thus, the appointing of Charles Trevelyan to oversee the relief efforts in Ireland fell in line with a Protestant attitude that the poor were not so much in need of economic help as moral re-education, be it in England or Ireland. He says as much, decrying in Scrooge-like terms the Irish reliance on government, which "eats like a canker into the moral health and physical prosperity of the people."[20]

Through a third year of Famine, Trevelyan zealously enforced the Gregory Clause (1847), which exempted from public relief anybody who occupied more than a quarter of an acre of land. The act all but assured the wholesale relinquishment of lands held by the last holdout of the Irish peasantry, which eventuated in the great immigration of 1847 as the absentee landlords further enticed the peasantry off the land with paid passages to America and Canada.

The foreign secretary to Ireland, the landed Lord Palmerston, acting on the advice of estate agents in 1847, eventually shipped some two thousand of his tenants to Canada aboard ships that one Canadian official compared to conditions on vessels used in the slave trade. If there was any doubt as to Palmerston's intent all along, during the early years of Famine, he circulated a memorandum among parliamentary colleagues adumbrating official British policy concerning agrarian reform in Ireland:

> It is useless to disguise the truth that any great improvement in the social system of Ireland must be founded upon an extensive change in the present state of agrarian occupation, and that this change necessarily implies a long continued and systematic ejectment of Small Holders and of Squatting Cottiers.[21]

The London *Times*, in assessing the expediency of the Gregory Clause, gleefully anticipated a second plantation of Ireland by "thrifty Scot and scientific English farmers, men of means, men with modern ideas... [further declaring] ... a Celtic Irishman will be as rare in Connemara as is the Red Indian on the shore of Manhattan."[22]

In so saying, one heard the ominous echo of a Malthusian providential endgame that characterized a wholesale assault on the disenfranchised, and not just the Irish. They simply fared worst in the great psychological realignment of a Protestant inspired capitalism.

The Silence of the Irish

What can I say? In reading, analyzing and summarizing the readings I did over a short period of time, I accessed the sentiment of the British body politic and an emergent political theory of economic advancement. I could almost look to a comedy, to Wilde's *The Importance of Being Earnest,* for the sheer lunacy of manners and earnest discourse on all things rational.

And yet, I was still without that elusive Irish voice, that plaintive emigrant evocation of all that was lost. I think the central issue is how to move through the realm of the conacre system and to discern an intellect, or let it speak, for how would that voice speak from the dung heap of a collapsing hovel or in the grip of Famine?

The closest I came to discerning that voice was an agrarian vernacular best explored by Patrick Kavanagh. Pushing against a prelapsarian Celtic revivalism of fable and folklore inspired by a "Protestant Ascendancy caste... outside the mainstream consciousness of the Irish [and] not the voice of the people,"[23] Kavanagh, asks of potato gatherers in the opening of *The Great Hunger*, "Is there some light of imagination in these wet clods?" and at the poem's end answers his own question:

> Patrick Maguire, the old peasant, can neither be damned nor glorified;
> The graveyard in which he will lie will be just a deep-drilled potato-field
> Where the seed gets no chance to come through
> Silence, silence. The story is done.[24]

So goes the plaintive lament of Patrick Maguire, who roars mid-poem, "O Christ! I am locked in a stable with pigs and cows for ever."[25] *The Great Hunger* here aligns less with the namesake Famine torment of deprivation, but with an agrarian system where matriarchal mothers survived into old age and kept their sons in a sort of indenture, forestalling them from marrying early, if at all. *The Great Hunger* is thus less concerned with historical imperial subjugation as much as a sublimated, individualized sexual longing as Maguire is left to:

Turn over the weedy clods and tease out the tangled skeins.
What is he looking for there?
He thinks it is a potato, but we know better
Than his mud-gloved fingers probe in this insensitive hair.[26]

The damnation of the land and a peculiar beholden Irish-Catholic servi-
tude eclipses any notion of political accusation toward the English. Rather,
Kavanagh counters the sentimentality of a nationalist revivalism, his narrator
damningly resorting to a simian metaphor that might as well have come from
the pages of the 19th century *Punch* Magazine:

No monster hand lifted up children and put down apes
As here.[27]

So much for national solidarity in the most harrowing of Ireland's great
epic poems. The crisis is existential, not political. Kavanagh is preoccupied
with the burden of family and the fear of becoming "some mute, inglorious
Milton,"[28] a sentiment his narrator tellingly intimates, stating,

Nobody will ever know how much tortured poetry the pulled
weeds on the ridge wrote
Before they withered in the July sun.[29]

And so it goes, *silence, silence.* The story is done in an "apocalypse of clay."[30] It
begs the question: can the voices of resignation, those wide-eyed victims of
deprivation, ever really speak? I think of the Famines in Africa through my
lifetime, the pitiful spectre of children with flies crawling around their eyes
and up their nostrils. Do they ever speak? Not really! It's the advocacy of
others. It's Bob Geldof! It's Band-Aid. There is no literature, no voice given
to those so brutalized and subjugated. How might they speak if they could?

Recently, I heard there has been enlivened talk of making a Famine
comedy series as a way of exploring the socio-political realities of the time.
How about a Kenny surrogate from "South Park?" Little Kenny who dies and

inexplicably is alive again in the next episode? The little baby who would die on the show—little famished Paddy—a petulant thorn in the side of England, his reconstituted parts forever assembling like hacked weeds that simply multiply. Or how about an incarnation of little Stewie from "Family Guy," a soothsayer who might deliver a palaver of political economic theory during an eviction whilst suckling on mother Moiré's rosebud tit? It's not without precedence. Monty Python applied a black comedic undertow to the Plague in "The Holy Grail," with its infamous skit depicting a near-dead old man feebly pleading, "I'm not dead!" as he's carried on the shoulder and thrown onto a cart by a presumed in-law.

I can somehow see the descending gallows humor of a new way of processing that which cannot be accessed otherwise. What I can say is that, in my earlier work, I borrowed from a tradition. *The Keepers of Truth* and the trilogy of books thereafter were Joycean, social realism inspired by Steinbeck, with an elixir of the crime genre for popular taste. The question remains: Where is that voice of the Famine? Where is that emergent tone, that way of speaking as they must have done—those denizens of the hinterland?

The nationalist writer John Mitchel refers to Ireland as succumbing to "death by discourse," an ignoble muted death. Mitchel laments how:

> If one should narrate how the cause of his country was stricken down in open battle, and blasted to pieces with shot and shell, there might be a certain mournful pride in dwelling upon the gallant resistance... but to describe how the spirit of a country has been broken and subdued by beggarly Famine... how her life and soul have been ameliorated and civilized out of her;—how she died of political economy, and was buried under tons of official stationery;—this is a dreary task, which I wish someone else had undertaken.[31]

And again, that question arises—where is that Famine voice? All is *silence*, or what emerges in our Famine-inspired literature is, at best, an elliptical casting of staccato thoughts in the wasteland of a stage or novel. One thinks of Beckett's ahistorical figures, moored to the dark cosmos, unbound, castoffs—Malone,

Molloy and Murphy—each seeking existential self-affirmation within a condition that Beckett aptly defines as *Unnamable*, the protagonist of "*The Unnamable*" declaring at novel's end:

> I'll go on, you must say words, as long as there are any—until they find me, until they say to me... you must go on, perhaps it's done already, perhaps they have said me already, perhaps they have carried me to the threshold of my story, before the door that opens on my story, that would surprise me, if it opens, it will be I, it will be the silence, where I am, I don't know, I'll never know: in the silence you don't know, you must go on, I can't go on, I'll go on.[32]

On my return to America after completing The National Famine Walk, I bought a copy of Sebastian Barry's celebrated *Days Without End* in which the protagonist, Thomas McNulty, a Sligo native, had endured and survived the Famine. Intrigued, I was again seeking a deeper understanding of Famine history, or a literary voice from which to borrow or extend, and yet what was most revealing in the creation of a character of sustained insight—who extends the narrative reach of so many great American novelists in detailing the expansion of the West—was how little McNulty revealed of his Irish past. He says, "I'll say quickly what happened to me and brought me to America, but I don't feel much in the way of saying too much..." [33]

McNulty then gives a summary of the coffin ships, a truncated, page-long telling, inferior to the reach and insights of his American experiences. Later, in coming again to the coffin ships, in describing the skeletal figures huddled in the ships' holds, McNulty struggles only to abruptly break off, declaring, "That's why no one will talk because it's not a subject. It makes your heart ache. Goddamn corpses.... That's because we were thought worthless. Nothing people. I guess that's what it was... Nothing but scum."[34]

What is it about that psychological wound of the Famine that so blunts our imaginative reach? We are, as yet, without that defining genre, that way of telling that can be borrowed and extended.

I might contrast that national amnesia, that unnamable, against the transnational clairvoyant understanding of Nazi Germany as intuited by Irish writer John Boyne, whose novel *The Boy in the Striped Pajamas* was written in a matter of days. He describes it as a novel that arrived fully formed in the fever-pitch of a needful telling. Seemingly, some histories live in the collective consciousness. There is a Concentration Camp Literature, a point of perspective that allows the victims to speak. It is there in the *Diary of Anne Frank* and in Elie Wiesel's *Night*. Even Irishman Liam Neeson was cast as Oskar Schindler in the academy award winning *Schindler's List*. The story is universal.

So what of our history? Our reflexive psychological trauma continues—that dark indictment of those inhumane years that reduced us to nothing, a historical moment that continues to outstrip even the most eloquent and celebrated of our novelists, and sees us forever bound to and recoiling from what befell us. And yet it is for us to make it a subject, to make it a trans-global story that connects with the plight of all those dispossessed of basic human rights, to reclaim a voice and deeper understanding of all that passed.

It is not easy, and yet, "You must go on, I can't go on, I'll go on."[35]

NOTES

1. Catherine Hall. *Macaulay and son architects of imperial Britain* (New Haven, CT: Yale University Press, 2012) p. 186.

2. Robert Blaisdell, *Great English essays: from Bacon to Chesterton* (Mineola, NY: Dover Publications, 2005), p. 27.

3. T. R., Malthus, *Essay on the Principle of Population, or, a view of its past and present: with an inquiry into...* (Los Angeles: Hardpress, 2013), p. 465.

4. Richard Whately, *Introductory Lectures on Political-Economy, delivered at Oxford, in Easter term MDCCCXXXI. With remarks on tithes and on poor-laws and on penal colonies* (London: J.W. Parker, 1855), p. 64.

5. Martin Luther, *Working for our Neighbor*. This was one of seven sermons delivered in 1522 in Wittenberg on the connection between faith and love for our neighbor.

6. Adam Smith, Joseph Black, and James Hutton. *Essays on I. Moral sentiments; II. Astronomical inquiries; III. Formation of languages; IV. History of ancient physics; V. Ancient logic and metaphysics; VI. The imitative arts; VII. Music, dancing, poetry; VIII. The external senses; IX. English and Italian verses* (London: Alex Murray & Son, 1872), p. 210.

7. Jean-Jacques Rousseau's, *Discourse on the Origin and Basis of Inequality Among Men* was first published in French in 1754.

8. William Edward Hearn, *Plutology, or the theory of the efforts to satisfy human wants* (Place of publication not identified: Rareclub, 2012), p. 20.

9. Thomas Boylan, *Political economy and colonial Ireland: the propagation and ideological functions of economic discourse in the nineteenth century* (London: Routledge, 2014), p. 141.

10. David Lloyd, 'Nomadic Figures: The "Rhetorical Excess" of Irishness in Political Economy,' *Back to the Future of Irish Studies: Festschrift for Tadhg Foley* (1st ed. Verlag der Wissenschaften. Peter Lang, 2010), p. 41.

11. Ibid., p. 10.

12. Charles Trevelyan, 'The Irish Crisis,' in *The Edinburgh Review* LXXXVII (1848), p. 110.

13. Ibid., p. 230.

14. Whately, op cit., p. 95.

15. Whately, op cit., p. 102.

16. William Neilson Hancock, *Three Lectures on the Questions: should the principles of political economy be disregarded... at the present crisis? and if not, how can they be?* (Montana: Kessinger, 2010), p. 51. This text was first published in 1847.

17. Ibid., p. 60.

18. Trevelyan, op cit., p. 1.

19. Charles Dickens, "Lit2Go," *A Christmas Carol | Charles Dickens | Lit2Go ETC* (N.p.: n.d. Web), accessed 12 July 2017, p. 8.

20. Trevelyan, op cit., p. 162.

21. Jenny P. Edkins, *Whose hunger?: Concepts of Famine, practices of aid* (Minneapolis: University of Minnesota Press, 2002), p. 82.

22. John Kelly, *The graves are walking* (London: Faber, 2012), p. 255.

23. Patrick Kavanagh and Antoinette Quinn. *Collected poems* (London: Penguin Books, 2005), p. xxi.

24. Ibid., p. 89.

25. Ibid., p. 84.

26. Ibid.

27. Ibid.

28. Ibid., p. xii.

29. Ibid.

30. Ibid., p. 89.

31. John Mitchel, *The crusade of the period: and last conquest of Ireland (perhaps)* (New York: Lynch, Cole & Meehan, 1878), p. 236.

32. Samuel Beckett, *The Unnamable*, a novel, was first published in 1954.

33. Sebastian Barry, *Days Without End* (London: Penguin, 2017), p. 23.

34. Ibid., p. 125.

35. Beckett, *Three novels: Molloy, Malone dies, the unnamable* (New York: Grove Weidenfeld, 1991), p. 407.

ABOUT THE CONTRIBUTORS

STEPHEN G. BUTLER is a lecturer in the Expository Writing Program at New York University and is an associate editor of *New York Irish History*, the annual journal of the New York Irish History Roundtable. He earned a PhD in Modern History and Literature from Drew University. His publication, *Irish Writers in the Irish American Press, 1882–1964* will be published by University of Massachusetts Press in late 2018.

Limerick-born author, **MICHAEL COLLINS** has written 10 works of fiction translated into 20 languages. His work was shortlisted for a Booker Prize and an IMPAC nomination, along with a Kerry Ingredients Irish Novel of the Year Award and Best Foreign Novel Published in France. A former captain of the Irish National 100k team and current masters national record holder, Collins extended his endurance in 2016, by retracing the 1847 journey of some 100,000 Irish who, upon arriving at Grosse-Île quarantine station in Quebec, began a 600 mile journey along the Saint Lawrence to Toronto. Collins wrote exclusively for the *Irish Times*, documenting his month-long marathon-a-day journey. Collins was educated at the University of Notre Dame and Oxford University and holds a doctorate in English.

MARITA CONLON-McKENNA is an award-winning writer of both adult and children's fiction. Her work includes *'Under the Hawthorn Tree,'* part of the international best-selling *'The Children of the Famine'* series. She is a winner of the International Reading Association Award (1993). Her other books include *'The Blue Horse'* (1992) and *'Safe Harbour'* (1995), *The Magdalen* (1999) and *'Rebel Sisters'* (2016).

SIMON GALLAHER is a PhD student at the University of Cambridge. His doctoral research is entitled 'The welfare of children and childhood under the Irish Poor Law, c. 1850–1914' and is supervised by Eugenio Biagini and Samantha Williams. He is interested in how prevailing ideas of childhood promoted and shaped the institutional care of children in Ireland.

JONNY GEBER is a lecturer in biological anthropology at the Department of Anatomy at the University of Otago in New Zealand. His research has a particular focus on the bioarchaeology of social marginalization and poverty, and the Great Irish Famine in particular. He is the author of *Victims of Ireland's Great Famine: The bioarchaeology of mass burials at Kilkenny Union Workhouse* (Gainesville, 2015).

CHRISTINE KINEALY is founding director of Ireland's Great Hunger Institute at Quinnipiac University. She has published extensively on 19th-century Irish history, with a particular emphasis on the Great Famine. Her latest research has focused on the abolition movement in Ireland, her publications in this area including, *Daniel O'Connell and the Anti-Slavery Movement. The Saddest People the Sun Sees* (London: Routledge, 2011), *Frederick Douglass in* Éirinn (*Baile Atha Cliath: Coiscéim*, 2016) and *Frederick Douglass and Ireland. In his own words* (2 vols. London: Routledge, 2018).

JASON KING is the academic coordinator of the Irish Heritage Trust which operates the National Famine Museum in Strokestown Park. He has held previous appointments as a postdoctoral researcher, lecturer and assistant professor at the National University of Ireland Galway, the University of

Limerick, the Université de Montréal, Concordia University, the National University of Ireland, Maynooth University and University College, Cork. He has an extensive track record of publications and he curates several exhibits and a digital archive on the Great Hunger and Irish Famine migration.

KORAL LAVORGNA holds a PhD in Education History from the University of New Brunswick. She began exploring children's culture after discovering the 1947 Chocolate Bar War, a spontaneous children's protest movement which united kids across Canada. She is currently developing "Detective Perspective," an educational program that teaches children to solve the puzzles of the past.

MARK G. MCGOWAN is professor of History and Deputy Chair of the History Department at the University of Toronto. He has written many books and articles on the religious and immigration history of Canada, particularly focused on the Irish diaspora in the 19th century. His seventh book, *The Imperial Irish: Canada's Irish Catholics Fight the Great War, 1914–1918*, was recently published by McGill-Queen's University Press.

E. MOORE QUINN is a linguistic anthropologist who teaches language, culture, and Irish Studies at the College of Charleston, Charleston, South Carolina. As someone who has published widely in anthropological and Irish Studies circles, Quinn currently serves as the elected Social Sciences representative for the American Conference for Irish Studies (ACIS). At the present time, she is co-editing a special issue of the *International Journal of Religious Studies and Tourism* on the question, 'What is Pilgrimage?' (2018).

GERARD MORAN is a researcher at the SSRC at NUI Galway, where he has lectured in the Deptartment of History. His areas of research include Irish emigration and the diaspora, the Great Famine, and land and political agitation in 19th-century Ireland. He is author of *Sending Out Ireland's Poor: Assisted Emigration to North America in the Nineteenth Century* (Dublin, 2004 and 2014) and is joint editor of *Mayo—History and Society* (Dublin, 2014).

MAUREEN MURPHY is Hofstra University Professor Emerita. She directed the Great Irish Famine Curriculum project for New York state and is the historian of the Irish Hunger Memorial in Battery Park City. She is the author of *Compassionate Stranger: Asenath Nicholson and the Great Irish Famine* (2015) and editor of Nicholson's *Annals of the Famine in Ireland* (1851).

SALVADOR RYAN is professor of Ecclesiastical History at St Patrick's College, Maynooth and has published widely on popular religion and ritual in late medieval and early modern Ireland and Europe. Recent publications include *Death and the Irish: a Miscellany* (Dublin: Wordwell Books, 2016); *The materiality of Devotion in Late Medieval Northern Europe* (with Henning Laugerud and Laura Katrine Skinnebach. Dublin: Four Courts Press, 2016); *Remembering the Reformation: Martin Luther and Catholic Theology* (with Declan Marmion and Gesa Thiessen. Minneapolis: Fortress Press, 2017); and *The Cultural Reception of the Bible: Explorations in Theology, Literature and the Arts* (with Liam M. Tracey. Dublin: Four Courts Press, 2018).

ROBERT A. YOUNG JR. is the Public Services Librarian at the Arnold Bernhard Library at Quinnipiac University. He provides assistance to scholars and researchers who wish to access materials in the Lender Family Special Collection, a repository of primary and secondary resources related to the history of the Great Hunger and Ireland. In addition, he assists the campus community with questions related to copyright and fair use, serves as library liaison to several academic departments, and has collaborated with Ireland's Great Hunger Institute on various projects and exhibitions.

INDEX

IRELAND'S GREAT HUNGER INSTITUTE
AT QUINNIPIAC UNIVERSITY

Ireland's Great Hunger Institute is a scholarly resource for the study of the Great Hunger, which is also known as *An Gorta Mór*. Through a program of lectures, conferences, course offerings and publications, the institute fosters a deeper understanding of this tragedy and its causes and consequences.

To encourage original scholarship and meaningful engagement, the institute develops and makes available the Great Hunger Collection, a unique array of primary, secondary and cultural sources, to students and scholars.

Ireland's Great Hunger Institute was established in September 2013 and its founding director is Professor Christine Kinealy.